MONTH-BY-MONTH GARDENING

MID-ATLANTIC

Quarto is the authority on a wide range of topics.

Quarto educates, entertains and enriches the lives of our readers—enthusiasts and lovers of hands-on living.

www.quartoknows.com

First published in 2015 by Cool Springs Press, an imprint of Quarto Publishing Group USA Inc., 400 First Avenue North, Suite 400, Minneapolis, MN 55401 USA. Telephone: (612) 344-8100 Fax: (612) 344-8692

quartoknows.com
Visit our blogs at quartoknows.com

Cool Springs Press titles are also available at discounts in bulk quantity for industrial or sales-promotional use. For details contact the Special Sales Manager at Quarto Publishing Group USA Inc., 400 First Avenue North, Suite 400, Minneapolis, MN 55401 USA.

10 9 8 7 6 5 4 3 2 1

ISBN: 978-1-59186-642-8

Library of Congress Cataloging-in-Publication Data

Weigel, George, author.
  Mid-Atlantic month-by-month gardening : what to do each month to have a beautiful garden all year / George Weigel.
    pages cm
  Includes index.
  ISBN 978-1-59186-642-8 (pb)
  1. Gardening--Middle Atlantic States. I. Title.
  SB453.2.M527W45 2015
  635.0974--dc23
                                   2015020781

Acquiring Editor: Billie Brownell
Project Manager: Alyssa Bluhm
Art Director: Brad Springer
Layout: S. E. Anglin

Printed in China

MONTH-BY-MONTH GARDENING

MID-ATLANTIC

What to Do Each Month to Have
a Beautiful Garden All Year

GEORGE WEIGEL

COOL
SPRINGS
PRESS
Home and Garden Experts™

MINNEAPOLIS, MINNESOTA

Dedication

To Suze, my lifelong love and "co-propagator" of our daughter Erin and son Andy, who's grown the family landscape to include daughter-in-law Julie and a little sweet pea named Leona Pearl.

Acknowledgments

Thanks, first, to Cool Springs Press for realizing the importance of regional gardening information and for helping gardeners know what to do when.

Also, kudos to the whole production team at Cool Springs for making this book happen, especially editor Billie Brownell, who somehow manages to juggle multiple book projects at the same time and keep them all organized and flowing.

And third, thanks to the army of info suppliers who contributed the many bits and pieces that make up this book—the assorted Master Gardeners, horticulturists, growers, garden-center folks, horticulture professors, public-garden staffers, Extension educators, home gardeners, and yes, even my own backyard bugs and voles who assisted with the Problem-Solve section.

Contents

Introduction

"When do I do what?"

Especially if you're new to the mid-Atlantic region—or new to gardening altogether—that's the perplexing question when trying to figure out how to care for a landscape.

Doing the wrong thing at the wrong time usually won't kill plants, but it could short-circuit a shrub's bloom, give you a post-pruning "chopped" look for way longer than is necessary, or increase the odds of winter or drought damage.

In short, getting the hang of timing is a key factor that separates the "green-thumbers" from the "horticulturally challenged."

Unfortunately, few people have any training in the fine art of yard care. Those without parents or grandparents who showed them what to do are basically left to wing it. That leads to wasted time, energy, and money on the trial-and-error trail, or to "landscape paralysis" as people fear they'll do the wrong thing at the wrong time and ultimately end up doing nothing.

Experienced gardeners know that's a recipe for jungledom. Mother Nature takes over quickly when a gardener turns his or her back for long.

Like it or not, those with a yard are faced with learning how to stay a step ahead of the weeds and porch-eating yew bushes. It's either that or hire out the job to chainsaw-toting crews who will be happy to bill you for the privilege.

Think of this book as a way to fast-forward through the trial-and-error years to make you a more confident yard care person. Though it touches on the basics of how-to, *Mid-Atlantic Month-by-Month Gardening* is primarily a when-to. Use it as a detailed playbook or honey-do list to refer to throughout the year. Mark it up or whittle it down into your own specific gardening planner based on your observations and timings learned from experience.

Once you go through it for a few years, our hope is that you'll just know what to do when and find yourself referring to these pages less and less often. At that point, congratulations! You'll be one of those green-thumbers.

GARDENING BY THE CALENDAR

Most gardening tasks are not difficult. The tricky part is the timing—knowing *when* to do them. Timing involves understanding how plants grow in a particular area and how factors such as weather, soil, light, moisture, and even insect and plant interactions affect that.

Learning these things would be easy if they stayed the same from year to year. None of them do, of course, which makes gardening fun and challenging to the avid gardener but maddening and "@%!*#!" to those who want to get the work done and get back to golfing.

Gardening involves making time when the time is right to do certain tasks. So, Lesson No. 1 is to be flexible enough to adapt to Mother Nature's whims.

Just as optimal task dates vary depending on where you live in the Mid-Atlantic, so do these dates vary season to season. A mild winter or an unusually early spring can advance care needs by two weeks or more. Similarly, a cold winter and slow start can push back jobs by two weeks or more.

GARDENING IN THE MID-ATLANTIC

Although it may not always seem so during a January ice storm or August heat wave, the mid-Atlantic region is one of America's best for gardening.

■ *One of the nicest parts about gardening in the mid-Atlantic region is the distinct change of seasons.*

HERE'S HOW

TO GUESSTIMATE YOUR GROWING SEASON

Each year's "growing season" is the time between when frost ends in spring and when frost returns in fall. That's especially important for annual flowers and tropicals because frost kills most of these in a single cold night. Knowing your likely frost dates is important for determining when to plant annuals and when to take tender houseplants back inside after a summer vacation on the patio.

Frost varies from year to year and is very local in nature. Even the same yard may experience frost in one part but not another on the same night. Following are the average spring and fall times for the mid-Atlantic region's six different USDA Plant Hardiness Zones. Keep in mind that it's not unusual for frosts to swing two weeks to either side of the average.

That means if you don't want to risk losing tender annuals on a frosty spring night, wait two to three weeks *after* the average date to plant. Likewise, if you have tender plants that you keep inside over winter, get them inside two to three weeks *before* the average first fall frost date. Also, watch your local forecasts to laser-target each season's frosts.

The seasonal changes, moderate winters, and usually plentiful rainfall (35 to 40 inches a year) add up to a wide palette of plant choices and favorable growing conditions. The climate is cool enough for brilliant spring-bulb shows and blazing fall foliage, yet warm enough to grow "Southern" plants, such as crape myrtle, camellia, and gardenia. Some spring and fall days are nothing short of glorious.

No area is idyllic, though, and mid-Atlantic gardeners get their fair share of nature's curveballs, including super-soakings from hurricane remnants,

FROST DATES

Zone 5b (east-central West Virginia, such as Elkins, Pendleton)
Average first fall frost: late September
Average last spring frost: mid- to late May

Zone 6a (far northwest Maryland, central to north-central West Virginia)
Average first fall frost: early October
Average last spring frost: mid-May

Zone 6b (northern Maryland; western mountains of Virginia, such as Winchester, Harrisonburg and Blacksburg, Virginia, southwestern West Virginia)
Average first fall frost: mid-October
Average last spring frost: late April

Zone 7a (most of Delaware—Dover, Newark, and Wilmington; Washington, D.C.; central Maryland, northern to central Virginia)
Average first fall frost: late October
Average last spring frost: mid-April

Zone 7b (southeastern coastal Delaware; southern and coastal Maryland, southern Virginia)
Average first fall frost: early November
Average last spring frost: early to mid-April

Zone 8a (southeastern coastal Virginia—Norfolk, Virginia Beach)
Average first fall frost: mid-November
Average last spring frost: late March

Source: National Oceanic and Atmospheric Administration

AVERAGE FROST-FREE GROWING SEASON

Zone 5b: 140–155 days **Zone 7a:** 185–200 days
Zone 6a: 155–170 days **Zone 7b:** 200–215 days
Zone 6b: 170–185 days **Zone 8a:** 225–240 days

Source: National Oceanic and Atmospheric Administration

AVERAGE ANNUAL PRECIPITATION

Delaware: 46 inches
Washington, D.C.: 40.8 inches
Maryland: 37.4 inches (far northwest) to 47.3 (east coast)
Virginia: 36.4 inches (western mountains) to 46.6 inches (east coast)
West Virginia: 38.7 inches (north) to 44 inches (central)

Source: National Climatic Data Center

To determine your USDA Plant Hardiness Zone, visit the USDA's zone map site online at www.planthardiness.ars.usda.gov and type your zip code in the "Find" box, or look at the map in this book. To see your city's average first and last frost dates, go to Dave's Garden website at www.davesgarden.com/guides/freeze-frost-dates and type in your zip code.

To see your city's month-by-month average precipitation totals, go to the U.S. Climate Data website at www.usclimatedata.com/climate/united-states/us and select your state, then city.

branch-snapping snow dumps when nor'easters work their way up the Atlantic coast, and plant-killing freezes when polar vortexes dip down from the North.

The region also has a variety of localized growing conditions—two major ones in particular. Along the Atlantic coastal lowlands, the soil tends to be coarse and sandy with humid summers and milder winters due to the ocean water's moderating effect. Move west, and the land transitions into the Piedmont uplands, characterized by rockier, clay-based loam soils and colder winters. The division is a "fall line" that runs north to south, roughly from Wilmington, Delaware, to Baltimore, Maryland, to Richmond, Virginia.

Generally, average temperatures cool as you head from east to west and from south to north. One way to measure that is by U.S. Department of Agriculture Plant Hardiness Zones, a rating system based on average winter lows.

The mid-Atlantic region encompasses six of these zones, ranging from average winter lows of -10 to -15 degrees Fahrenheit in the mountains of

■ *Nasturtiums grow along this stone wall, which is an example of a microclimate.*

West Virginia (Zone 5b) to average winter lows of 10 to 15 degrees Fahrenheit in the southeastern corner of Virginia (Zone 8a). Most of the region falls in moderate Zones 6b to 7a, meaning winter lows bottom out somewhere between -5 degrees and 5 degrees Fahrenheit.

Knowing your zone helps time your jobs and pick plants wisely in the first place. Keep in mind, though, that these USDA hardiness ratings are *averages.* It's entirely possible to have abnormally hot or abnormally cold seasons.

MICROCLIMATES: GROWING LOCALLY

Even within a regional climate, other subtle but important local influences can affect gardening success. Growing in northern Maryland, for example, is not the same as growing in the state's southeastern coastal region. Even the same yard can include several different growing conditions.

These *microclimates* are influenced by soil type, light, wind, rainfall amount, how well that rain drains, and high and low temperatures.

Here are a few examples:

- Hilltops tend to be colder and windier, while frost tends to collect in valleys and low-lying areas.
- Urban areas can be 5 to 10 degrees warmer than surrounding suburbs and rural areas because of heat trapped by concrete and asphalt.
- Gardens near waterways such as rivers, bays, and streams as well as the Atlantic Ocean tend to stay warmer in winter and are slower to heat in summer.
- Plants along south- and west-facing walls get extra warmth in winter but also are more prone to sun and heat stress in summer.
- Plants along eastern walls or on the east side of hedges usually weather cold winter wind best because they're protected from northwesterly winter winds.

The better you're able to observe, recognize, and address these microclimates, the better your plants will survive and perform.

KNOW A PLANT'S NEEDS

The first step in plant care is to pick an appropriate plant for each particular site. A good strategy is to match each plant's natural environment as closely as possible. Most flowering bulbs, for example, prefer sun and well-drained soil. Astilbe, sedge, and turtlehead, on the other hand, would rather be in damp shade.

You'll have much better success with less work by identifying your conditions and matching plants to them than by buying whatever catches your eye and then trying to modify your conditions to meet their needs.

To use this approach, sketch a map of your yard. Include existing plants. Then observe each area, and mark them by differing conditions. This will help you determine what to plant where, or in the case of struggling or troubled plants, what to *move* where.

Pay attention to:

Light. Where is it sunny and where is it shady? At what time of day is it sunny and for how long? Note that afternoon sun is more potent than morning sun.

HERE'S HOW

TO CHECK THE QUALITY OF YOUR SOIL

Drainage test. Before planting, dig a hole as big as the rootball of the plant you want to plant. Fill it with water and give it twenty-four hours to drain. Then fill it again, and watch to see how many inches it drains per hour.

If it's not going down by at least 1 inch per hour, plan to "uncompact" it by adding compost or similar organic matter or by building raised beds.

Soil-texture test. Dig a tablespoon of soil and add enough water that you can roll it into a ball. If you can't form a ball, the soil is sandy.

Next, squeeze the ball between your thumb and index finger to make a ribbon. The longer the ribbon goes before cracking, the more clay you have. Less than 2 inches is a good composition. More than 2 inches means the soil is clayish and would benefit from compost or similar organic matter.

Jar test. Dig 2 to 3 cups of soil from 6 to 8 inches deep in your planting bed. Dry it on newspaper for twenty-four hours. Use a sieve or colander to sift out rocks, roots, and other debris.

Pour 2 cups of the sifted soil into a quart jar or clean mayonnaise jar and add 1 tablespoon of powdered detergent. Fill the jar with water, seal, and shake vigorously for three minutes.

After one hour, the biggest sand particles will settle into a bottom layer. After two hours, the slightly smaller silt particles will settle into a second layer. After twenty-four hours, the smallest clay particles will settle into a third layer.

Measure the thickness of each layer and the total depth. To figure the percentage of each layer, divide that layer's thickness by the total depth. (Example: If all three layers total 3 inches and 2 inches of that is the clay layer, then about 66 percent of your soil is clay.)

Ideally, all three layers will be about the same. If any exceed 60 percent, that type is becoming undesirably dominant, and amending with organic matter is advised.

Moisture. Are some areas damper than others? Where does water run in a rain? How long does it take to dry afterward? Are overhangs or structures blocking any areas of rain? Do any low-lying areas collect rain?

Soil. You may not have consistent soil quality or nutrition throughout the landscape. Do a soil test in differing areas to get a read on major plant nutrients as well as each area's acidity level (pH).

Also do one or more do-it-yourself checks of your soil's quality and drainage ability. (See "Here's How to Check the Quality of Your Soil.")

Wind. Succulents and other plants adapted to dry and windy climates do fine out in the open. Others need wind protection, especially borderline-hardy broadleaf evergreens that can take a beating in windy spots during a cold winter.

What's nearby. Scope out the surrounding area and make note of features that impact your plants and their care. This includes hot spots such as driveways and asphalt roads; nearby trees with encroaching roots; utility boxes that might limit plant choices; trees such as walnut or butternut that inhibit the growth of many species; and the presence of deer, rabbits, groundhogs, voles, and other plant-raiding critters.

SELECTING PLANTS

Don't fall for a plant simply because it's trendy, on sale, or gorgeous! Maybe you'll get lucky and guess right. Maybe not. Increase your success odds by replacing guesswork with homework.

Aim for many different kinds of plants—trees, shrubs, bulbs, perennials—and lots of varieties of each. The more diverse your plant selection, the more host plants you'll have for beneficial organisms and insects that protect plants from predators.

Start with plants rated for your USDA zone. Plant borderline-hardy species in your most protected microclimates. Or accept that these may die back to the ground or croak some years.

Lean toward varieties that have been bred or selected for bug- and disease-resistance. This alone can go a long way toward eliminating spraying.

Choose plants that solve landscape problems rather than create new ones, such as species that will grow over into your neighbors' space or block your view as you back your car out of the driveway.

■ *Plants, such as these hostas, soften the look of and add color to rock walls.*

And pick plants that match the available size so you don't end up spending more time with your pruners than your significant other. Most pruning work isn't done because the plant or the gardener enjoy it; it's done to keep a too-big plant from overgrowing a too-small space.

DON'T CALL ME DIRT

Many homes built since the 1950s are on land that's been heavily graded. During construction, topsoil is often removed, saved, and reapplied only several inches thick after the home is built. While that may suit home construction, it results in layered, compacted soil that's difficult for plants.

Whether your soil flunked the good-soil tests for that reason or another, you may need to amend it by adding nutrients and air spaces that allow roots to "breathe."

■ *The soil in many subdivisions has been compacted during construction—a trait that's good for building but not so good for plant roots.*

The best way to do that is by working 2 to 3 inches of compost, mushroom soil, chopped leaves, rotted cow manure and/or similar organic matter into at least the top 10 or 12 inches of the existing soil. That works out to about 20 to 25 percent "good stuff" worked into your lousy existing stuff.

It's best to prepare whole beds rather than dig individual holes for each plant. That results in uniform soil throughout, allowing plant roots free reign to spread unimpeded in all directions. When you're done, you'll have slightly raised beds that taper down to ground level around the edges.

If you're planting a single tree or large shrub in a hole instead of planting a bed, add no more than 10 percent organic matter. Why? If you greatly improve the soil in a small hole, tree and shrub roots will grow out until they hit the unimproved "real-world" soil, then turn back inward where the going is easier. Also, water can back up in the improved hole when it hits the surrounding slower-draining, compacted soil, leading to rotted roots. If you must plant in a single hole, make the hole at least three times as wide as the rootball.

Follow these four ways to keep the soil in good shape in the long run:

- Maintain the soil's acidity and nutrition at optimal levels.
- Avoid digging/tilling soil when it's wet.
- Annually top garden beds with mulch, compost, leaves or similar organic matter.
- Limit use of herbicides, fungicides, insecticides, and other "cides" to what's absolutely necessary.

DIGGING: WHEN TO DO IT

Digging new beds can be done anytime the ground isn't frozen or wet enough that you'll ruin the soil structure.

Fall is one of the best times. The ground is typically warm and fairly dry, plus it's more pleasant then for the gardener than during a 99-degree summer heat wave.

Spring is another good time to prepare a new bed. Just wait long enough so the soil is not too cold and wet from snow melt or spring rains.

Midsummer isn't ideal for planting because of the heat and usually drier conditions, but that doesn't mean you can't dig then. If you don't mind the heat, do your digging and soil work to get the beds ready in summer. Add mulch, and walk away to plant later when the heat breaks in September.

The September to October time frame is one of two ideal planting windows in the mid-Atlantic region. The other is early-to-mid spring—from right after the ground thaws through May.

Plants grown in containers can be planted anytime from early spring through October, or maybe longer if fall is warm. Be sure to keep any summer-planted fare well watered. Consistently damp soil is critical in those first six weeks after planting.

Most plants do well whether planted in spring or fall. The exceptions are cold-sensitive species that would rather not experience a cold winter until their roots are more fully established. These include camellia, crape myrtle, nandina, cherry laurel, osmanthus, cedar, sweetbox, aucuba, skimmia, or any plant with which you're pushing the winter-hardiness envelope. Spring planting is better for those.

WATCH THE SIZES

Don't space plants based on how they look now. Consider eventual sizes. Unlike sofas and tables in your indoor designing, a new plant doesn't stay that size for long.

Gauge plant spacing by the mature sizes listed on the plant tag. Keep in mind that these are sizing guides at a fixed point in time, often five or ten years down the road. Plants may slow in growth rates as they age, but *they never stop growing*—until they're dead.

A few spacing guidelines:

- When planting next to a wall or property line, take the listed width and divide in half. Plant no closer than that distance. (Example: A holly that will grow to be 8 feet around should be planted a *minimum* of 4 feet away from a wall.)

■ *The plants in this landscape are an appropriate size for the house.*

■ *Don't waste water by sprinkling more on pavement than on the lawn or garden beds.*

- To determine how close to place plants to one another, space them the mature width apart. (Example: Plant 4-foot-wide spireas no closer than 4 feet apart.) If two plants of differing sizes are going next to one another, add the two mature widths together and divide in half to determine minimum spacing. (Example: A 6-foot-wide viburnum and a 4-foot-wide spirea should be planted no closer than 5 feet apart. 6 + 4 = 10 ÷ 2 = 5.)
- Planning for height is easier. If your windowsill is 3 feet off the ground and you don't want to obstruct the view, look for plants that list out at 3 feet tall—unless you plan to do regular trimming.

In borders and foundation plantings, arrange your plants so that the tallest plants are in the back and the shorter ones in front. In an island bed in which you'll be able to view your plants from all angles, go with the tallest plants toward the middle and the shorter ones around the perimeter.

PLANTING
Past planting advice often suggested heavily amending planting holes, adding a layer of stone for drainage under the rootballs, and immediately pruning top growth to balance out with roots lost in digging and transplanting.

Current tree-planting advice now suggests planting in unimproved soil (unless it's atrocious, as described in this introduction), digging holes no deeper than the rootball, planting on solid ground without stones underneath, and *not* pruning off any healthy, unbroken limbs.

More emphasis is also being placed on way-too-common counterproductive practices, such as planting too deeply, failing to correct matted or circling roots before planting, failing to remove potentially strangulating ropes and strings, and packing mulch high up against trunks. (See March's "Here's How To Plant a Tree" for more tree-planting details.)

WATERING
Even though the mid-Atlantic region usually receives adequate rainfall over the year, rain doesn't always fall at regular intervals. That means supplemental watering is often necessary.

Plants' moisture needs vary, and soils vary in their ability to hold it. Changing weather is another variable. More water is needed during hot, dry, windy spells than during cool, cloudy spells.

That's why the answer to the question, "How much should I water?" is, "It depends."

Keep these principles in mind:

- New plants need more frequent watering than mature ones because their root systems haven't yet spread to "mine" moisture efficiently.
- Water enough so that the soil is damp beyond the reach of the roots and to just below their depth. Young plants need less total water, and they need it fairly close to the plant's base. Maturing plants need more total water over a wider area. It does little good to wet just the mulch or top inch of soil.
- Don't water at such a high rate that the water runs off instead of soaks in. Slow it to a trickle if necessary to keep it all on target.
- Don't overdo it. The goal is consistently damp soil, not soggy soil (unless you're growing bog plants).
- Water the *soil* rather than the plant. Wet leaves encourage disease.
- Sandy soil dries faster and requires more frequent watering. Clay soil holds water longer and requires less watering, but it's more at risk of leading to rotting roots.
- Water lawns deeply but not often—if you water them at all. Lawns often go brown and dormant in mid-Atlantic summers, but established ones usually recover well even after a month of no water in a dormant state.

FERTILIZING

One size does not fit all here. The only sure way to know what particular fertilizer your landscape needs (if any) is to test the soil. Inexpensive test kits are available at garden centers and County Extension offices. These give important information on your soil's acidity level (pH) and nutrient status, such as if it contains enough phosphorus, potassium, and calcium.

These are some good fertilizing principles:

- Maintain the correct soil pH to ensure optimum effectiveness of fertilizer.
- Every year, topdress your garden beds and lawns with organic material such as bark mulch, compost, pine needles, or leaves.
- Use slow-acting fertilizers for long-term, consistent nutrition over many weeks.
- Fertilize just before or during the growing season, not when plants are dormant or when the soil is frozen.
- Recognize that different plants have different nutrient needs and therefore may need different fertilizers. That's where your soil test helps.

PRUNING, PRIMPING, PROTECTING

Pruning done at the correct time fosters thick growth and prolific blooming and fruiting. It can bring back a plant from old age, forestall disease, or create an espaliered work of art.

When done improperly or at the wrong time, pruning can ruin the next bloom season or even kill a plant. Woody plants such as trees, shrubs, and vines are most often pruned to control size, but the irony is that pruning incorrectly can stimulate plant growth.

A few pruning principles to note are:

- *Always* have a pruning goal, and time the procedure correctly. The month-by-month pruning tips throughout this book will help you keep track of this.
- Keep your pruners, loppers, saws, and mower blades sharp.
- Remove injured and diseased plant parts promptly.
- Disinfect pruning equipment used on diseased plants. A mix of 1 part bleach to 9 parts water is an effective homemade solution.
- Move plants that need constant size-control pruning to a larger space.

Besides pruning off or cutting back branches, landscapes can be kept in peak form by several other types of "cuts."

One is *deadheading*, which involves snipping off spent flower heads. This neatens the look of the garden, prevents unwanted seeding, and encourages repeat bloom. (See August's "Here's How To Deadhead Flowers.") Snipping off ratty leaves throughout the season is another good primping endeavor. It also aids plant health by getting rid of foliage that was discolored due to disease.

Most perennial flowers benefit from periodic division. This involves digging up plant clumps that are dying in the center or spreading into unwanted areas. The dug clumps are divided into healthy, smaller clumps, then replanted to keep plant spread in check or to expand a variety into a new area. (See April's "Here's How To Divide Perennials.")

One other form of cutting is using a sharp tool to "edge" garden beds. This involves trimming off grass or weeds that are encroaching mulched and planted beds. Long-handled, half-moon-shaped edging tools are available to do this deed, but a flat edged spade or a power edger also works well.

Finally, think about protection for plants that need some extra TLC. Good plant selection will limit the need for much of this, but even the toughest native plants aren't exactly "native" to the contrived environment that is now your yard.

Some protection examples include:

- Stake plants that are vulnerable to injury by wind, rain, and people.
- Know which potential pest problems affect your plants. Be ready to use controls when necessary.
- Observe and inspect plants regularly for pest problems and signs of stress.
- Separate temporary or cosmetic plant problems from serious ones, and treat the serious ones as soon as possible.
- Fence out critters.
- Mulch plants to buffer soil-temperature extremes around their roots.
- Overwinter tender plants in frost-free areas, and protect borderline-hardy ones with burlap wind barriers.

- Acclimate plants gradually to indoor or outdoor sites rather than suddenly moving them.

That'll do it. Now you're ready to get out there and whack, deadhead, and dig with the best of them, but more important, to sniff, ogle, and enjoy what you (and Mother Nature) have created.

■ *Keep sidewalks clear by using a power edger to cut a sharp edge along the grass.*

HOW TO USE THIS BOOK

Try not to look at *Mid-Atlantic Month-by-Month Gardening* as a very long to-do list. You won't/don't have to do everything listed, and nothing cataclysmic will happen if you fail to carry out the exact details at the assigned time.

The idea is to help you garden more efficiently and become more confident in knowing your way around the yard. You'll get best use of the book by referring to each section as needed as the months go by.

Once you get through it two or three times, you'll likely need to refer to the book less and less. You'll just *know* what to do when—which is good because the book should be dirty and dog-eared by then.

Under each month, the work is divided into six main categories:

PLAN covers the getting-ready or "cerebral" part, such as prioritizing new projects, deciding on plants to be added or moved, and gathering supplies.

PLANT gives you details on when to plant which plants and how to do the deed correctly.

CARE tells you what do to keep your yard and plants looking their best, including mulching, controlling weeds, and knowing when and how to prune.

WATER is a rundown on how to deliver the right amount of moisture to each type of plant in the different seasons, both indoors and out.

FERTILIZE tells you when to fertilize which plants and how to know what kind and how much nutrition to deliver.

PROBLEM-SOLVE helps you figure out what might go wrong, which problems you can ignore, what to do about ones you shouldn't ignore, and early signs of trouble.

Under each of those six categories are seven sub-categories that break down the basic jobs, plant type by plant type.

The **All** category covers the more general tasks, while the five other categories cover **Annuals & Tropicals** (including annual vines), **Bulbs** (both winter-hardy and tender summer bloomers), **Lawns, Perennials & Groundcovers** (including ornamental grasses), **Shrubs** (both flowering and evergreen as well as roses and woody vines), and **Trees** (both flowering and evergreen).

The back of the book offers a few additional details, including how to determine how many plants and how much soil or mulch you need and a glossary to help you decipher gardening terms.

USDA PLANT HARDINESS ZONES

The U.S. Department of Agriculture divides the United States into Plant Hardiness Zones based on each area's average lowest winter temperature.

The four states (Virginia, West Virginia, Maryland, Delaware) and District of Columbia covered in *Mid-Atlantic Month-by-Month Gardening* encompass six of those zones, ranging from average lows of -10 to -15 degrees Fahrenheit in the mountainous reaches of West Virginia (Zone 5b) to the "balmy" average lows of 10 to 15 degrees above zero in the southeast coastal area of Virginia (Zone 8a).

Most of the mid-Atlantic region falls in the moderate Zones 6b to 7a, meaning winter lows typically bottom out no lower than a range of -5 to 5 degrees Fahrenheit.

Keep in mind those are *averages* and that the current 2012 USDA map is based on temperatures recorded between 1976 and 2005—levels that were warmer than in the previous 30-year measurement period. Many winters never reach even those lows, meaning it's possible to grow plants rated for warmer zones. However, it's also possible for a rogue winter to go *below* the average, killing plants that normally survive.

To determine your exact USDA Plant Hardiness Zone, visit the USDA's Plant Hardiness Zone Map site online at www.planthardiness.ars.usda.gov and type your zip code in the "Find" box at the top, or check out this map.

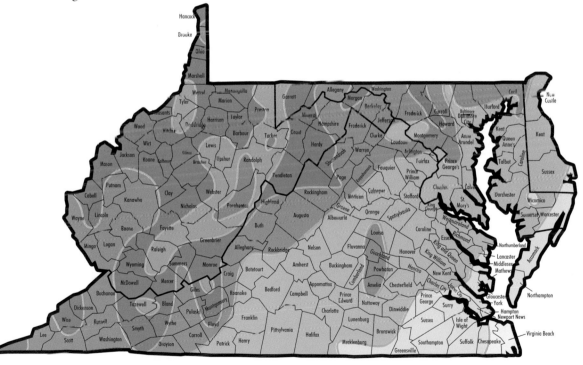

ZONE	Average Minimum Temperature	ZONE	Average Minimum Temperature
5A	-15 to -20	7A	5 to 0
5B	-10 to -15	7B	10 to 5
6A	-5 to -10	8A	15 to 10
6B	0 to -5		

January

January is downtime in the mid-Atlantic landscape . . . for the most part. Some years, when the heart of winter delivers a thaw and periods of temperatures in the 50s and 60s, it's possible to get out and get a few "gardeny" things done.

Winter weeds can be pulled. Broken branches and other debris can be whisked away. And edging the beds is a breeze in thawed, winter-softened turf. Other times, it's either too cold to stay out for long, or our plants are buried under a layer of frigid, white "mulch."

Though mid-Atlantic gardeners might not always welcome it, snow is generally a good thing for plants—in reasonable amounts. Snow makes an excellent insulator to protect plant crowns, roots, and broadleaf evergreen foliage from the damaging blows of polar-vortex intrusions. The occasional snow dumps that happen when a nor'easter storm meets polar air, on the other hand, are a different story. The weight of this heavy snow can cause our Leyland cypresses to sag and our white pine branches to snap.

Worse still are sporadic ice storms that can bring down whole trees. Trying to remove snowy and icy burdens not only is difficult or futile, the effort may do more harm than good. Whacking ice-laden junipers with a shovel (yeah, it's been done) is likely to snap off branches rather than rescue them.

That's why veteran gardeners usually figure that January is most productive when devoted to planning. It's a good month to curl up next to a fireplace with a how-to book or seed catalog and dream about the garden-to-be.

Use this time to think back to last year's successes, failures, and postponements. Assess what worked, what didn't, and what you can/should do differently.

- Sketch out some ideas on paper.
- Make a to-do list to help you hit the ground running when the white mulch gives way to green grass.
- Jot down plants you'd like to try.

Put this out-of-garden time to good use. Especially as you age, you might become grateful for a slower-paced mid-Atlantic January.

PLAN

ALL

Start a garden journal. Items to record throughout the year are: the weather, what blooms or leafs when, new plants and their names, lessons learned, ideas to consider, and sketches of what's planted where.

Tackle jobs you'll be too busy to do come spring. Clean and sharpen those tools. Catch up on that pile of gardening books and magazines. Clean your stored pots to get them ready for spring planting. Paint wooden tool handles a bright color so you're less likely to lose them in the bushes.

Study your winter landscape from inside various windows. How can you improve this overlooked fourth season of the landscape? How about winterberry hollies and red-twig dogwoods in front of that evergreen screen planting? Maybe an arbor or bench could add hardscape winter interest. Or maybe you just need a few more evergreens to add winter life to the dormant perennial gardens.

ANNUALS & TROPICALS

Inventory leftover seeds and determine which ones are good for another year. Most will last two or three years if they're kept dry and away from temperature extremes. To test viability, roll up a few in a damp paper towel, place the towel in a plastic bag, and set in a warm area for the germination time listed on the seed packet. If few to none have sprouted when you open the towel, toss the pack and buy fresh.

Buy or order seeds—both those to be started inside and those to be direct-seeded in spring. The best selection is now. Some of the easiest annual flowers to start from seed are marigolds, zinnias, sunflowers, bachelor buttons, nasturtiums, cosmos, cleome, and hyacinth beans.

It's a little early to start most seeds inside in most of the region (cold-tolerant species such as pansies, calendula, and snapdragons excepted), but you *can* get ready. Clean and sterilize used trays and seed-starting packs in a solution of 1 part bleach to 9 parts water. Or buy new ones. Are your lights in working order? Do you have enough seed-starting mix? Are your plant labels ready?

BULBS

Some of the earliest spring bulbs, such as snowdrops and winter aconite, may bloom this month, especially in the region's warmer Zones 7 and 8. If you don't have any, make note to plant some this fall to add color to next year's winter landscape.

Summer-flowering bulbs, such as lilies, dahlias, and cannas, operate on a different schedule. They're best planted in spring rather than fall. Check the catalogs for any you'd like to try.

LAWNS

If you didn't already do it at the end of last season, clean your mower, sharpen the blades, change the oil, and get a new sparkplug. The gas tank was drained, right?

Are you tired of mowing? Consider turning some lawn into tree-covered sitting spaces or gardens for wildlife.

PERENNIALS & GROUNDCOVERS

Check your notes from last season, and nail down specifics of what perennial flowers and groundcovers are to be moved or added this spring. Make a list for plant-shopping time.

■ *Too much lawn to mow? Consider converting some of your green ocean into garden beds.*

HERE'S HOW

TO START SEEDS INSIDE

You don't need a greenhouse, light contraption, or even special "grow lights" to start plants from seed.

1. Clean and label plant trays or used plastic containers, such as margarine tubs or cut-off milk containers. Drill eight or ten small holes in the bottom of each for drainage.

2. Fill each container two-thirds full with vermiculite (light, fluffy, water-holding stuff available at garden centers). Scatter seeds over the surface, and cover with a light layer of more vermiculite. Seed packs will tell you the depth to cover the seeds.

3. Place the containers on a clean foam meat tray from the grocery store or in a plastic seedling tray. *Gently* sprinkle with water until the vermiculite is saturated and draining out the bottom.

4. Lay plastic wrap over the containers. Set the trays near a sunny window at room temperature. For varieties that prefer warmer germination temperatures, use a store-bought seedling heat mat or set it on top of a water heater or refrigerator. Within five to seven days, some varieties will emerge. Others may take up to three weeks. Check moisture every few days and lightly re-wet the surface if it's drying.

5. Once the first set of leaves unfurl, use a pencil or similar pointy object to transfer each seedling into labeled, individual pots filled three-quarters full with moistened, lightweight potting mix from the garden center. For smaller plants, use recycled plastic six-packs from past plant purchases. Clean and soak these in a 10-percent bleach solution for fifteen minutes before using. For bigger plants, use recycled 4-inch pots. (When moving the seedlings, handle by the *leaves*, not the stems.)

6. Set the planted packs and pots in plastic seedling trays under fluorescent workshop lights for about fourteen hours per day; a timer makes it automatic. A cool basement or room with temperatures in the 50s is ideal for most seedlings and promotes stocky growth. Hang the lights from chains and hooks so you can keep the lights 2 or 3 inches above the plants.

7. Add water with a balanced, water-soluble fertilizer mixed at quarter-strength to the trays, not over the tops of the plants. Add enough so the plants soak up the water in fifteen or twenty minutes. This "bottom-watering" is less disturbing to roots and less likely to promote disease. Check every few days and add more water when the surface is drying and the tray's weight is noticeably lighter.

8. Once the seedlings reach transplant size, take them outside to "harden off." Set them in shade for a couple of hours the first day, then gradually give more light and more time out until they're outside round the clock for two or three days before planting.

SHRUBS

Evaluate your landscape's winter-interest shrubbery, both by taking a walk around the yard and looking out key windows. Can you even *see* shrubs out the windows, or are they crowded up against the house?

Do your shrubs have ornamental features to relieve winter bleakness, such as berries, cones, interesting bark, and/or colorful evergreen foliage? Do you have a variety of sizes and shapes? Are there enough evergreens, or are you leaning too heavily on flowering shrubs that drop their leaves in winter?

Evergreen shrubs are useful both for screening unwanted views and for blocking cold winter winds. The north and northwest exposures of your house are the best locations for blocking those arctic prevailing winds.

Don't overlook roses in the landscape. They come in many different types, colors, sizes, and habits. Not all require high care. New varieties of hybrid teas are more disease resistant than ever. Shrub types perform well on sunny banks and other hot spots. Climbers are naturals on arbors. And miniature roses are worthy choices for balconies and window boxes.

Vines on a trellis add screening where you need height but don't have much horizontal space. Examples are narrow side yards between homes, between decks in condo and apartment complexes, in skinny beds along sidewalks, and around heat pumps and trashcans.

TREES

Spruce, fir, pine, arborvitae, holly, and Japanese red cedar are choices that can grow tall enough to give wind protection even to the second floor of your house. Evergreen trees provide wind protection for a distance twice as far out as their height. For example, a line of 25-foot spruces can protect areas up to 50 feet away on their down-wind side.

Do you have a few "specimen" evergreens to add winter interest and focal points out key windows? Good examples are weeping Alaska cedar, Japanese umbrella pine, weeping Norway spruce, and golden Hinoki cypress.

Consider ornamental trees with interesting bark for winter interest. Examples include stewartia, birch, crape myrtle, and paperbark maple. Others offer interesting branching patterns when the tree is bare, such as Japanese maple, weeping beech, and Kousa dogwood.

PLANT

ALL

Other than burying those forgotten bulbs from fall (see Bulbs, below), January is not prime time for planting anything else. You might see landscapers inserting trees or shrubs. Plants will do their best to survive this timing, but the survival odds are lower in winter than when the soil is warmer and when water (the unfrozen kind) is more available to roots.

ANNUALS & TROPICALS

■ *Don't overlook the houseplants section of your favorite retailer—they often have many tropicals that can be acclimated to the outdoors later.*

Visit the houseplant section of your favorite garden center. Not only is it a warm, bright and plant-filled getaway, but houseplant selection and sales are abundant this month. Many houseplants serve double-duty by brightening your living room in winter, then becoming an outdoor flowerpot centerpiece in summer.

BULBS

Uh-oh! Found a few packs of spring-flowering bulbs that you bought but forgot to plant in fall? Better to get them in the ground ASAP rather than wait until spring or next fall. They'll likely dry out and die by then. Plant them now, even if you have to hack through frozen ground.

It's not too late to force amaryllis or paperwhite narcissus bulbs indoors. These need no chill period (as do the bulbs you planted outdoors in fall), and you might find post-holiday bargains at stores. (See December's "Here's How To Grow Amaryllis Inside.")

LAWNS

Winter-sowing of cool-season grass seed (Kentucky bluegrass, perennial ryegrass, and tall or fine fescue) isn't optimal but is possible if the soil is thawed. (Seed scattered over the surface of frozen soil can wash away in a heavy January rain.) Scratch the seed into the surface and top lightly with straw. The seed won't germinate until the soil warms to about 50 degrees Fahrenheit in spring, assuming birds didn't eat it.

PERENNIALS & GROUNDCOVERS

Enjoy your perennials that stay evergreen most winters (helleborus, coral-bells, and dianthus, for example), but wait until early spring to transplant existing ones or plant new ones.

SHRUBS

Cut branches taken late this month from early-blooming shrubs such as forsythia, fothergilla, witch hazel, and bridal wreath spirea can be "forced" into blooming in a vase inside for winter color. (See "Here's How to Force Shrub Cuttings.")

Roses that were forced into bloom for holiday sales shouldn't go in the ground yet. Grow them as houseplants next to a sunny window the remainder of winter, then plant outside in late April through mid-May after gradually acclimating them over a seven- to ten-day period.

Install trellises, arbors, and similar vine supports when the soil is thawed over winter, but wait until spring to plant the vines.

TREES

Cut branches from early-blooming trees such as cornelian cherry dogwood and filbert also can be forced to bloom in a vase inside.

Wait until late March or April to plant new trees. They'll establish better. One exception: if you bought a live, balled-and-burlapped evergreen as a Christmas tree, get that in the ground as soon after Christmas as possible.

CARE

ALL

If you don't have at least an inch or two of mulch over your garden beds, and snow isn't insulating the

HERE'S HOW

TO FORCE SHRUB CUTTINGS

"Forcing" branches is the technique of cutting live branches from trees and shrubs and causing them to bloom inside in winter in a vase.

1. Plants that work best are those that naturally flower before May, such as fruit trees, azalea, dogwood, redbud, witch hazel, forsythia, and fothergilla. These are species that produce their flower buds the previous year.

2. On an above-freezing day, cut 1- to 3-foot sections off the ends of branches that are a ½-inch in diameter or less. Look for wood with plump buds, which are flowering buds. (Leaf buds are skinnier.)

3. Plunge the cut ends into a bucket with 6 to 8 inches of very warm water—100 to 110 degrees Fahrenheit is ideal. Soak for at least six hours.

4. After soaking, cut an inch off the bottoms at an angle and arrange the branches in a water-filled vase at room temperature. Maximize display life by adding floral preservative or antibacterial mouthwash (diluted to 1 tablespoon of mouthwash per quart of water).

5. Change water and preservative every three or four days. Most branches will bloom in two to four weeks, with the earliest natural bloomers taking the least amount of time to open.

ground, consider January mulching (if you can get mulch now). Your neighbors will think you're nuts, but mulching frozen ground helps *keep* it frozen, sidestepping the fluctuating temperatures that can cause plants to "heave" upward and expose roots.

Can't get mulch? January is a good month to chip saved yard trimmings if you have a chipper-shredder.

Take advantage of thaws to edge garden beds. Turf cuts easily when it's soft and damp in winter.

Go easy on rock salt used to melt ice. The salty runoff can end up in lawns and planted beds where excess sodium impedes water uptake. That can lead to browning of leaf tips and leaf edges, especially in hot, dry weather. Instead of rock salt, consider manually removing ice or improving traction by scattering gritty material, such as sand. Do not use potentially polluting fertilizer as an ice-melt.

ANNUALS & TROPICALS
Pinch back annuals you've potted for overwintering indoors if they're getting spindly (that is, "leggy.") These like bright windows or supplemental light.

BULBS
Don't panic if crocus, daffodil, or other bulb foliage is emerging. There's no need to pile more mulch on the foliage for protection. At worst, freezing temperatures might brown the foliage tips, but the bulbs will develop additional leaves and bloom just fine. Hardy bulbs have a lot of experience with winter weather.

When amaryllis bulbs finish blooming, cut off the flower stalks. Treat it as a houseplant the rest of winter—watering when the soil goes dry, displaying it next to a sunny window, and fertilizing monthly with a balanced houseplant fertilizer (10-10-10). After danger of frost, gradually acclimate the plant to the outside over seven to ten days, then either grow it as a potted plant outside or plant it in the ground over summer. If you *don't* plan to keep your amaryllis, toss the bulb when the flower show ends.

LAWNS
It's normal even for cool-season turfgrasses to lose their rich green color in winter. The lawn will turn green when warm weather returns. Fertilizing now is not the answer.

Avoid walking on frozen grass. You may smash the frozen blades and damage the crowns, which is the point from which new blades emerge.

Stay off soggy or wet lawns in winter to the extent possible to avoid compacting the soil.

Don't worry if your zoysia-grass lawn looks dead. It's a warm-season grass and can spend five or six months of the year dormant and looking straw brown in cold-winter climates. It'll be green by May.

■ *Certain lawn grass varieties, like zoysia, are dormant in the winter.*

PERENNIALS & GROUNDCOVERS
Newly planted perennials and groundcovers are particularly prone to heaving during winter freezes and thaws. They're not yet fully rooted. During January thaws, check for perennial clumps sporting exposed roots and tamp them back down. Add an inch or two of mulch or fallen leaves around them to lessen the odds of a repeat.

Let perennials and ornamental grasses stand for another month or two. Seedheads offer a food source for overwintering birds, while dried grass stems are a favorite nest-building material. If blades are blowing around and driving you crazy, go ahead and cut the clumps to a stub.

SHRUBS

Limit pruning to injured and broken branches. Make clean cuts back to where the branch joins with a larger branch or main stem. Don't gouge into wood on the main branch or trunk. Leave the wound as is to heal in the air. No need to paint or apply tar.

If heavy snow is sagging apart your yews, boxwoods, rhododendrons, hollies, and other evergreens, it's usually best to do nothing. Most plants will spring back from moderate snow-load pressure when the snow melts and the weather warms. If you're crossing the line from sagging to snapping, use a soft implement such as a broom to *gently* release the snow with an upward motion.

Climbing roses can be pruned this month.

Clip broken branches from woody vines anytime. Clean cuts prevent further tears on the bark and heal faster.

TREES

Evergreen trees may brown around the leaf edges during cold blasts, while wind gusts that follow ice storms can rip off limbs, especially from brittle-wooded species such as white pine, birch, flowering pear, Chinese elm, poplar, willow, and locust. There's not much you can do about any of that, other than remove some of the low-hanging snow loads that you can reach from the ground (with that same upward motion of the broom that you used on the shrubs).

Cut broken branches that you can reach from the ground back to healthy joints. No ladder-and-chainsaw attempts! Call a trained, insured pro to handle any higher hanging limbs—as soon as possible for ones over areas of heavy traffic.

Prune deciduous trees that get "sappy" when you cut them in spring. Six that fall into this category are maple, birch, dogwood, yellowwood, snowbell, and elm. (See February's "Here's How To Prune a Tree.")

WATER

ALL

Hoses can be safely packed away most winters. The exception is an unusually dry, windy winter with little to no snow. In that case, some landscape plants benefit from a soaking or two during thaws. Broadleaf evergreens (which lose more moisture in winter than any other plant) are tops on the list, followed by needled evergreens and also trees, shrubs, vines, and perennials that you've planted in the last year or two.

Gauge water needs by inserting the probe of a water meter into the soil, about 6 inches deep. Or check by inserting your index finger into the thawed ground.

Indoors, dry air from heating systems can be eased by a room humidifier, by clustering plants closer together, by setting dry-sensitive plants in the kitchen or bathroom, or by setting plants on shallow trays of damp gravel.

ANNUALS & TROPICALS

Water houseplants, overwintering tropicals, and potted annuals when the soil surface dries and your pots feel noticeably lighter. Once a week usually does it. Don't overwater. Water demands go down in the low-light, slow-growing conditions of winter. Soggy soil is the leading cause of houseplant death.

Misting plants doesn't counteract dry indoor air. It might keep them clean (and encourage leaf disease),

■ *If heavy ice is weighing down the branches of your evergreens, leave them alone. The danger of branches snapping from the weight is too great to try to remove it.*

but research has found misting offers little to no benefit when it comes to a plant's humidity needs.

■ *Setting indoor plants on a bed of gravel with water can slightly increase humidity.*

BULBS

Water indoor potted bulbs such as amaryllis, paperwhites, and hyacinths when the soil surface dries and the pots become noticeably lighter, assuming you plan to keep them going. If not, toss the bulbs when the flowers finish.

There's no need to water bulbs planted outdoors.

LAWNS

No water is needed, even in a dry January. Turfgrass is dormant.

PERENNIALS, GROUNDCOVERS, SHRUBS, TREES & VINES

Those planted in the last year or two might benefit from a soaking during a January thaw if the soil is unusually dry and snowless. That's especially helpful for broadleaf evergreens, such as cherry laurel, aucuba, nandina, osmanthus, holly, hardy camellia, and sweetbox.

FERTILIZE

ALL

Put away the fertilizer for outside plants until at least the end of winter. It's wasteful to your wallet and harmful to waterways to apply fertilizer over frozen ground, only to have it carried away by winter rains or melting snow.

Indoors, fertilizer needs are low during this limited-light, slow-growing time. Overfertilizing plants that don't need it is also wasteful and potentially counterproductive to healthy growth.

ANNUALS & TROPICALS

A balanced fertilizer once a month is typically adequate for your houseplants and overwintering tropicals. This includes poinsettias, which should continue holding their color all month.

BULBS

Bulbs come packaged with their own "fertilizer" in the form of stored energy. Those that are potted for forced bloom will have enough to produce blooms this season. If you plan to keep potted bulbs for another season or plan to plant hardy ones outside in spring (hyacinths, tulips, or daffodils, for example), fertilize monthly with a balanced, water-soluble fertilizer formulated for bulbs.

LAWNS

Wait until the ground thaws in March to apply the season's first treatment, if needed. Lawn fertilizing is banned in Maryland this month and anytime the ground is frozen.

PERENNIALS, GROUNDCOVERS, SHRUBS, TREES & VINES

No fertilizer is needed now; wait until the end of winter.

PROBLEM-SOLVE

ALL

January is one the worst months for deer browsing—especially when snow cover hides alternative food sources and makes landscape plants the main dish. If you're depending on repellents to keep hungry deer from eating favorites such as arborvitae, yew, azalea, rhododendron, and even jaggy hollies and roses, reapply your favorite product according to label directions.

ANNUALS & TROPICALS

Stressed indoor plants are more vulnerable to bug damage. New seedlings and young plants are especially at risk if pest insects managed to ride

■ *Hungry deer will eat anything and everything.*

inside over winter. Cold drafts, insufficient light, and dry air from hot-air heat are three key indoor plant stressors.

Whiteflies, aphids, scale, mites, and mealybugs are the main five threats. Try controlling them by rinsing infested foliage and stems under the faucet or under the shower. (Yes, some gardeners regularly give their houseplants showers.) Water can wash away their waste and interrupt the insects' life cycle.

If you catch a problem early, pinch off infested or diseased leaves. Or wipe away pests with a soft rag slightly dampened with rubbing alcohol.

For major infestations, take plants outside on above-freezing days long enough to spray them with insecticidal soap, horticultural oil, or other insecticide labeled for houseplant use. Get them back inside as soon as the spray dries. Follow all label directions.

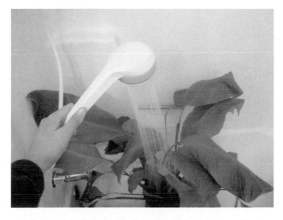

■ *Houseplants and (nearly) anything you're overwintering indoors can take a "shower" to wash off pests.*

BULBS

Check stored dahlias, callas, cannas, gladioli, and such to make sure they're not too damp and rotting. If your storage medium feels wet, replace it with drier sawdust, peat moss, or sand. Toss any bulbs showing signs of rot. Move them to a drier storage spot. If the medium is so dry that the bulbs are shriveling, slightly dampen the medium and look for a storage spot with higher humidity.

LAWNS

Voles could be doing surface-tunnel damage under a snow cover, but spring is the time to patch that with new seed. Set out cage traps or snap traps baited with peanut butter near fresh surface tunnels to capture or kill voles.

PERENNIALS & GROUNDCOVERS

Perennials and groundcovers that don't die back to the ground in winter are potential targets for deer and rodent damage over winter. Favorites are wintercreeper euonymus, strawberry, hardy geranium, spurge, and sometimes even ivy. Protect vulnerable plants by spot-fencing them with wire or plastic cylinders or by spraying repellents. Alternate repellents for best results instead of repeatedly using the same one.

SHRUBS & TREES

As food choices dwindle, deer may damage trees and shrubs they ignored earlier. It's not too late to erect fencing around targeted plants or to apply deer repellents.

Signs that deer are lurking include tender new growth nibbled from branch tips, leaving slightly ragged versus sharply cut ends; the lower stems of shrubs and trees stripped of foliage, up to the height of, say, an adult deer with its neck extended; small piles or clumps of bullet-shaped dark-brown pellets (deer poop), and/or tall weeds flattened where deer are bedding.

If you haven't done so, wrap tree trunks with plastic spiral wraps or hardware cloth to keep rodents from chewing the bark. Make sure it's high enough to account for snow that may give rodents extra lift.

February

February is when stir-crazy mid-Atlantic gardeners can be found wandering aimlessly around the houseplant section of garden centers, trying to fend off chlorophyll deprivation.

It's been three to four months now since fall frost ended the growing season. Depending on your location and winter's mercy, figure on another month until significant botanical life returns.

That doesn't mean you're reduced to twiddling your catalog-ink-stained thumbs all month. Thaws can lead to pockets of outdoor opportunity, such as pruning, bed-edging, cleaning up dead perennials, and chasing rabbits away from the overwintering parsley. Even when we're stuck inside, February is a time for getting ready. Once the weather warms enough to go outside, a flurry of job demands hit all at once.

Are your tools ready for it? Are you stocked up on fertilizer, crabgrass preventer, plant protectors, and other early-season supplies? Have you nailed down plans on what plants you're going to move, remove, or add?

Seed-starting is one actual hands-on gardening activity that hits full stride this month. It's not as hard as you might think, and you don't need expensive equipment or elaborate lighting for young flower and vegetable seedlings.

Home and garden shows pop up this month and next, offering more chlorophyll-deprivation therapy. These are like horticultural robins—the first sign that spring is near. And while you're waiting for warmth to return and the deer to find lunch elsewhere, think about public gardens you'd like to visit this year.

Choices for these inspiring, plant-idea places abound, including the coastal gem at the Norfolk Botanical Garden, Richmond's diverse Lewis Ginter Botanical Garden, Maryland's unique Ladew Topiary Garden, the native plants at Delaware's Mt. Cuba Center, and the assorted plant collections at the D.C. region's Brookside Gardens, U.S. Botanic Garden (with its native-plant-filled National Garden) and U.S. National Arboretum, the last three of which offer free admission.

Finally, be patient. Rest a spell. We're getting there. One day soon we'll be outside again in our own little botanical gardens.

PLAN

■ *Snowdrops* (Galanthus nivalis) *have earned their name!*

■ *Take this time to plan which annuals and perennials you want to plant in your borders and gardens.*

ALL

Thinking of hiring professional help for a design, a planting job, or a new paver patio this season? Make your calls now, and get on their calendar. If you wait until April like everybody else, you might run into a months-long backlog. Early-bird bid prices also may be lower.

February is a good time to assess "microclimates"— areas that are warmer, colder, drier, wetter, windier, and so forth than other parts of the yard. A masonry wall where snow melts first gives a good clue about prime spots for borderline-hardy species, for example. Snow drifts and leaf pile-ups show you where the wind blows.

ANNUALS & TROPICALS

Decide which annuals to start from seed and which you're going to buy in plant form later. Acquire your seeds now if you don't have them already.

BULBS

Snowdrops and winter aconite are the first bulbs out of the gate and should be poking up this month. What? You don't have any? Make a note to add a patch or two this October.

If you don't have a map of where hardy bulbs are planted in the yard, make one this spring as their bloom season unfolds. It'll be useful come fall planting time.

Plan where to site tender, summer-blooming bulbs later this spring, such as dahlias, gladioli, and callas. You can order these now in addition to seeds.

LAWNS

Take the lawn mower and other lawn-care equipment to the shop for servicing while it's a slow period. When grass-cutting season starts, everybody will be there, and you'll wait longer.

PERENNIALS & GROUNDCOVERS

Perennial flowers are versatile; some options include classic perennial borders with taller species

■ *Seed displays are up in February and are usually well stocked for the coming season.*

toward the back and shorter ones in front; mixed gardens or island beds of interplanted shrubs and evergreens; clusters in house-foundation beds; mass-plantings under trees, in rock gardens or in meadows; or a block-planted cutting garden of species that bloom in succession.

SHRUBS

Are some of your shrubs getting too big or are in the wrong place (not thriving, for example)? Plan to move the smaller, younger, manageable ones and to scrap and replace the hopeless hulks.

Other shrubby points to ponder: Is this the year to throw in the trowel on species the deer keep eating? Is it time to add privacy with a new hedge? What shrubs encourage birds? Do some of those new colorful-leafed beauties deserve a spot in the yard? How about some summer and fall bloomers to pick up the slack after the spring bloomers finish?

Valentine's Day is a good reminder to think about roses in the landscape. Roses come in many forms (shrub types, climbers, uprights, and so forth), and they're not limited to a dedicated rose garden. Other possibilities include colorful hedges, anchoring a mixed flower border, covering an arbor or pergola, controlling erosion on a slope, replacing lawn as a groundcover, and accenting island or border beds.

TREES

Winter is a good time to evaluate tree health because trunks and limbs are easier to see when leafless. Address signs of failure, such as newly leaning trunks, expanding cracks (especially at the juncture of large limbs or V-shaped double leaders), and rotting or sunken wood. Hire a certified arborist or experienced tree professional if you're not sure.

Is it time to remove street trees that are pushing up sidewalks, driveways, curbs, and the streets themselves? Simply sawing off big roots and replacing the concrete compromises the tree's stability. Before removing, check your municipality for street-tree rules. Some require approval for removal, and some have strict rules on which species are allowed in curbside tree lawns (if any).

Check your pruning equipment. Sharpen loppers and saws for the new season.

PLANT

ALL

Wait until next month to plant when the soil temperature becomes more agreeable to root growth.

ANNUALS & TROPICALS

Start seeds of annual flowers inside this month for annuals that you want to have ready for planting outside after frost. Allow six to ten weeks total for sprouting, grow time and gradually acclimating seedlings to the outside. That translates into early- to mid-February starts for Zones 7 and 8, and late-February to early-March starts for Zones 5 and 6. (See January's "Here's How to Start Seeds Inside.")

Seeds of fragrant sweet peas, an annual that doesn't like hot weather, can go in the ground in Zones 7 and 8 and early next month in Zones 5 and 6.

Take cuttings from last year's overwintering annuals or tropicals, such as geraniums, coleus, and begonias. Clip 3- to 4-inch stems with at least two sets of leaves. Strip off all but the top set of leaves, dip the bottom in rooting powder (available at garden centers), and plant in a lightweight, soilless mix with

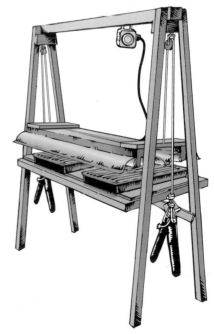

■ *It's not difficult to construct a light stand that can be adjusted as seedlings grow.*

the top set of leaves sticking out. Keep the mix damp, and you'll have rooted "babies" in a few weeks.

BULBS

Transplant or thin snowdrops and winter aconite once they're done blooming. Do it next month if the ground is frozen now.

PERENNIALS & GROUNDCOVERS

Some perennials can be started from seed—either directly in the garden in spring or ahead of time inside. Many perennials take longer to germinate and/or need a longer growing time than annuals, so February isn't too early to start most inside. Among the easier perennials to start from seed: rudbeckia, columbine, balloon flower, purple coneflower, statice, yarrow, dianthus, and Shasta daisies. (See January's "Here's How to Start Seeds Inside.")

SHRUBS & TREES

Branches cut in early February from early-blooming woody species can be "forced" to bloom in a vase for winter color indoors. Examples are apple, cherry, crabapple, ornamental pear, azalea, PJM rhododendron, dogwood, and redbud. Cuttings from beech, birch, Japanese maple, lilac, magnolia, quince, red maple, serviceberry, mock orange, and willow can be taken from mid-February on to add flower and leaf color to vase arrangements. (See January's "Here's How to Force Shrub Cuttings to Bloom Indoors.")

Although it's too early to plant roses outside, it *is* time to order roses. Suppliers ship bare-root roses starting in March.

CARE

ALL

Winter annual weeds germinate in the cold of fall and even winter, including chickweed, henbit, purple deadnettle, speedwell, and prickly lettuce. These are ones you might see looking hale and green already. Dig them as soon as you're up to it.

HERE'S HOW

TO WINTER-SOW SEEDS

Some seeds can be started outside in small containers, side-stepping the need for lighting equipment inside. It's a technique known as "winter-sowing."

1. Save gallon or half-gallon clear-plastic jugs, cut in half except at the handles to create "flip-top" containers.

2. Cut small holes or slits at the base of each corner with an X-Acto knife for drainage.

3. Add about 4 inches of seed-starting mix to each container. Dampen the mix with water, and scatter seeds on the surface. Lightly cover the seeds with the amount of mix recommended for each variety on the seed packet. Label what you've planted.

4. Use pieces of duct tape, placed vertically on two of the sides, to secure the container and create a mini-greenhouse. Set them outside with the caps off.

5. Open to sprinkle with water every few days if it's dry. As the weather warms, the seeds will sprout, and young plants will grow that can be planted in the garden.

Good annual flowers for winter sowing: Ageratum, sweet alyssum, snapdragon, calendula, celosia, cosmos, diascia, sunflower, nicotiana, cosmos, cornflower, browallia, larkspur, nigella, Joseph's coat, tithonia.

Good perennial flowers for winter sowing: Aster, astilbe, baby's-breath, gaillardia, liatris, coreopsis, gaura, penstemon, phlox, black-eyed Susan, coneflower, Shasta daisy, yarrow, carnation, coral-bells, baptisia, hollyhock, salvia, veronica.

Thawed winter soil is soft, making it easy to edge your garden beds. If you didn't get to that in January, February is another good opportunity.

During non-frigid spells, pick up twigs on lawns and debris in garden beds. Avoid walking on beds and lawns if they're wet or soggy. That compacts the soil, which impedes root growth.

■ *Chickweed is one of the earliest weeds to emerge between late winter and early spring.*

■ *Deadnettle is another common early-season weed. Pull it as soon as it emerges and before it goes to seed.*

ANNUALS & TROPICALS

Maximize houseplant bloom by displaying them away from hot spots like heater vents, TVs, and computer monitors. Also, don't display them near the fruit bowl. Ripening apples and other fruits give off ethylene, a natural gas that growers use to accelerate flower development.

Lightly trim back outdoor winter-hardy pansies and violas that are looking leggy or that have gone out of bloom over winter. These soon will flush out

with new growth and new flowers as days lengthen and temperatures warm.

To promote sturdy stems and a compact habit in cuttings taken from annuals and tropicals, pinch leggy stems. These pinchings can be rooted for even more plants.

BULBS

Don't worry if a sudden cold snap or snow arrives after you've noticed bulb tips emerging. Even early bloomers such as snowdrops and winter aconite are adapted to snow and winter cold. A scattering of leaves over the foliage protects them a bit, but the worst thing that will happen is the leaf tips will brown. The bulbs won't die.

Check stored tender bulbs such as cannas, dahlias, and gladiolas. Discard any that are mushy or dried. In another month to six weeks, you'll have the option of potting some of these inside so you'll have growing plants ready to set outside after frost.

Colchicum foliage (fall crocus) usually appears this month. The bright green leaves yellow and die back by June, then flowers poke up in September.

LAWNS

Sharp mower blades cut grass foliage cleanly rather than bludgeon its tips. Ragged tips turn brown, increase moisture loss, and make grass more prone

■ *Sharp mower blades cut the grass rather than tearing it. It's worth the effort to sharpen your mower's blades (after every twenty-five hours of use or so).*

to disease. Use February downtime to sharpen your mower blade (if you haven't done it already) so it'll be ready when the grass starts growing. Resharpen after every twenty-five hours of cutting time.

PERENNIALS & GROUNDCOVERS

Check perennials planted last fall to make sure the rootballs haven't "heaved" partly out of the ground due to freezing and thawing. Tamp them down if they're coming up. Add mulch around heaving plants if you don't have 2 inches over the soil.

Another good reason to have 2 inches of mulch over perennial beds is to prevent premature growth during a sunny, warm spell over winter. Mulch moderates temperature swings and keeps the soil more consistently cool until spring warmth arrives for good.

If you haven't cut back ornamental grasses, now's when the blades often start blowing around the yard. Let one or two clumps stand as nest-building material for birds.

SHRUBS

If heavy snow threatens to snap shrub branches, use a broom and gentle, upward motions to release snow from them. No whacking down on them with a shovel or you'll do more harm than good. Remove snow from the lower branches first so you don't overburden them by dropping more snow from the upper branches.

Removing ice from shrub branches is more difficult. You're better off letting them alone and hoping the ice doesn't build up enough to cause snapping. Ice-laden shrubs may surprise you. They may look threateningly saggy when the ice is piling up, but they usually spring back soon after the ice melts.

If the weather's decent, February is a good time to prune summer-flowering shrubs (especially in the warmer Zones 7 and 8) as well as woody vines that bloom on new wood in summer. That includes summer-flowering clematis (as well as the fall-blooming sweet autumn clematis), climbing hydrangea, climbing roses, Japanese hydrangea vine, ornamental (hardy) kiwi vine, trumpet vine, and American bittersweet. (See March's "Here's How to Prune Flowering Shrubs.")

HERE'S HOW

TO CUT ORNAMENTAL GRASSES

1. Tightly bundle grass clumps about halfway up with jute, rope, or similar strong ties.

2. Use gas-, electric-, or hand-powered shears to cut the bundle to a stub about 2 or 3 inches high. For big or tough grasses, you may need to use a chainsaw. For smaller ones, pruners are fine.

3. Bundling causes the clump to drop like a tree, keeping the blades from blowing around. Discard the bundles or run the blades through a chipper-shredder or compost or mulch.

Some wisteria varieties bloom on wood that grows in the current season; those are best pruned in winter. Some bloom on last year's growth *and* new same-season wood. And some gardeners like to prune *any* wisteria both in July and over winter to limit size. For winter wisteria pruning, thin out excess branches back to the main stem. Then shorten each "keeper" stem to 2 or 3 inches so it has two to four buds.

TREES

Check trees that were staked when planted last year. Sometimes alternate freezing and thawing loosens the soil and the supporting stakes. Pound the stakes back down if they're coming up. Also make sure the ties aren't rubbing the tender young bark. Loosen them if they are—or replace them with the wider bands you should've used in the first place.

Shade trees and species that don't flower in spring are candidates for dormant-season pruning. The branches are easier to see when leafless. If a young tree has a double trunk, cut away the less dominant one, creating a single strong trunk that lessens the likelihood of splitting. (See February's "Here's How to Prune a Tree.")

WATER

ALL
Most watering this month involves houseplants, overwintering potted annuals, and the first few "babies" you've started inside from seed. Consistently damp soil is good. Don't overdo it and rot roots. Remember, growth is slow over winter, and water demands are low.

Outside, the only time you'll have to think about watering is in an unusually dry winter with no snow cover. Then a soaking or two during thawed conditions benefits newly planted trees and shrubs, especially broadleaf evergreens.

ANNUALS & TROPICALS
Water houseplants, overwintering tropicals, and any young plants you've rooted from cuttings when the soil feels dry about 1 inch down. Water until it drains out the holes in the bottom. Pour off any standing water.

Another good way to water seedlings and rooted cuttings is by setting the pots in a tray of water. Add enough water so that the soil soaks it up within fifteen or twenty minutes. This "bottom-watering" is less disturbing to young roots and less likely to foster leaf disease than watering over the top.

Give an occasional small drink to any semi-hardy plants you're overwintering in pots in the garage, such as tender salvia, gardenia, or jasmine. The roots can use just enough moisture to keep them from drying but not enough that they attempt to push new growth yet.

BULBS
Hardy bulbs (daffodils, hyacinths, crocuses, and so forth) planted out in the yard in mulched beds need no supplemental water even if winter rain and snow are limited. Those planted in window boxes and aboveground outdoor planters are a different story. Moisture evaporates faster from those. Soak weekly when the soil is thawed and dry. Make sure containers have drainage holes so excess water or melting snow can drain.

PERENNIALS & GROUNDCOVERS
Dormant perennials use very little water. Most years, melting snow or winter rain does the deed.

SHRUBS & TREES
Mulched and established flowering trees and shrubs need no water while dormant over winter. The only exception for leaf-dropping species (lilac, weigela, hydrangea, dogwood, and so forth) is a first-year planting in an unusually dry winter when the soil isn't frozen.

Evergreens—particularly broadleaf types such as cherry laurel, camellia, and osmanthus—continue to lose moisture through their foliage all winter. They're more susceptible to dry winter soil. If the ground is dry and snowless during thawed periods, retrieve the stored hose (or a bucket) and give these a good soaking weekly until moisture returns. Newly planted broadleaf evergreens and those in windy sites are most susceptible to dry-soil trouble over winter.

FERTILIZE

ALL
It's still too early to fertilize landscape plants, such as trees, shrubs, and perennials. Definitely do *not* apply fertilizer to frozen ground. If a winter rain comes along while the product is sitting on the icy surface, it'll wash away into the sewer system, streams, rivers, and so forth.

ANNUALS & TROPICALS
If you didn't add slow-acting fertilizer to your pots of rooted cuttings, mix a liquid, balanced fertilizer into the water every other watering. Half-strength is usually plenty this time of year.

Seeds carry their own energy for early development. Newly emerged shoots need no fertilizer until new sets of leaves are growing and your seedlings are in their individual containers. Then, a half- or quarter-

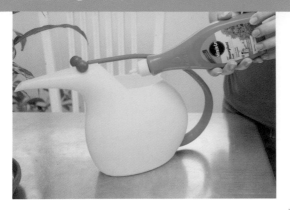

■ *Get your fertilizer ready to go as a new season approaches.*

strength dose of balanced liquid fertilizer is fine to add to the trays of seedlings every watering or two when you're bottom-watering (adding water to the trays and letting the soil take it up from the bottom).

BULBS

For amaryllis and other indoor potted bulbs that you plan to continue growing for additional seasons, apply a half- or quarter-strength dose of balanced liquid fertilizer every other watering.

LAWNS

Wood ashes from the fireplace or woodstove are a good source of potassium and calcium, which usually benefits lawns. Save them for scattering in March or April, especially if your soil is acidic. Ashes make soil more alkaline (raises the pH).

Lawn fertilizing is banned this month in Maryland and anytime the ground is frozen. The season's first fertilizer can go on lawns late this month in warmer

■ *Wood ashes from the fireplace can be used to raise soil pH and add potassium to lawns, gardens, and compost piles.*

Zones 7 and 8 if the ground isn't frozen and grass is starting to green.

PERENNIALS & GROUNDCOVERS

For perennials you've started inside from seed, start applying a dilute fertilizer as soon as the second set of leaves starts growing. Add a dose of quarter- to half-strength liquid, balanced fertilizer to your water every other time you water.

PROBLEM-SOLVE

ALL

If you're spraying dormant oil this month to smother insect eggs on leafless trees, shrubs, and roses, use a separate sprayer for oil and pesticides— *not* the same one you used to spray weeds last season. If you use herbicides to spray for weeds, keep that sprayer for that use only.

Most bugs are still inactive outside, but many animals (deer, rabbits, voles and, as winter winds down, groundhogs) are active and getting hungrier

■ *Snap traps aren't just for indoor use. Bait them with peanut butter and place them outside to trap voles.*

in a diminished food environment. Be sure fencing and plant wraps are still in place and not being violated. Groundhogs climb as well as they dig and deer can out-perform Olympic high-jumpers (8 feet up and over isn't unusual).

ANNUALS & TROPICALS

A common indoor bug this month is the fungus gnat. The adults are mostly just annoying, but the soil-borne larvae can cause wilting and leaf-yellowing from root feeding. New generations can occur every two to three weeks through winter. Since

■ *Sticky traps are a non-chemical way to control indoor bugs.*

this bug thrives in damp soil, water infrequently (soakings as needed instead of daily sprinklings), and cover the soil with an inch of sand or gritty material to keep the surface dry, scratchy, and less hospitable to egg-laying. Fabric softener sheets laid over the soil seem to repel them. Yellow cards coated with a sticky substance (such as petroleum jelly) work like a fly trap. Or kill the larvae by drenching the soil with a product containing Bti (*Bacillus thuringiensis* var *israelensis*) or one of several insecticides labeled for fungus gnat control on houseplants.

Aphids and whiteflies are two other indoor pest bugs that often reach a crescendo in February. Aphids are tiny, pear-shaped green or black bugs that cluster on stems, leaving behind a sticky black substance. Whiteflies are small, white, flying insects that can be seen flitting around the leaves. Controls include rinsing infested foliage and stems under the faucet or under a shower; wiping away bugs and eggs with a soft rag dampened with rubbing alcohol; and spraying with insecticidal soap, horticultural oil, or another insecticide labeled for houseplant use. Ideally, spray outside on an above-freezing day, and get plants back inside as soon as the spray dries.

BULBS

Squirrels *love* early crocuses. Discourage them by laying chicken wire over the beds before the shoots emerge. The shoots will poke through the openings.

Deer browse on most crocuses, but they love tulips even more. They'll often nibble the buds off tulip flower stalks even before the flowers open. The earliest tulips will bud soon, so get repellent sprays on the plants ahead of time.

LAWNS

Voles are still the biggest threat this month as they tunnel into areas where they normally wouldn't go without cover of snow. Set out cage traps or snap traps baited with peanut butter near fresh surface tunnels. Deal with the existing damage by seeding killed areas next month.

PERENNIALS & GROUNDCOVERS

Those sneaky voles also will eat the roots out from underneath selected perennials, sometimes killing them. Some of their favorites are foamflowers, coral-bells, foamybells, dianthus, hostas, and lilies. Set out cage traps or snap traps baited with peanut butter to capture them. Or turn a cat loose. Tamp down and firm soil around any plants you've discovered that are partially eaten; if enough roots are left, they may reroot.

SHRUBS

If you haven't done so, erect tall cages of metal or plastic fencing around plants deer are attacking or around vulnerable ones you don't want eaten. Renew deer-repellent spray.

You wouldn't think animals would eat thorns, but rabbits and deer are notorious for nibbling roses in winter when other food is scarce. To protect branches, surround rose bushes with wire cages tall enough so deer can't reach inside and/or spray stems with a critter repellent. It is not too late. If snow gets deep, animals can reach higher than usual.

Mice and voles find rose roots tasty. They may chew on bark as well. To prevent this in the future, delay mulching until after the ground freezes to encourage the rodents to nest elsewhere. For now, spray stems with a critter repellent.

Spray egg-smothering horticultural oil on the bare, stubby stems of roses that have a history of insect problems. Follow the directions on the product label. Spray heavier dormant oil only before leaves appear.

TREES

Spray heavier dormant oil on fruit trees and other leafless trees subject to scale and other insect pests with overwintering eggs or larvae on the bare branches. Use dormant oil only before foliage and flower buds emerge.

March

It's here. A new gardening season semi-officially gets under way this month as the snow and cold retreat and the first new leaves appear on landscape shrubs.

March is a changeable month in the mid-Atlantic region. It often brings the year's first 70-degree days, but it also can bring a last snowfall or ice storm. Occasionally, it's 70 degrees one day and snowing the next.

Erratic though it is, March isn't too daunting for a smattering of stoic bloomers. It's a time when white and brown give way to the first pinks of Lenten rose, the welcome gold of witch hazel and forsythia, and, of course, the beginning of a string of favorite spring-blooming bulbs, such as Siberian squill, crocus, glory-of-the-snow, and early daffodils and tulips.

Aren't you glad you planted all of those bulbs back in October? If you didn't, now you're stuck with buying more expensive potted bulbs for your winter-ending hurrah.

On days when you don't risk getting blown away in a March gale, you'll be able to get outside and start spring cleanup. This involves removing last year's dead perennial foliage, clearing out any leaf excesses, raking debris off the lawn, and yanking weeds that laughed off winter.

While you're down on the ground, pay attention to what's coming up. You'll likely see all kinds of little shoots poking up and tiny buds poking out, making it a favorite time of hope and optimism for many a soil jockey. Take some time to admire these demure pleasures.

By mid- to late March, it's usually warm and dry enough throughout most of the region to start planting. Stick with planting only the hardier landscape fare this time of year—winter-surviving trees, shrubs, evergreens, and perennials. Wait until all danger of frost is past in April or May to plant those tender annual flowers and to move your houseplants and tropicals outside.

We're not fully there yet ... but at least things are looking better than they did in mid-January.

PLAN

ALL

■ *Clean your pots and get your planting supplies ready now for peak planting time.*

Use the USDA Plant Hardiness Zone as a gauge to determine what plants to try in your landscape. Gardeners in the Zone 8 region of the Norfolk/ Virginia Beach area, for example, can grow more cold-sensitive species, such as gardenia, fringe flower, and camellia, than gardeners in the colder-winter Zones 5b and 6a regions of West Virginia and northern Maryland. Local garden centers usually stick with fare suitable for their zones, but plant labels and mail-order listings almost always list hardiness zones to confirm temperature suitability.

Get organized before things get too crazy. Locate trowels, shovels, and rakes. Sharpen pruners and garden scissors. Check your supply of stakes, wire cages, garden twine, plant labels, fertilizer, potting mix, and whatever else you regularly use.

ANNUALS & TROPICALS

Finish perusing catalogs to order annual flower seeds and plan what varieties to seek out in plant form at the garden center in spring.

BULBS

The spring bulb-bloom show gets under way in earnest this month. Bulbs can be tricky to use well because they flower at one time of year but get planted at another. Jot down successes and deficiencies this spring so you'll have something to jog your memory come bulb-planting time in fall.

LAWNS

Are you hiring out lawn care or mowing? Decide what you'd like someone else to do and get bids now so you have an action plan in place at the end of March or early April when work should begin.

If you didn't do it at the end of last season, get your mower ready. Replace the spark plug. Clean

■ *Change the oil in your mower and get it cleaned and ready for grass-cutting season.*

gunk and grass clippings from the engine, fan, and undercarriage. Clean and sharpen the blade. Replace the fuel filter and clean or replace the air filter. Change the oil. Drain old gas and add fresh gas before cutting for the first time.

PERENNIALS & GROUNDCOVERS

The season's first perennials begin blooming as winter winds down. Since perennials typically only bloom for several weeks out of the year, the best way to get season-long color is to pick varieties that bloom at different times throughout the season. Here's a guide to peak bloom in Zones 6 and 7. Times are slightly earlier in Zone 8, and slightly later in Zone 5.

■ *Primrose tolerate cool weather and are one of the first flowers to bloom in spring.*

March: Lenten rose

April: Barrenwort, bergenia, bleeding heart, bloodroot, brunnera, columbine, creeping phlox, euphorbia, foamflower, lamium, primrose, pulmonaria, rock cress, Virginia bluebell

May: Amsonia, bachelor button, baptisia, candytuft, catmint, creeping Veronica, dianthus, foamybell, forget-me-knot, fringe-leaf bleeding heart, geum, goat's beard, hardy geranium, Jacob's ladder, lamium, lily-of-the-valley, meadow rue, peony, poppy, salvia, snow-in-summer, sweet woodruff, Solomon's seal, thrift, trillium

June: Astilbe, bellflower, catmint, coral-bell, coreopsis, daylily, delphinium, evening primrose, filipendula, foxglove, gaillardia, gaura, hardy geranium, hosta, knautia, lady's mantle, lamium, lavender, lupine, penstemon, red hot poker, rodgersia, rose mallow, scabiosa, Shasta daisy, shooting star, silene, spiderwort, tiger lily, verbascum, Veronica, yarrow, yellow corydalis, yucca

■ *Russian sage (Perovskia atriplicifolia) is a long-blooming perennial that especially helps the late-summer garden.*

July: Agastache, Asiatic and Oriental lilies, baby's breath, balloon flower, beebalm, black-eyed Susan, blackberry lily, butterfly weed, cimicifuga, coreopsis, crocosmia, garden phlox, heliopsis, hollyhock, hosta, Jupiter's beard, liatris, obedient plant, purple coneflower, Russian sage, sea holly, soapwort, stokesia, veronicastrum

August: Aster, cardinal flower, goldenrod, Japanese anemone, Joe-pye weed, leadwort, ligularia, liriope, monkshood, perennial sunflower, purple coneflower, reblooming daylily, Russian sage, sedum, sneezeweed, turtlehead

September: Aster, boltonia, catmint, gaillardia, goldenrod, Japanese anemone, mum, salvia, sedum, toad lily, turtlehead

October: Aster, goldenrod, mum, Nippon daisy

SHRUBS

New shrubs start showing up at the garden center this month, so finalize plans for which ones you plan to add. Some key uses are color for house foundations; focal points in garden beds; softening house corners; hedging to mark off property lines or different parts of your yard; flanking doorways; food and shelter for wildlife; flowers in three potential seasons; fall foliage; screening for heat pumps, trash cans, and other "uglies"; and enclosure for patios.

Look for big, bare walls around the landscape that could be dressed up with the addition of vine-covered trellises. Even if you're planting leaf-dropping vines, the trellises themselves can add wintertime interest.

TREES

Use of native species in home landscapes is on the rise. Some of the more "yard-worthy" tree species native to the mid-Atlantic region include American fringe tree, American hornbeam, American and pagoda dogwoods, American beech, American larch, American linden, blackgum, chokecherry, hop hornbeam, red maple, redbud, red and white oaks, river birch, sassafras, serviceberry, sweetbay magnolia, witch hazel, and sweetgum.

Match your tree choices to the size and site conditions you have, and lean toward bug- and disease-resistant species. Among useful purposes besides just the sheer beauty: shade for a patio; blocking noise from a nearby road; screening unwanted views; marking property lines; creating a future shady getaway area, and in the case of a line of tall evergreens along the north or northwest exposure, blocking cold winter wind.

PLANT

ALL

March is the beginning of planting season, toward early to mid-month in the warmer Zones 7 and 8 and later March in Zones 5 and 6. Container-grown and field-dug trees, shrubs, and evergreens that are balled and burlapped start showing up at the garden centers, and mail-order vendors begin shipping bare-root stock. You'll also find the first greenhouse-grown perennials, already leafed out.

March can be mud month. Melting snow and early spring rains conspire to turn even great garden soil into sticky slop. Don't ruin your soil's structure by digging too soon. Working wet soil

forces out air particles and leaves you with something akin to concrete.

Try this soil-wetness test: Squeeze a handful of soil, and see if it crumbles when you release it. If water drips as you squeeze, or if it's a solid, sodden ball when you open your hand, wait until it dries before digging. Some years you'll be able to get an early start in March. Others years, you won't.

ANNUALS & TROPICALS

Fresh pansies and their Johnny-jump-up and viola cousins can be planted whenever the soil is thawed. Plant 6 to 8 inches apart in a sunny area for fullest coverage. Or plant some in pots and window boxes for early-season color.

■ *Pansies* (Viola × wittrockiana) *are ready for planting and usually come in cell packs.*

Seeds still can be sown indoors for annual flowers that you'd like to plant outside later in spring. Allow seven to fourteen days for most seeds to germinate, then another six to eight weeks of growing time indoors. Gradually acclimate your seedlings by increasing light and time outside over seven to ten more days before planting them in the ground.

Some biennials (plants that sprouted and developed leaves last season and that will flower this season) may start popping up in March. Once thawed soil can be dug, thin these seedlings and/or transplant them to where you'd like them to grow.

Retrieve geraniums that you stored bare-root over the winter in the basement or attic. Examine them and pot them in a soilless potting mix if they're in good condition.

BULBS

If you didn't plant your own hardy bulbs last fall, buy already-blooming potted tulips, daffodils, and hyacinths from the garden center. Either remove the bulbs from the pots and plant them in the ground, or plant them next month after you've displayed the flowering bulbs in the pots.

Snowdrops, winter aconite, and other early bulbs that have finished blooming can be dug, divided, and transplanted late this month or in April. Gently dig up masses, and shake away excess soil. Tease apart individual bulbs, and discard any that are damaged or diseased. Replant some of the bulbs in the original spot, and plant the rest where you'd like to spread the colony.

LAWNS

If temperatures are mild and the soil is not too wet, patch bare spots in the lawn with either pieces of sod cut to fit or with grass seed. Loosen the bare soil, and scratch in granular, slow-acting fertilizer before seeding or sodding. If spring rains are lacking, water daily to keep the patched areas constantly moist.

PERENNIALS & GROUNDCOVERS

Most perennial flowers and groundcovers can be planted outside this month beginning early to mid-month in Zones 7 and 8 and later in the month in Zones 5 and 6. Ideally, plant new perennials on a cloudy day, in the evening, or when rain is in the forecast to reduce transplant shock.

Give store-bought perennials a few days outside in their pots before planting to make sure they're acclimated. Most perennials are grown in greenhouses, and when you buy at the very beginning of the season, the plants may not have been displayed for very long outside yet.

■ *Didn't get your hardy bulbs planted last fall? Don't worry; it's fine to buy potted spring bulbs and plant them later in the ground once they've had their show.*

■ *Shrubs and trees can be sold bare-root, balled-and-burlapped, and container-grown.*

SHRUBS

Most flowering and evergreen shrubs also can be planted this month as soon as the ground thaws and dries enough that it's no longer soggy. (See "Here's How to Plant a Shrub.")

Mail-order vendors sell and ship bare-root shrubs beginning this month. These are field-grown plants that are dug when dormant and sold with roots devoid of soil to reduce shipping costs. Garden centers occasionally sell some varieties of bare-root shrubs, although most now have gone strictly with container-grown and field-dug, balled-and-burlapped options.

Roses are among the most common plants sold bare root. These typically arrive with roots covered in moist sawdust, sphagnum moss, or shredded paper, all covered by a plastic bag with air holes. Some bare-root roses are packaged in boxes. Plant as soon as you can after delivery. In the meantime, keep the packing material intact and damp,

HERE'S HOW

TO PLANT A BARE-ROOT ROSE

1. Set the plant in a pail of water so its roots are immersed for at least eight hours prior to planting but no more than three days. (Change water daily if you soak roots for more than one day.) Clip off any damaged or broken roots.

2. Dig a hole about as deep as the roots are long, and at least 2 feet wide.

3. Form a mound in the middle of the hole so you can set the rose on it with its roots draping down the sides. Use a yardstick or

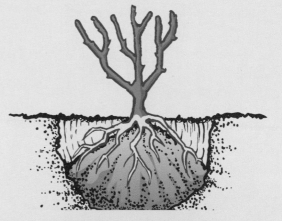

flat board to determine the height of the mound. With grafted roses, the bud union (the knobby joint where the stem meets the roots) should be planted 2 to 4 inches below ground level. For roses growing on their own roots, the point where the stem splays out into the roots should go at ground level.

4. Mix compost or similar organic matter into the removed soil (about 1 part compost per 4 parts existing soil). Also mix in a scattering of slow-acting, granular fertilizer formulated for roses. Use this to backfill the hole, firming it gently around and over the roots.

5. After planting and firming the soil, soak well to settle the soil around the roots. Cover the ground with 2 inches of bark mulch.

HERE'S HOW

TO PLANT A SHRUB

1. Dig a hole at least three to five times as wide as the rootball but no deeper than the rootball's height.

2. Mix the excavated soil with 10 to 20 percent compost or similar organic matter. If your soil is reasonably good and not compacted clay or subsoil, skip this.

3. For container-grown plants, remove the plant from the pot, and fray out the roots, especially if they are circling. It's okay to disturb or remove some of the soil to do this. If you can't free the roots by gently pulling them, make three or four vertical cuts in the rootball to break up the tight mat.

4. For plants that are balled and burlapped, set the shrub in the hole, and cut off and remove as much of the burlap as you can. Also cut apart or remove wire baskets and any rope or strings tied around the trunk or roots.

5. Set the shrub on solid ground so that the crown of the plant (where the emerging stems transform into the roots) is sitting an inch or two *above* grade (at grade in sandy soil). Remove or add soil to adjust to this planting depth. Do not plant with the crown below grade.

6. Adjust the plant so the "good" side (if there is one) is facing the way you want. Check the plant from all angles to make sure it's in the ground straight. Backfill halfway with soil, tamp, recheck for straightness, water, then finish backfilling and tamp again.

7. Cover the ground with 2 to 3 inches of bark mulch or wood chips and then water again.

and store the dormant roses in a cool, above-freezing, dark place. (See "Here's How to Plant a Bare-Root Rose.")

Bare-root shrub planting is similar to planting a bare-root rose. Dig the hole and improve the soil in the same manner. If your soil is reasonably good and not compacted clay, use less or no compost. A key exception is that since almost all flowering and evergreen shrubs are grown on their own roots, the planting depth should be so that the crown (where the emerging stems transform into the roots) is at or slightly above ground level.

Do *not* plant shrubs with the crown below the soil grade.

Once the soil thaws, it's also a good time to *transplant* most shrubs that need to go to a new location. Early spring is good for moving shrubs because the plants are still dormant and leafless but the soil is warming enough to encourage root growth. Early spring is also usually damp and cool—ideal for giving a transplanted plant time to recover from the root loss and damage that's inevitable any time you dig an established shrub. (See May's "Here's How to Transplant a Tree or Shrub.")

HERE'S HOW

TO PLANT A TREE

1. Dig a hole three to five times as wide as the rootball but no deeper than the rootball's height. Planting on solid ground will ensure the soil doesn't settle and cause the tree to end up too deep in the ground (one of the leading causes of tree death).

2. Mix the excavated soil with 10 percent compost or similar organic matter (1 part compost to 9 parts existing soil). If your soil is reasonably good and not compacted clay or subsoil, skip this.

3. For trees grown in containers, remove the tree from the pot, and fray out the roots, especially if they are circling. It's okay to disturb or remove some of the soil to do this. Make a few cuts if necessary to free circling roots if you can't tease them apart with your fingers.

4. For field-dug, balled-and-burlapped trees, set the tree in the hole and cut off and remove as much of the burlap as you can. Also cut apart or remove wire baskets and any rope or strings tied around the trunk or roots.

5. Set the tree so that its crown (where the trunk flares at the base to transform into the roots) is sitting about 2 inches *above* grade (at grade in sandy soil). Remove or add soil to adjust to this planting depth. Never plant a tree with its crown below grade. There's also no need to line the bottom with stones as was once recommended.

6. Check the plant from all angles to make sure it's in the ground straight and situated as you like. Backfill halfway with soil, tamp, recheck for straightness, water, then backfill and tamp again.

7. Cover the ground with 2 to 3 inches of bark mulch or wood chips and then water again.

8. Staking is *not* necessary unless you've planted a large tree with a comparatively small root ball, or if you've planted on a slope or in a windy area. If staking is needed, hammer two or three stakes in the ground, and secure the tree with a wide band or strap at chest to shoulder level. Tie securely but not so tight that the tree can't move at all. Don't use wire or rope, which can cut into the bark. Remove the staking after one year.

TREES

Most trees can be planted starting in early March in Zones 7 and 8 and starting in late March in Zones 5 and 6. Wait until the ground is thawed and not soggy. As with shrubs, trees are now primarily grown in containers or field-dug and wrapped in burlapped balls. (See "Here's How to Plant a Tree.")

Mail-ordered trees, on the other hand, are almost always sold as bare-root varieties to hold down shipping costs. Bare-root tree planting is similar to the bare-root planting of roses and shrubs. (See Plant, Shrubs, and "Here's How to Plant a Bare-Root Rose.")

CARE

ALL

For roadside plants that got blasted with salty snow-plowings or salt runoff this winter, give them a deep soaking with a hose if spring rains don't do the deed for you. Sodium in road salt can burn foliage, but more insidiously, it impedes water uptake by plant roots, leading to symptoms of brown leaf tips and margins during hot, dry spells in summer. Ample rain flushes salts out better than anything, but scratching a layer of gypsum (calcium sulfate) into the soil surface can counteract the effects of sodium overload in the ground.

Weeds increasingly appear now anywhere there's bare soil. Not only do perennial ,weeds begin to emerge from their roots, but annual weeds that germinate in cool weather also pop up this month. Pull them, dig them, or spray them as soon as possible. It'll only get worse if you don't.

Another weed-fighting strategy is weed preventers, also called "pre-emergent herbicides." These are granular products that don't kill existing weeds but that do stop many new weeds from sprouting. Ones with corn gluten meal offer a marginally effective alternative to synthetic chemicals, although it's likely the product was made from genetically modified (GMO) corn, rendering it technically *not* "organic."

Weed preventers don't harm most existing plants and can be applied over top of perennials and underneath shrubs and trees. Check the label for the few species that are susceptible to damage by weed preventers. Most are effective for eight to ten weeks. Ideal timing for applying weed preventers is when forsythia has reached peak bloom. That's early March in warmer zones to early April in cooler zones most years.

ANNUALS & TROPICALS

Adjust fluorescent lights over young annuals being grown indoors from seed to within 2 or 3 inches of the tops of the plants as they grow. This will keep the stems sturdy. One method is to hang your lights on chains, which allows you to raise the lights gradually as needed. Another method is to set seedling trays on blocks or scrap wood, then remove the blocks as needed.

Rotate seedlings growing on a windowsill every few days so that light falls on every side. This keeps them from leaning in one direction.

Research suggests that gently brushing tender tops of seedlings a couple of times a day with your fingertips or open hand helps them develop sturdy stems. Annual seedlings also grow fuller and bushier by pinching off the tips of their stems periodically.

BULBS

Do not cut back, tie, or otherwise disturb outdoor bulb foliage while it is still green! This interferes with its job of collecting sun for energy for next year.

There's no need to pinch off the faded flowers of small bulbs, such as Siberian squill, anemone, and snowdrops. Spent flowers of larger bulbs, such as daffodils, early tulips, and hyacinths, are more noticeable, so it helps to neaten the garden by snipping off their entire flower stalks. Eliminating flower stalks prevents bulbs from wasting energy trying to produce seeds.

Allow the foliage of potted bulbs to mature in a sunny window. Then plant them outdoors either late this month or in April.

Check stored, tender bulbs (dahlias, callas, gladioli, and so forth) one more time this month to be sure they haven't dried or rotted. You'll be able to plant them outside after danger of frost. Or start them four weeks in advance of that in pots inside (mid- to late March in Zones 7 and 8, early April in Zones 5 and 6).

LAWNS

If your lawn has a chronic crabgrass problem, consider using a crabgrass preventer. These products kill crabgrass as the seeds germinate, stopping it before it gets started. Most crabgrass preventers should go on the lawn before crabgrass begins germinating, which most years is early to mid-March in Zones 7 and 8 and late March to early April in Zones 5 and 6. When forsythia hits peak bloom is a good indicator. Most preventers work for only eight to ten weeks. So in cool, damp springs, a second application might be needed in late spring to control late-sprouting crabgrass.

A few crabgrass preventers, such as ones containing the chemical dithiopyr, both prevent and kill young crabgrass, so they can go down as late as May. Most crabgrass preventers also stop several other annual weeds from sprouting in lawns, including foxtail, barnyard grass, and spurge.

If your soil is acidic and you forgot to lime the lawn last fall, early spring is another good time.

PERENNIALS & GROUNDCOVERS

Don't fret if a sudden and unusually cold spell browns the tips and edges of newly emerged perennial foliage. The plants will almost always grow new leaves to replace the cold-zapped ones. Pick or snip off the brown leaves if that happens.

Take advantage of nice days to get outside and start cleaning the perennial beds. Rake out debris and excess leaves. Cut browned-out ornamental grasses and liriope back to 2 or 3 inches if you haven't already done that. And remove the browned-out foliage from last year's perennials, except for those that are "evergreen perennials" (ones that keep their foliage all year long). (See April's "Here's When to Cut Which Perennials.")

SHRUBS

End of winter is a good time to cut back some overgrown shrubs. Species that flower *before* mid-June are almost all ones that form their flower buds the season before, and so they should be left to flower first before pruning. Species that flower *after* mid-June generally produce their flower buds on that season's new growth, and so they're best pruned heading into a new season—now. (See "Here's How to Prune Flowering Shrubs" and April's "Here's When to Prune Which Shrubs and Trees.")

Sometimes a big or neglected shrub benefits from "coppicing"—cutting back an entire shrub to

within a few inches of the ground. Not all species tolerate that, but many respond by producing fresh, healthy growth from the stubs or roots. Butterfly bush, spirea, redtwig dogwood, forsythia, beautyberry, burning bush, caryopteris, ninebark, summersweet, and Virginia sweetspire are among those that accept coppicing without complaint. As the plants regrow, remove weak or "directionally challenged" shoots.

■ *Rejuvenation pruning is a way to encourage fresh new growth on an old or overgrown shrub.*

Rejuvenation is another shrub-pruning option. This involves bringing an overgrown shrub under control over a three-year period and then keeping it that way. First, cut back one-third of the oldest, thickest, woodiest stems to 3 or 4 inches above the ground. Do the same the following year and the year after. By the fourth year, you'll have a whole young shrub again. Keep doing the one-third thin-outs each year to constantly encourage young wood, which flowers better and has better disease-resistance than old wood. Old-fashioned French lilacs are best pruned this way, but it's also a good way to maintain mock orange, bridalwreath spirea, forsythia, sweetshrub, weigela, chokeberry, beautybush, and most viburnums.

For evergreen shrubs, late March to early April is a good time to thin, cut back, or shear holly, boxwood, euonymus, nandina, cherry laurel, yew, and Japanese plum yew. To control size, cut before new growth occurs. Trim hedges so that the bottoms are wider than the tops.

Several other evergreens also can be pruned heading into a new season, but they *don't* push new growth

HERE'S HOW

TO PRUNE FLOWERING SHRUBS

Summer-flowering shrubs (ones that bloom after mid-June) are best pruned at the end of winter. Spring-flowering shrubs (ones that bloom before mid-June) are best pruned immediately *after* they flower so as not to cut off that season's flower buds that formed the fall before.

1. First remove any dead, broken, or rotting wood back to live, healthy branches or buds.

2. With loppers or a handsaw, thin out up to one-third of the biggest, oldest stems. Cut as close to the ground as you can. Skip or reduce this if the shrub has been flowering well, hasn't been suffering from disease, and you prefer maximum denseness.

3. If necessary for size control, shorten "keeper" branches back to branches or buds facing the desired direction. Make angled cuts facing down and away from the branches or buds. For most shrubs, remove no more one-third of the total wood.

4. Shrubs being grown in a hedge setting or in cases where dense growth is desired (abelia, boxwood, yew, or photinia, for example) can be sheared instead of hand-pruned. Limit removed wood to one-third in most cases.

very well when cut back severely. Juniper, globe arborvitae, birds' nest spruce, and dwarf cryptomeria are examples of species that should never be cut back beyond green growth on the branch ends.

Remove winter protection and mounded mulch from any plants that needed a little precautionary cold TLC, such as grafted roses, fig, bay laurel, osmanthus, skimmia, and gardenia.

Begin pruning roses as the buds swell and are about ready to open. That's usually early to mid-March in Zones 7 and 8 and late March to early April in Zones 5 and 6. First, remove any damaged, broken, or winter-killed wood. Then thin out excess canes and shorten the "keepers" by cutting about one-quarter of an inch above buds or shoots pointing in the desired direction (usually outward-facing).

Some rose-pruning specifics:

- For hybrid teas, floribundas, and grandifloras, select three to six healthy, finger-sized canes evenly spaced around the bush and cut them back to 12 to 18 inches tall.
- For long-armed landscape roses, thin out one-third of older canes and weak branches, then reduce the length of remaining canes by one-third.

- For miniature roses, prune back stems to 3 to 5 inches and clip off twiggy growth, especially from the center.
- For groundcover and shrub roses, shear all growth back to between 6 and 12 inches.
- For climbers and ramblers, prune off canes that are two years or older back to the base, and shorten the remaining side branches by two-thirds of their length. Select and tie new young main shoots at 45-degree angles.

Summer-blooming vines such as climbing hydrangea, Japanese hydrangea vine, ornamental kiwi, trumpet vine, American bittersweet, and some clematis can be pruned this month before new growth begins.

TREES

March is a good month to prune most deciduous (leaf-dropping) trees. They're still dormant and leafless; it's much easier to see the branches and less messy than pruning with leaves in the equation. One thing to keep in mind if you prune spring-flowering trees such as dogwood, redbud, and cherry now: You'll reduce the number of this season's flowers. Prune spring bloomers right *after* they flower if you want to maximize flowers. This isn't a concern for shade trees or summer-flowering trees that bloom on this year's wood

HERE'S HOW

TO PRUNE EVERGREENS

1. First remove any dead or snapped limbs. Make a clean cut back to live growth or back to just outside the branch collar (the ringed area where a branch attaches to the trunk) in the case of a whole lost limb.

2. Pine, spruce, and fir grow in clusters of shoots called "whorls." When their size reaches the desired maintenance level, these are best maintained by letting the new season's shoots grow and then snipping all or most of it off. Best timing is mid- to late spring.

3. Arborvitae, yew, cedar, false cypress, juniper, hemlock, holly, cryptomeria, Hinoki cypress, and Douglas fir are best pruned at the end of winter, just before new growth begins. Avoid cutting back so far, though, that you're into the bare inner part of the branches. This timing lets new growth quickly hide your pruning cuts. Lighter maintenance trims also can be done again in early to midsummer.

4. Species that tolerate shearing and even harder cutbacks into bare wood include holly, boxwood, yew, hemlock, nandina, photinia, and euonymus. Still, it's best to cut back no farther than where green growth intersects with bare wood. Best timing is end of winter through midsummer.

5. Avoid all pruning of evergreens from late summer through mid-fall. That's when dormancy is beginning. Late-season pruning can encourage new growth that won't "harden off" before winter, making it more susceptible to cold kill.

(crape myrtle, *Hydrangea paniculata,* and seven-son flower, for example).

Some evergreen trees can be pruned or sheared for size control starting this month, so long as you don't cut back so severely that you're into the bare inner wood. Examples are arborvitae, Leyland cypress, cryptomeria, Hinoki cypress, cedar, and false cypress. American holly trees also can be pruned in March, including back into bare wood, if necessary. Wait until late May or June after new growth finishes to prune fir, spruce, and pine.

Branches of leaf-dropping conifers such as dawn redwood, larch, and bald cypress can be thinned out or shortened now before new growth begins.

The lowest limbs of all trees can be removed this month if you need more space to sit or walk under or if you just want to expose more of the trunk. You might also find that the lower limbs of aging evergreens are dying; these can come off now, too. The rule of thumb is never remove branches more than one-third of the way up.

For trees you've been staking since last spring, remove the stakes late this month or next. One year is long enough.

WATER

ALL
Winter-ending snow melt and/or cold, early-spring rain means soil is usually wet enough this time of year. Occasionally, though, a dry spell following a snowless late winter might mean a soaking is needed for newly planted pansies, sweet peas, or anything that's less than a year old and not yet well rooted.

ANNUALS & TROPICALS
Use a water meter or test using your finger to keep tabs on the soil moisture of indoor potted cuttings, especially in terra cotta pots. Indoor air is dry as long as the central heating is still on.

Keep seedlings moist, but don't cross over into sogginess. It's okay if the soil dries out slightly between waterings. Many annuals are adapted to a wet/dry cycle. If seedlings are drying very quickly, that's a sign they need to be repotted into a larger pot. Water seedlings with tepid water, not water directly from the cold-water faucet.

BULBS
Normal rain or melting snow is enough moisture for bulbs. In a rare end-of-winter dry spell, soak bulb beds after the ground has thawed. Then water is needed only if that rare spring dryness continues.

LAWNS
Lawns need no water so long as they're still dormant in winter. You'll only need to think about a watering if it's unusually dry and warm once the grass starts to green—if even then. Newly seeded or newly sodded lawns are more in need of early-season water than established lawns.

PERENNIALS, ROSES, SHRUBS, TREES & VINES
None of these should need March watering in a typical year. The exception is a dry spell following a snowless late winter, and in particular, plants that are less than a year old. Otherwise, winter moisture and a 2- to 3-inch layer of mulch around these plants are usually enough to maintain adequate soil moisture.

FERTILIZE

ALL
Wood ashes from the fireplace or woodstove are a good source of plant nutrients, especially potassium. They also increase soil alkalinity (raises the pH), a side benefit when the soil is too acidic. Test your soil pH to determine whether applying wood ashes is a good idea or not. Most of the time, it's a benefit to lawns and gardens but not a good idea around hollies, azaleas, dogwoods, blueberries, and other plants that prefer acidic soil.

ANNUALS & TROPICALS
Continue adding a half- to quarter-strength dose of balanced liquid fertilizer to the trays of your indoor annual flower seedlings every watering or two.

The brightening days of March signal the beginning of a new growing season for houseplants and overwintering tropicals. Increased growth means it's time to ramp up fertilizing. Use a balanced fertilizer at about half-strength every other time you water.

BULBS
If you're planning to yank your tulips after their first year (many of them go downhill in ensuing years), there's no need to fertilize them. But for spring bulbs you'd like to keep going for years, lightly scratch a granular fertilizer into the soil surface sometime this month or early April. Use a product with a balanced nutrient breakdown or one labeled specifically for bulbs.

LAWNS
Improper lawn fertilizing is a significant source of water pollution, which led Maryland to enact rules that ban fertilizer applications on frozen soil, ban the routine application of bay-polluting phosphorus in lawn fertilizer (okay only if a soil test indicates a need), and limit the amounts of nitrogen (maximum nine-tenths of a pound of total nitrogen per 1,000 square feet or seven-tenths of a pound of water-soluble nitrogen). It also requires fertilizer spilled on walks to be swept, bans the use of fertilizers to melt ice, and bans homeowner lawn-fertilizing between November 15 to March 1 or within 15 feet of a waterway. Those practices usually are solid ones throughout the rest of the region as well.

The three optimal times to fertilize a lawn are: mid- to late spring, end of summer, and mid-autumn. That's assuming you want to push growth to near-peak performance. Most lawns do reasonably well with minimal fertilizer. If you haven't done it in a while (or ever), test your lawn's soil before adding anything.

If you're going with a commercial "four-step" lawn-fertilizer plan, the four times are: early spring, late spring, late summer, and mid-autumn. Do you really want or need that much? If so, late this month or early April is time for the first application.

March is a good month to apply either wood ash or pelleted lime to the lawn if a soil test indicates your soil is too acidy (low on the pH scale). Wait until the ground has thawed to apply it. A pH reading of neutral to slightly alkaline (7.0 to 7.5) is ideal.

If you didn't spread fertilizer on the lawn last fall, spread a quarter-inch layer of compost or a granular, slow-acting lawn fertilizer late this month after the ground has thawed as your first treatment.

If you *did* spread slow-acting fertilizer last fall, it will begin to kick in this month and last until late spring to early summer. No need to apply another dose now.

PERENNIALS & GROUNDCOVERS

Late March through April is the best time of year to scatter a dose of organic or slow-acting granular fertilizer over the beds of blooming perennial flowers. Lightly scratch it into the soil or mulch for best results. Spring rains will carry the nutrition to the roots just as nutrient demands rise.

Groundcovers and perennials being grown for their foliage usually don't need supplemental fertilizer. Fertilize these only if the growth rate or color is poor, or if a soil test indicates a nutrient deficiency.

SHRUBS & TREES

Established trees and shrubs that are growing well usually need no supplemental fertilizer, especially if the lawn around the plantings is being fertilized.

If the growth rate is not up to par or the leaf color and size is not normal, first test the soil. The result will tell whether a nutrient deficiency is a problem, and if so, exactly what and how much is needed. Otherwise, you're guessing.

A soil test will indicate whether the soil's acidity level (pH) should be adjusted. Lime or wood ash will raise the pH (make the soil more alkaline). Sulfur will lower the pH (make it more acidic). Most shrubs and trees prefer neutral to mildly acidic soil. Holly, camellia, mountain laurel, azalea, rhododendron, blueberry, dogwood, birch, and most needled evergreens prefer moderately acidic soil.

Roses are heavy feeders and perform best when they're fertilized regularly throughout the growing season. March is the time to get started. For those with organic leanings, a layer of compost, a granular organic fertilizer formulated for roses, and/or a scattering of aged manure will do the trick. Many a rosarian buries banana peels around roses to supply potassium; others scatter a half-cup of Epsom salts around each plant this month to supply magnesium. For chemical gardeners, scatter granular rose fertilizer according to label directions, or water in the season's first application of liquid rose fertilizer, also starting in late March.

Do *not* encourage large, fast-growing vines such as wisteria or trumpet vine by fertilizing. These hardly ever need nutrition help. Most other woody vines (climbing hydrangea, clematis, honeysuckle, and so forth) also usually get all of the nutrition they need from average soil. If poor growth, poor color, or a soil test indicates a particular nutrient is needed in any of these, late March is a good time to apply it.

PROBLEM-SOLVE

ALL

Rabbits are active all winter, and with little else to eat, they often chew young tree and shrub bark, low-to-the-ground twigs, bulbs (especially tulips) and selected plants that hold their leaves in winter. Fencing works best if you don't mind the Fort-Knox look. Otherwise, spot-protect young trees, shrubs, and perennials by surrounding them with wire-fencing or hardware-cloth cylinders. Or regularly apply one of the many commercially available rabbit repellents. Pansies and violas are particular favorite bunny desserts.

ANNUALS & TROPICALS

That thin white crust growing over the soil surface of your houseplants or overwintering tropical is fertilizer salt and/or minerals left behind by evaporated water. Both are harmless to plants in small amounts and can be scraped off if it bothers you. To head off buildups, some gardeners give their houseplants periodic showers (yes, in the tub) to wash out salts being left on the surface by fertilizer. Another option is to repot your plants in fresh potting mix at winter's end—now.

"Damping off" is the bane of seedlings. It's caused by a soilborne pathogen and is aggravated by an overly wet medium. The telltale symptom is a stem that darkens near the soil surface and then keels over. To prevent damping off, use a sterile, soilless planting medium and water by adding water to the tray, not over tops of plants. Dump any water that's left standing in the tray after fifteen minutes.

If your seedlings are getting "leggy" (long and skinny instead of stocky), that's usually due to insufficient light. Move your lights closer. Also helpful is to grow in cooler conditions instead of room-temperature 70 degrees Fahrenheit.

If indoor leaves look mottled or speckled with yellow dots, inspect for tiny bugs called spider mites. A telltale sign is fine webbing on the stems and leaves. Spider mites are almost too small to see without a magnifying glass. If you have them, spray or wash the foliage with tepid water several times a week to remove and disrupt the mites. Use insecticidal soap on stubborn infestations, following label directions.

BULBS

Both deer and rabbits are fond of tulips and some crocuses and will nibble emerging shoots and the flower buds before they open. Fence beds of vulnerable bulbs or apply deer and/or rabbit repellent. Or switch to daffodils, hyacinths, Siberian squill, glory-of-the-snow, and other bulbs that are less tasty to four-legged pests.

Mice and voles are threats to eat bulbs (especially tulips) by tunneling underground. Cover the bed with chicken wire and a light layer of mulch to prevent tunneling. Or try trapping rodents with snap traps or cage traps baited with peanut butter.

LAWNS

Snow mold is a term for two fungal diseases that occur in turfgrass that suffers prolonged cold, wet conditions or compacted snow cover in winter. After spring thaw, patches up to 2 feet in diameter may be covered with a white or gray fungus or with matted, dead grass that is pink in color. To prevent it, avoid overdosing the grass on nitrogen, and remove thatch if it's more than

a half-inch thick. Make a note to cut the grass short (about 2 inches) for the last cut of the season. Avoid piling shoveled snow into large mountains on the lawn. If you get snow mold anyway, rake off the dead grass and wait for warmer, drier weather to solve the problem for you. There's no need to treat with a fungicide.

PERENNIALS & GROUNDCOVERS

Slugs—those slimy snail relatives without the shell—often become active in March. They overwinter in moist, acidic, organic debris in shady areas in the yard and especially favor hostas. Set out traps to catch the first arrivals. Use a shallow pie plate or a commercial slug "bar" trap filled with beer (yeast attracts them) near vulnerable plants. Check it daily for slug bodies to pinpoint when they start feeding. Set out more traps (a slight distance from vulnerable plants) to lure more slugs once you know they are active.

Watch for rot diseases that can cause some low growing groundcovers to mysteriously "melt away." Bugleweed (*Ajuga*) is especially prone to this in cold, wet winter soil. Add compost or similar organic matter to improve drainage in the bare areas, then either transplant living groundcover plants or add new ones.

SHRUBS

Brown needles on Hinoki cypress, dwarf pines, arborvitae, and other evergreens are not necessarily cause for alarm. So long as the browning is limited to the inner needles, this is aged foliage that is giving way to new replacement foliage farther out on the branches. It's normal but can be more pronounced following dry years, extra-cold winters, and similar stresses. If the tips are green and growing, don't worry.

TREES

Birds are allies in the campaign against pest insects in trees. Woodpeckers and flickers dig borers and beetles from tree bark. Robins enjoy tent caterpillars. Wrens favor tiny insects. Invite birds to set up housekeeping in your yard by putting up birdhouses or nesting boxes and by planting plenty of trees and tall evergreens to give them high shelter.

April

Widespread blooming glory emerges from the erratic cold and wind this month in the mid-Atlantic landscape.

Lengthening days and warming temperatures trigger a symphony of color, ranging from the familiar dogwood and redbud show overhead to a stream of bulb blooms and early-season perennials underneath. Color is everywhere … or at least it *should* be if you thought to plant some of the many species that peak in April.

Flowering pear, flowering cherry, saucer magnolia, and those dogwoods and redbuds are trees that peak this month. Camellia, forsythia, fothergilla, and some spireas and viburnums are among the first shrubs to color. Barrenwort, brunnera, creeping phlox, candytuft, bleeding heart, and foamflower are perennials that bloom almost as soon as new leaves begin growing. And, of course, spring bulbs hit full stride, especially daffodils, early tulips, and one of spring's most fragrant flowers, the Dutch hyacinth.

The threat of frost usually comes to an end early this month in the warmest coastal Zone 8 gardens, by mid-April in Zone 7, and by late April to early May in Zone 6. That opens the door to adding the season's first annual flowers. Sorry, Zone 5'ers. You'll usually have to wait until mid-May before your frost threats end.

Days typically start to reach into the 60s and 70s this month. Evenings are cool but pleasant. Showers come regularly enough to water new plantings and green the lawn. Overall, it's one of the nicest months, both for plants and the gardeners tending them.

Speaking of that, April is a busy time in the garden. It's time to weed and edge the beds in preparation for new mulch. It's time to finish cutting back roses, summer-blooming shrubs, and some of those overgrown evergreens. It's time to plant those new trees, shrubs, and perennials you've been drooling over in the catalogs all winter.

But most of all, it's time to look around, sniff, admire, and otherwise enjoy all of the fresh beauty that verifies that winter is now officially gone.

PLAN

ALL

Transfer your winter ideas and sketches to the ground outside by using a hose or rope to mark off new or changed garden beds. Then dig and improve the soil in advance of your future beautiful new planting. (See "Here's How to Turn Lawn into a New Garden Bed.")

Clean stored garden accessories (birdhouses, feeders, birdbaths, statues, fountains, etc.), and return them to the outside. Make repairs to anything that got banged up in the move. Also clean your pots, and get hanging baskets ready for a new season of duty.

Reset and secure stones in walls, walks, and terraces that may have been moved by freeze-and-thaw cycles in the soil over the winter.

ANNUALS & TROPICALS

Annual flowers start filling the garden centers this month. Some varieties tolerate frost (pansy, viola, dusty miller, snapdragon and dianthus, for example) and can be planted outside when nights still might dip below freezing. Others are sensitive to below-freezing temperatures and will die if a frost comes along after you plant them. These include petunia, marigold, zinnia, vinca, begonia, impatiens, and coleus.

There's a difference between *average* last killing dates in spring and *all-time* late killing-frost dates. Average last-frost dates tell you that in half of the years, you'll be "safe" planting those frost-tender annuals. The other half of the time, though, those zinnias could get zapped. That's why most gardeners play it safe and wait to plant summer annuals until after all danger of frost passes.

So-called "safe" annual-planting times are usually early this month in Zone 8, mid- to late April in Zone 7, late April to early May in Zone 6, and mid-May in Zone 5. Check your local ten-day temperature forecasts before planting as an extra season-by-season precaution.

The trend in annuals has been using them for *spots* of color as opposed to massed displays, particularly in pots and baskets. Annuals offer season-long bloom, a wide choice of colors, versatility (choices for sun, shade, wet, dry, even climbing up supports), potential use as cut flowers, fragrance (some), and attractiveness to birds, butterflies, bees, and other pollinators.

BULBS

Pay attention as bulb plantings bloom. Note which beds need to be "beefed up" with additional bulbs, which ones need some rearranging, and which bare areas of the yard would benefit from some new daffodils, snowdrops, glory-of-the-snow, and so on. The information will come in handy at bulb-planting time in fall.

Two overlooked spots for spring bulbs are in plantings of low groundcovers, such as pachysandra, creeping sedum, sweet woodruff, leadwort, and hardy ginger, where the bulbs will poke up and bloom over top, and among perennials, where the bulbs flower as the perennials are just waking up. The perennials then hide the bulb foliage as it fades, taking over the space as the bulbs go dormant.

Some other potential bulb areas to scope out include along a fence, around a light post, around a water garden, under trees, and along bare walls.

LAWNS

Get the mower ready (sharp blade, new spark plug, fresh gas), and get your fertilizer, crabgrass preventer, and other supplies on hand. The lawn will green up quickly now.

All grass may *look* green and bladed, but five distinct turfgrass types make up most mid-Atlantic lawns. Four are "cool-season" grasses—ones that grow best in spring and fall, go dormant most of winter, and often temporarily brown in a hot, dry summer. The fifth type—Zoysia—is a "warm-season" grass that grows densely in summer but goes brown and dormant all winter.

Kentucky bluegrass. It has medium-textured blades and dark green color. Pluses: spreads well; recuperates quickly from drought and injury; good tolerance to cold, heat, and drought; takes foot traffic well. Minuses: not good in shade or wet soil; fairly heavy feeder; prone to thatch (spongy

■ *Kentucky bluegrass is a popular and attractive type of grass that does well in full sun.*

buildup underneath); slow to sprout from seed; moderate risk of bugs and disease.

Perennial ryegrass. It's finer textured than Kentucky bluegrass and slightly darker green in color. Pluses: germinates and establishes quickly; tolerates foot traffic, heat, and cold well; less prone to thatch than Kentucky bluegrass. Minuses: doesn't recuperate as quickly from drought and injury as Kentucky bluegrass; only moderate shade and drought tolerance; somewhat prone to bugs and disease.

Fine fescue, which includes chewings, hard, creeping red, and sheep fescues. These have the finest texture and medium green color. Pluses: best shade tolerance; light fertilizer demand; recovers

■ *Most lawns include one or more types of fescue grass.*

quickly from drought or injury; does well in drought and acidy soil. Minuses: doesn't appreciate heavy foot traffic; fairly prone to thatch.

Turf-type tall fescue. Has the coarsest foliage, to the point of looking too rough sometimes when used with the above three finer-bladed grasses. Pluses: excellent heat, drought, and foot-traffic tolerance; more shade-tolerant than Kentucky bluegrass or perennial ryegrass; minimal thatch problems. Minuses: slow to establish and recover from injury; not as attractive as narrow-bladed types.

■ *Zoysia grass is durable in the heat but goes brown and dormant in winter.*

Zoysia. Medium to fine texture and medium-green summer color. Pluses: very thick grower, making it excellent for choking out weeds; recuperates quickly from injury; good drought-tolerance; light feeder. Minuses: overtakes other grasses, including into the neighbor's yard; turns brown at first frost and stays brown most years until April or May; expensive to establish (planted by plugs, not seed); prone to thatch.

PERENNIALS & GROUNDCOVERS

Pay attention to your yard's microclimates. You can't put just any perennial anywhere. An astilbe, for example, may do fine in the damp shade along your eastern foundation but probably will fry by your sunny driveway. Read those plant labels, and match the preferences to your specific sites. If you guess wrong and find that a new perennial suffers, don't hesitate to move it to a more suitable spot.

The trees are leafing out, making this a good time to evaluate shady spots. In addition to eastern exposures, shady spots around the yard include the north foundation and any area to the east or north of a fence, building, or screening of tall evergreens. Shade-tolerant perennials include astilbe, Japanese anemone, woods aster, barrenwort, bleeding heart, brunnera, cimicifuga, coral-bell, foamflower, hosta, foamybell, Japanese forestgrass, lamium, ferns, Lenten rose, variegated liriope, lungwort, woodland phlox, variegated Solomon's seal, turtlehead, and Virginia bluebells.

SHRUBS

You should be seeing a nice selection of shrubs blooming by now. If not, you're missing the boat. Think about adding such early bloomers as forsythia, fothergilla, viburnum, early types of spirea (especially bridalwreath and 'Ogon'), spicebush, sweetbox, mahonia, PJM rhododendron, and winter hazel.

Vines are good choices to hide "uglies" around the yard—crumbling walls, downspouts, heat pumps, the neighbor's junk pile, and so on. Either buy a trellis or build your own support so it's in place for prime time planting of vines this month and next.

■ Vines are useful for hiding "uglies" in the landscape.

Clematis is a good vine choice to ramble up a tree. So are shade-preferring and semi-shade annual vines, such as black-eyed Susan vine, Rex begonia vine, and moonflower. Climbing hydrangea and Japanese hydrangea vine are two other good shade-tolerant, woody, perennial vines for growing up trees; just keep them pruned enough that the vine leaves don't cover tree leaves and shut off sunlight to them.

TREES

Arbor Day is in April for good reason. It's an ideal month to plant new trees and a time when more trees flower than any other. If you're not cashing in on this color show, consider adding such early-blooming species as magnolia, dogwood, flowering cherry, flowering pear, flowering plum, redbud, serviceberry, and crabapple.

PLANT

ALL

Planting on a slope? Instead of planting on a downward angle along the original grade, loosen the soil and level it to a "terrace" of 1 to 2 feet across for a perennial or 2 to 3 feet across for a tree or shrub. Then taper the bed down in front, and finish it off with mulch, making sure the roots are covered. These little platforms will catch rainwater, and allow it to soak into the roots instead of running straight down the hill.

ANNUALS & TROPICALS

Finally! It's time to plant at least some annual flowers. Frost-tolerant pansy, viola, dusty miller, snapdragon, and annual dianthus can go in the ground throughout the mid-Atlantic region this month. Wait until all danger of frost passes to plant frost-wimpy summer annuals. (See Plan, Annuals and Tropicals.)

Some annuals start well from seed planted directly in the ground, a less expensive option than buying transplants. Loosen the soil, scatter the seed, and follow the packet label to determine how deeply to cover the seeds with soil. Then keep the soil damp to aid germination. Cold-tolerant species such as larkspur, annual poppies, cleome, and sweet alyssum can be planted three to four weeks before your zone's

■ *Late winter to spring is the time to direct-seed some flower species right into the ground.*

last-frost dates. Wait until all danger of frost passes to direct-seed summer annuals, including cosmos, four-o'-clocks, portulaca, bachelor's buttons, flax, marigold, calendula, nasturtium, sunflower, nigella (love-in-a-mist), nicotiana, zinnia, black-eyed Susan vines, moonflower, and purple hyacinth bean.

Start "hardening off" annual flowers you've started inside before planting them outside. This involves giving young seedlings gradually more light and outdoor exposure over a seven- to ten-day period to help them acclimate to outside conditions. Use your zone's last-frost date as a hardening-off timing guide, starting with cold-tolerant species four to five weeks before the last frost date and frost-sensitive ones about one week before. (See Plan, Annuals & Tropicals.)

BULBS

Bulbs that are done blooming can be dug, divided, and transplanted. Division usually improves the performance of too-crowded bulb plantings. Now is a good time because you can see where the bulbs are; the foliage is still attached. Gently dig up masses, shake away the soil, and tease apart individual bulbs. Toss damaged or diseased bulbs. Replant immediately with the foliage attached,

unless it's already started to yellow. In that case, cut it off and replant. The correct depth is three times as deep as the bulb is tall. Good spacing is three times apart as the bulb is wide.

Get a jump on dahlias, cannas, calla lilies, tuberous begonias, and other tender bulbs by starting them in pots inside early this month rather than waiting to plant directly in the ground after frost passes. First cull out injured, diseased, or shriveled bulbs. Divide ones that have formed clusters. Plant in a soilless potting medium with a scattering of granular, slow-acting fertilizer mixed in. Water them, and set the pots in a bright room. By the time frost-free planting time arrives, they'll be sprouted and growing.

LAWNS

April is one of the best months to seed a new lawn as well as patch bare spots in a thin lawn. Two important steps: loosen the soil surface so you have good seed-to-soil contact (no scattering seed over a compacted surface), and keep the seed and young grass consistently moist to help it germinate and establish. (See September's "Here's How to Seed a New Lawn" and "Here's How to Overseed a Thin Lawn" for step-by-step tips.)

As with flowers and vegetables, grass comes in many varieties within each grass species. Some varieties perform markedly better than others, especially in drought tolerance, bug- and disease-resistance, and color. Universities in each state perform turfgrass variety trials. Results are posted on the National Turfgrass Evaluation Program website at www.ntep.org. Select the State Data button, then hit your state on the map. You'll get a current list of top-rated varieties in each species that you can use when scouring garden centers and online vendors for seed.

PERENNIALS & GROUNDCOVERS

April is prime time for planting almost all new perennials, groundcovers, and ornamental grasses. It's also when you'll find the best selection in garden centers. (See "Here's How to Plant Perennials.")

Perennial spacing varies depending on the size of the plant, how fast each variety spreads, and your patience. A good general rule is somewhere between 18 to 24 inches apart. Larger perennials, such as Russian sage, hardy hibiscus, baptisia, ornamental grasses, and large-leafed hostas, can go 3 or even 4 feet apart.

When you're planting a new bed, space the pots over the ground before planting anything. This gives you a chance to make minor spacing adjustments without having to go back and dig anything up. An alternate plan is to use sticks or bamboo stakes to mark off planting spots.

If your existing perennial beds are getting crowded, weedy, or generally going downhill, it's time for a renovation. This involves digging the plants, removing weeds, improving the soil with compost, dividing large clumps, and replanting. Most perennial plantings benefit from this every five to ten years. April is a good month to do it, especially for perennials that aren't yet in bloom.

SHRUBS

April is an excellent month to plant new shrubs, roses, and woody vines including widely available

HERE'S HOW

TO PLANT PERENNIALS

1. Perennials perform best in soil that has been loosened to 10 or 12 inches deep and improved by incorporating an inch or two of compost, rotted leaves, rotted manure, or similar organic matter into it. If you're planting in individual holes, loosen as deep as the rootball and at least two to three times as wide. Work in a handful or two of the above organic matter.

2. Remove the plant from the pot. Fray out the roots, including cutting three or four vertical slits to free a badly circled root mass, if necessary. It's okay to remove most of the soil in the process.

3. Open a hole and set the plant so that it's at the same level as in the pot. Be careful not to bury the crown of the plant (the point from which the stems emerge).

4. Tamp soil firmly all around the plant and cover the ground with an inch or two of bark mulch or pine needles. Keep the mulch from touching the base of the plant.

5. Water well and keep the soil consistently damp through the first season via soakings once or twice a week when rain doesn't happen.

container-grown ones as well as larger-sized, field-dug, balled-and-burlapped plants. (See March's "Here's How to Plant a Shrub.")

Potted hydrangeas, azaleas, and miniature roses that were holiday gift plants can be planted in the ground outside this month. Get them used to the outside first by giving them increasing sunlight and wind exposure over a seven- to ten-day period. Then plant.

TREES

Warning: Sometimes new trees and shrubs are already buried too deeply in their pots or burlap bags. Check by looking for a slight widening where the trunk turns into the roots (a point known as the "root flare"). When the tree is planted, this flare should be slightly *above* grade. If you can't locate it, gently remove soil until you find the flare. That's your guide for gauging tree depth in the hole. (See March's "Here's How to Plant a Tree.")

Skip adding a layer of rocks to the bottom of your planting hole "for drainage." According to current research, that old bit of advice is actually counterproductive and leads to poorer drainage.

Remove burlap, cages, and any other protective material from around your tree's roots once the tree is in the hole. Those materials are used to secure trees in transport, but they're no longer needed once a rootball is safely in the ground. Burlap eventually will decay, but in the short term can impede root spread. Burlap or fiber pots left above ground can wick moisture out of a rootball. Ropes and ties are slow to decay, can constrict roots and trunks, and may imbed in the wood, causing a weak spot that's prone to snapping. Bottom line: remove anything that goes between your roots and the soil or that could constrict roots and shoots.

CARE

ALL

Weeds love warming weather and plentiful rain as much as the desirables. Pull them when they're young, especially after a rain moistens the soil. Dig weeds such as dandelions and thistle that have deep taproots. Or spot-treat weeds with an herbicide. Tenacity now will save much work later.

■ *Staking a new tree usually isn't necessary, unless you're in a windy area or planting a tree that's unusually top-heavy. Remove burlap and other materials from the rootball before backfilling with soil.*

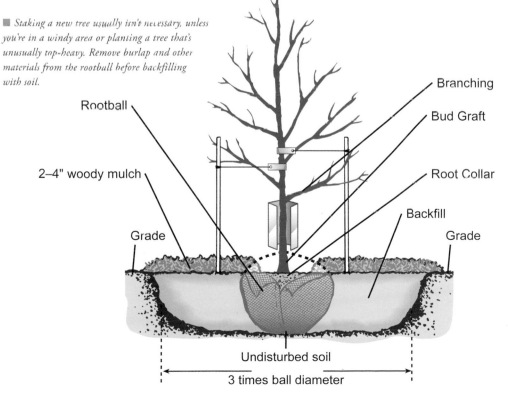

Rootball

2–4" woody mulch

Grade

Branching

Bud Graft

Root Collar

Backfill

Grade

Undisturbed soil

3 times ball diameter

April is a good month to add mulch to garden beds. Don't be too quick to put it down, though. Let the soil warm and dry a bit if it's been cool and rainy. Mulching too soon can trap moisture and keep the soil colder longer, slowing root growth.

ANNUALS & TROPICALS

Get your beds ready for planting by clearing out weeds, remaining dead plants from last year, and debris from winter. Dig in a light layer of compost, and rake the beds smooth so you'll be ready to plant once frost is done.

Do *not* dig the soil where you want self-seeded plants from last year's dropped seed. Self-sowers include cleome (spider flower), nigella (love-in-a-mist), larkspur, snapdragon, four-o'-clocks, calendula, cosmos, and sometimes gloriosa daisy, zinnia, marigold, and petunia. Don't mulch over the tops of these areas either. Seedlings will be popping up shortly, if not already.

BULBS

You may be tempted to remove the leaves of bulbs that already have bloomed. *Resist the urge* even if the foliage is flopping. It's okay to snip off faded flowers and spent flower stalks, but let the leaves continue to soak in sunlight to recharge the bulbs for next year's flowering. Wait at least until the leaves turn yellow to cut them.

No braiding or tying the bulb foliage either. That also cuts down the surface area of leaves available to soak up sunlight. There's plenty else to do this time of year than give your bulbs a hairdo.

LAWNS

Grass growth kicks into high gear this month. Don't scalp your grass this year. Keep the blades a minimum of 2½ to 3 inches tall. Taller grass retains soil moisture, chokes out sunlight to weeds, and provides more chlorophyll for stronger grass-root growth. Try mowing higher and see if it's the levelness that you like, not necessarily the shortness. The exception is zoysia grass, which should be maintained at 2 inches or slightly less.

Sharpen the mower blade if you didn't do so over winter. Sharp blades make clean cuts instead of the ragged, brown tips left behind by dull mower

■ *Cutting the lawn too short can lead to thinning and more drought/heat stress on the grass.*

blades. Ragged tips also lose more moisture and are more prone to disease. Resharpen blades after every twenty-five hours of cutting.

Mow only when the grass is dry to minimize compaction and fungal disease. As for frequency, mow often enough that you're never removing more than one-third of the grass blades at a time.

It's not too late to apply crabgrass preventer if you've had a problem with this weed in the past. It's also not too early to begin killing weeds in the lawn by applying a broadleaf weed-killer formulated for lawns. These kill non-grassy plants only. Spot-spray a liquid broadleaf weed-killer to control occasional weeds, or apply a granular broadleaf weed-killer if they're everywhere. Hand-pick or dig larger lawn weeds.

■ *Use a screwdriver or similar long-handled weeding tool to dig up larger lawn weeds.*

PERENNIALS & GROUNDCOVERS

April is a good month to dig and divide most perennials and groundcovers that are getting too crowded or outgrowing their allotted space. The exception is plants blooming this month or those in bud and about the bloom. A good rule of thumb is to divide species in the *opposite* season from which they bloom (spring bloomers in fall and fall bloomers in spring, with most summer bloomers tolerating either spring or fall). (See "Here's How to Divide Perennials.")

Once the soil has warmed and dried, mulch the perennial beds. It's easier to get good coverage before the perennials grow and spread in the coming weeks.

Cut back any remaining dead foliage from last season if you haven't already done it. (See "Here's When to Cut Which Perennials" for a list of what gets cut, how, and when.)

Some perennials hold their leaves all year and just need some neatening snips to get rid of winter-

HERE'S HOW

TO DIVIDE PERENNIALS

1. In spring, first cut back last year's dead foliage if you haven't done so already, except for species that hold their leaves all year long. In fall, green growth should be left intact so long as it's healthy and alive.

2. Dig down in the soil and around the clump until it dislodges. Lift the entire rootball out of the ground.

3. Using a spade, ax, or similar sharp tool, cut the clump into pieces at least the size of a fist. Some species, such as daylilies and garden phlox, have roots that can be pulled apart into smaller clusters. Discard any dead sections, and make sure each piece has roots of its own.

4. Replant one of the pieces at the same depth as before, and water well. Use the remaining pieces to expand your planting elsewhere, or give them away.

5. Another option for most plants (and ones that aren't dying out in the center) is to use a spade to cut, separate, and remove pieces from the perimeter of the mother plant without digging up the whole thing.

HERE'S WHEN

TO CUT WHICH PERENNIALS

Perennials fall into one of four categories when it comes to when and how to cut them back each year:

1. **Cut to the ground after frost browns foliage in fall:** Anemone, armeria, aster, balloon flower, baptisia, beebalm, bleeding heart, boltonia, brunnera, catmint, centaurea, cimicifuga, columbine, corydalis, coreopsis, crocosmia, daylily, filipendula, garden phlox, goat's beard, goldenrod, hardy hibiscus, helianthus, hosta, iris, lily, lysimachia, obedient plant, penstemon, peony, salvia, sneezeweed, spiderwort, verbascum, Veronica

2. **Cut to the ground in early spring before new growth begins:** Acanthus, amsonia, asclepias, astilbe, black-eyed Susan, campanula, coneflower, creeping phlox, delphinium, echinops, epimedium, eupatorium, ferns, foamflower, Frikart's aster, gaillardia, geum, heliopsis, hollyhock, Jacob's ladder, lamb's ears, leadwort, liatris, ligularia, liriope, lobelia, lupine, lychnis, monkshood, mum, poppy, rose mallow, sea holly, sedum, sundrops, stokesia, turtlehead, yarrow

3. **Cut back to 2 or 3 inches in early spring before new growth begins:** Artemisia, baby's breath, candytuft (right after blooming), gaura, hardy geranium, Jupiter's beard, lady's mantle, ornamental grasses, red hot poker, Russian sage, scabiosa, thyme

4. **Don't cut, just trim off ratty foliage as needed:** Ajuga, bergenia, coral-bells, dianthus, evergreen ferns, foamybells, lamium, Lenten rose, ornamental strawberry, pulmonaria, snow-in-summer, verbena

injured or ratty leaves. These include Lenten rose, coral-bells, ajuga, dianthus, and bergenia.

If a groundcover of evergreen ivy, pachysandra, or vinca is getting overcrowded, diseased, or losing vigor, an April mowing can renovate the planting. Mow or cut the planting down to about 2 to 3 inches. Remove large or excess cuttings. Then scatter a light, ½-inch layer of compost over the bed. Water if it does not rain within a day or two. In a few weeks, the groundcover will generate fresh new foliage.

SHRUBS

Prune early-spring-flowering shrubs right after they finish blooming. This includes witch hazel, forsythia, bridalwreath spirea, and fothergilla. *Do not* prune flowering shrubs now that will bloom later this spring, or else you'll cut off the flower buds before they open (azalea, lilac, weigela, bigleaf hydrangea). (See "Here's When to Prune Which Shrubs and Trees.")

Summer-blooming shrubs, such as butterfly bush, rose-of-Sharon, and caryopteris, are best pruned at the end of winter. If you didn't do it last month, these can still be clipped if they need it. Do it as soon

■ *Prune dead wood first, then shorten the branches of "keeper" wood.*

as you can this month. You're wasting the plant's energy by letting growth happen and then cutting it off. Plus, if you wait too long into the season to prune summer bloomers, they may not flower at all.

When mulching around shrubs, keep the mulch a few inches back away from their trunk(s). Mulch can trap moisture against the bark and encourage rotting.

For evergreen shrubs such as holly, boxwood, globe arborvitae, euonymus, nandina, cherry laurel, yew, and Japanese plum yew, early April is still a good time to prune or shear. Wait until spring growth finishes to cut spruce, fir, and pine.

Finish pruning roses this month if you didn't get to it in March. Your ideal cue is when the leaf buds start elongating from the canes.

TREES

Now that grass and weeds are growing fast, you'll likely be spending much time with the weed-whacker. Be careful you don't whack tree bark! Also don't run into tree trunks with mowers. Both can open wounds and lead to infection. This is one of the many reasons why it's good to maintain mulched circles around the base of trees.

Remove staking from trees planted last spring. One year is enough. While you're at it, check other more recently staked trees to make sure the ties aren't too tight.

Early-spring-flowering trees (star magnolia, redbud, and cornelian cherry dogwood, for example) can be pruned right after they're done flowering. Wait to prune late-spring bloomers so you don't cut off this year's flower buds that haven't yet opened.

April also is fine to prune most evergreen trees, including arborvitae, Leyland cypress, cryptomeria, Hinoki cypress, cedar, holly, and false cypress. Wait until May or June after new growth finishes to prune fir, spruce, and pine. Dead wood can be cut off anytime from any species.

WATER

ALL

Watering is one of the last things you'll need to worry about in April. The soil usually starts out moist from winter snowmelt, then frequent showers make this month largely hoseless.

It's always a good idea, though, to "water in" anything newly planted to help the soil settle around the roots. Then just watch to make sure rain keeps the soil consistently damp in the early going.

HERE'S WHEN

TO PRUNE WHICH SHRUBS AND TREES

Shrubs and trees that are best pruned in late winter to early spring, i.e., heading into the growing season: Abelia, arborvitae, barberry, beautyberry, boxwood, burning bush, butterfly bush, caryopteris, cherry laurel, clematis (summer bloomers), coral-berry, crape myrtle, dogwood (shrub types), euonymus, false cypress, gardenia, heather, hemlock, holly, juniper, nandina, oak, panicle hydrangea, photinia, potentilla, privet, most roses, rose-of-sharon, skimmia, St. John's wort, seven-son flower, smooth hydrangea, spirea (most), summersweet, snowberry, vitex, yew

Shrubs and trees that are best pruned right after they bloom: Aucuba, azalea, beautybush, bigleaf hydrangea, bittersweet, bridalwreath spirea, camellia, Carolina jessamine, chokeberry, flowering cherry, clematis (spring bloomers), cotoneaster, daphne, deutzia, dogwood (tree types), enkianthus, flowering almond, fothergilla, forsythia, fringe tree, fringe flower, heath, honeysuckle, kerria, lavender, leucothoe, lilac, magnolia (most), mahonia, mock orange, mountain laurel, ninebark, oakleaf hydrangea, pearlbush, pieris, flowering plum, pyracantha, quince, redbud, rhododendron, Scotch broom, serviceberry, smokebush, snowbell, spicebush, sweetshrub, viburnum, weigela, winter jasmine, witch hazel

ANNUALS & TROPICALS

Newly planted annuals benefit from watering two to three times a week (whenever it doesn't rain) to help them establish. The roots of new annuals are small and shallow, so they're more prone to drying when the soil surface goes dry. This is a rare case in which frequent shallow waterings are better than infrequent deeper ones, as with trees and shrubs.

BULBS

Unless it's unusually dry, you won't need to water spring bulbs. Bulbs in pots dry faster, though, so you may need to water those every day or two.

LAWNS

Established lawns almost never need water in April. Newly seeded lawns are a different story. Keep seed continually moist with frequent (even daily) light sprinklings until it sprouts. Then water the young growth a little deeper every two to three days in the absence of rain. The goal is consistently damp soil in the top 4 to 6 inches to encourage the young grass roots to penetrate downward.

Newly sodded lawns also need regular water. Soak well after planting, then water every two to three days in the absence of rain to keep the soil consistently damp in the top 4 to 6 inches. Be sure to apply enough water that it's soaking through the sod layer and down into the soil.

PERENNIALS & GROUNDCOVERS

April showers are usually enough to satisfy established perennials and groundcovers. Give them a weekly soaking if it's unusually dry. Newly planted perennials and groundcovers should be soaked twice a week if rain doesn't do the deed for you.

SHRUBS & TREES

Established woody plants seldom need April watering, especially if you've maintained a 2- to 3-inch mulch layer around their base. The exceptions are the ones that have less than two years in the ground. The roots of these are still young enough that a deep soaking once or twice a week is beneficial if rain isn't watering for you. The goal is to keep the soil consistently damp all around the growing rootball and just under it.

FERTILIZE

ALL

The beginning of a new growing season is prime time for giving the soil new nutrition. However, the idea of fertilizing is to supply the soil with *adequate* amounts of each of the nutrients the plants in that bed need. More isn't better. Plants will take up what they need, and the rest goes unused, leaches out, or runs off.

The only sure way to determine your soil's nutrition status is to do a soil test. Do-it-yourself kits are available at County Extension offices and most garden centers. Send in your soil sample, and the lab returns a report on key nutrient levels, the soil's pH (acidity level), and recommendations on type and amount of fertilizer needed (if any).

■ *A soil test gives you exact fertilizer needs and recommendations; otherwise, you're just guessing.*

If your plants are growing well and showing no signs of poor color, stunted growth, or other symptoms related to a nutrition deficiency, they probably don't need fertilizer.

Organic gardeners often top their soil each spring and/or fall with a light layer of compost, mulch, or similar organic matter, which adds nutrition as it breaks down.

ANNUALS & TROPICALS

Annuals are relatively heavy feeders and benefit from rich, loose soil. Work compost into the soil before planting each year, and consider adding a small amount of granular, organic flower fertilizer or a granular, slow-acting flower fertilizer to gradually release nutrients through summer.

BULBS

If you're planning to yank the tulips after their first-season performance (many of them go downhill in ensuing years), no fertilizer is needed. But for daffodils, hyacinths, crocuses, and other spring bulbs you're keeping, lightly scratch a granular fertilizer into the soil surface if you didn't already do that in March. Use a product with a balanced nutrient breakdown or one specifically formulated for bulbs.

LAWNS

If you already spread a slow-acting granular fertilizer last fall, there's no need to do so again until May or early June.

If you *didn't* spread fertilizer on the lawn last fall and didn't do it in March either, this month is still okay. A soil test will tell you the exact breakdown and amount your lawn needs, if any. Generally, a granular organic lawn fertilizer or one high in slow-release nitrogen and low in phosphorus is preferred. Lawns usually need no phosphorus at all (the second number on those three-digit bag labels).

For zoysia grass being fertilized twice a year, April is prime time for the first treatment. (June is the other.)

Remember, Marylanders: Phosphorus in lawn fertilizer is banned unless a soil test indicates it's needed. The state's lawn-fertilizer rules also limit the amount of nitrogen and require you to sweep any spills from hard surfaces. See March, Fertilize, Lawns for more details on the state's regulations or check the Maryland Department of Agriculture's website at www.mda.maryland.gov/Pages/fertilizer.aspx for current rules and additional details.

Another fertilizer option is to skip granular products and sprays and instead spread a light layer of compost over the soil surface in spring and/or fall.

Avoid heavy doses of fertilizers high in water-soluble ("fast-release") nitrogen. They green a lawn quickly but also can increase the growth rate to undesirable levels. That means more mowing and more energy going into excessive blade growth instead of strong root growth. Excess nitrogen also can pollute water and increase the likelihood of some lawn diseases. Fertilizer bags usually list the percentage of water-soluble versus water-insoluble ("slow-release") nitrogen.

PERENNIALS & GROUNDCOVERS

Groundcovers seldom need supplemental fertilizer. Fertilize those beds only if poor growth or a soil test indicates a deficiency.

Many established perennials also do fine with existing soil nutrition, boosted by nutrients coming from each season's decaying mulch and/or compost. Some gardeners like the "insurance" of scattering granular organic or slow-acting flower fertilizer over the perennial beds each April, just as new growth is taking off.

SHRUBS & TREES

Most of these don't need routine fertilizer. Especially for woody plants growing in or near lawns, their roots will grab fertilizer being applied to the lawn. Decaying mulch also supplies nutrition.

A good rule of thumb: skip fertilizer unless poor growth or a soil test indicates it. Rather than guess and buy something unnecessary, it's best to test the soil and act based on the report.

Mophead and lacecap hydrangeas can switch bloom color between pink and blue, depending on soil acidity. Add granular sulfur in spring and fall to lower the pH and turn flowers blue. Add lime in spring and fall to raise the pH and turn flowers pink.

Roses are heavy feeders and usually benefit from a scattering of granular, organic or slow-acting rose fertilizer as growth begins in a new season. Apply that now if you didn't do it in March.

PROBLEM-SOLVE

ALL

The key to healthy plants is keeping them stress-free. That starts with getting the right plant in the right location—a site that provides the preferred soil type, adequate moisture, correct light, and room to grow. Well-placed plants have healthy immune systems that are better able to defend against insect and disease attacks.

Don't guess about perceived problems and wing it with treatments. Identify a problem first and target your response, *if* one is even needed. Routinely spraying the entire yard for insects and diseases "just in case" is wasteful, polluting, and harmful to beneficial or harmless organisms, which make up the majority of landscape life.

Ask yourself these problem-solving checklist questions: Does your plant *really* have a problem, or are those yellowing, dropping needles and flaking bark normal? If it is a bug, disease, or other insult, is it a threat to the plant's health and life, or is it just a cosmetic issue that'll resolve on its own? If it *is* a serious threat, exactly what's causing it? What can be used to solve the problem without causing damage to off-target organisms or the environment? And when is the correct time to apply it?

ANNUALS & TROPICALS

Deer and rabbits are fans of tender, newly planted annuals. Fencing defeats the purpose of ornamental plants, so your best bet is to apply scent or taste repellents. Reapply them as frequent spring rains wash them off.

Spot-fencing young plants being targeted by marauding animals works well—if you don't mind looking at the fence.

BULBS

Deer and rabbits also like the flower buds of some spring-blooming bulbs—especially tulips. Keep a repellent spray on them if you're running into trouble. Or consider erecting a fence around them.

Tulip fire (*Botrytis tulipae*) is a disease that attacks tulips growing in the same place for several years, deforming their flowers. Dig and discard infected bulbs, and avoid tulips in that soil for at least four years. The disease will die out on its own.

LAWNS

That brown zoysia grass isn't dead. It's still waking up. Your neighbors might not like how it's creeping

into their now-green cool-season lawn, though (zoysia elbows out most other grasses). To keep zoysia within your borders, sink a plastic, metal, or concrete barrier down at least 3 or 4 inches deep and also 2 or 3 inches above grade to keep runners from spreading. Anything that's already spread has to be dug out or sprayed with a non-selective, kill-everything herbicide such as glyphosate.

Thatch is the spongy layer of decomposing organic matter (mostly dead grass roots) at the soil surface. A ½-inch layer or less is normal, but some grass types and some practices encourage it to thicken to levels that impede oxygen, moisture, and nutrition to the roots. Letting grass clippings on the lawn doesn't cause this problem. To deal with excess thatch, use a power rake or dethatching attachment to the mower to rip up and remove this mat. Dethatching is best done in early fall for most grasses, in early spring for zoysia grass.

Red thread is one of the season's first lawn diseases. It's caused by a fungus that prefers cool, damp conditions, and it shows up as a pinkish, thready look at the tips of grass blades. Fertilizing usually fixes it, as does warmer, drier weather. It's usually not severe enough to kill grass.

PERENNIALS & GROUNDCOVERS

Slugs are often a problem this month. These slimy crawlers prefer shady areas and are especially fond of hosta. Set out homemade traps, such as a shallow pie pan filled with beer. Or buy commercial slug traps or repellents.

■ *A ½-inch or less layer of thatch in the lawn is normal and not harmful.*

■ *Set out beer traps to capture slugs.*

Other ways to deter slugs are to go out at night when they're most active and sprinkle them with salt; scatter sand, gravel, or a similar scratchy material over the ground (their soft bodies are sensitive); set boards or cantaloupe half-shells over the ground at night and check underneath in the morning for hiding slugs; or surround the bed with copper wire or strips (which apparently give off enough of an electric charge to make sensitive-skinned slugs uncomfortable).

Deer, rabbits, groundhogs, and voles may nibble the tender foliage of emerging perennials. They each have particular favorites. Watch for chewing damage, and either spot-fence the plants or use repellents. Once the growth thickens, this early damage often dwindles.

One of the season's first bug pests are aphids, which are small, pear-shaped green or black bugs sometimes called "plant lice." Lady beetles and other predator bugs often clean up aphid infestations without you doing anything. But if it's getting out of hand, and you're not seeing beneficials, sprays of insecticidal soap or Neem oil are controls.

SHRUBS
If you're seeing brown tips and edges on broadleaf evergreen leaves, such as cherry laurel, nandina, sweetbox, and aucuba, it's most likely "windburn"

from cold, winter winds. Wind and frozen soil team up to dry these leaves over winter, starting with the extremities (tips and edges). Assuming the branches are alive, the brown leaves will drop, and fresh growth will fill in. Dead branches and branch tips should be pruned back to live growth.

Roses, honeysuckle, and several other shrubs are also prone to aphids, which tend to cluster on tender new tip growth and suck the chlorophyll out of the leaves and needles. You may see ants running along stems because they like the sweet "honeydew" that aphids secrete. If aphids are out of control and causing noticeable damage, try blasting them with a stiff spray of water, or spray them with insecticidal soap or Neem oil.

Watch out for a fairly new and deadly rose disease called "rose rosette disease." It's caused by a virus that's thought to be spread by a mite. Symptoms include elongated canes that are thicker than usual, deformed flowers, mutated new growth that's often red in color, and excessive thorns. Have a sample diagnosed by your Extension office or a trusted garden center to rule out bugs, herbicide injury, or other possibilities. If you have rose rosette disease, there's no effective cure. The recommended treatment is to remove the diseased rose.

TREES
Aphids may cluster at the tips of some tree branches, too. Use the same strategy as with shrubs.

Tent caterpillar nests are visible in tree branches this month. Either cut off the branches they are attached to and put them in the trash, or poke the tents open with a long stick so birds can eat the eggs and young caterpillars.

Woolly adelgids are a serious bug pest of hemlock. These aphid-like bugs suck the chlorophyll out of hemlock needles under the protection of little, white, cottony balls. This cottony growth can be seen forming at the base of hemlock needles now. You've got two treatment options: apply a liquid adelgid-killer, such as imidacloprid, to the soil in late March or early April for season-long control, or spray the foliage twice two weeks apart in early spring and early fall with a chemical adelgid-killer or with horticultural oil or insecticidal soap.

May

May is the best time to be a gardener in the mid-Atlantic region. Fragrant lilacs scent the air, crabapple flowers glorify cobalt-blue skies, and fresh summer annuals add colorful new life to your front yard.

Even the weather is generally well behaved. March winds and April clouds and showers give way to frequently pleasant, sunny days in May that kick plant growth into high gear. The threat of overnight freezes that ended last month in the southern and coastal areas disappears this month even in the region's coolest reaches of western Maryland and the West Virginia mountains. Summer is knocking on the door.

The arrival of frost-free time means the widespread planting of annual flowers—the petunias, zinnias, lantana, and begonias that color our landscapes until frost returns in fall.

There's no need to wait for those to thrive though. The Mid-Atlantic's biggest concentration of tree, shrub, and perennial flowering also happens in succession throughout May, ranging from native Virginia bluebells to the gazillions of Asian-bred azaleas and rhododendrons that decorate so many house walls. The spring bulb show joins in with its last main hurrah, in particular the tulips but also late daffodils, Spanish bluebells, and the year's peak month for ornamental onions (*Allium*).

It all adds up to a delightful and diverse setting at a time that's usually not too hot or too cold and not too wet or too dry. But don't sit on that bench under the tree gawking for too long. There's *plenty* for the gardener to do to maximize the current display and set the stage for the rest of the growing season.

Those early-blooming shrubs will need to be pruned once their flowers fade. The yellowing bulb foliage will need to be cut. And your new plantings should go in the ground before it gets too hot in June and beyond.

Yeah, it's a busy time for gardeners—one of our busiest. But you won't hear much complaining.

PLAN

ALL

This is like Christmas season for garden centers. Everybody swarms to buy plants this month. Do your buying on a weekday, if you can, to avoid peak crowds, lines, and spats over who gets that last dark-leafed elderberry.

■ *Garden centers are at their peak inventory this time of year.*

You'll be less confused if you arrive at the garden center already knowing what you want to buy.

You don't necessarily need a detailed drawing for your shopping (although that helps), but at least know basics such as how much space you have to work with, what kind of light you have, and any particular site challenges (wet soil, tree roots nearby, lurking animals, and so on).

ANNUALS & TROPICALS

Wait until all danger of frost passes if you don't want to risk losing newly planted cold-sensitive annual flowers. So-called "safe" annual-planting times arrived last month in warmer Zones 7 and 8. The threat of overnight frost typically ends early this month in Zone 6 and by mid-May in Zone 5.

If you're a gambler and don't mind the risk of losing plants some years in a late frost, annuals can go in the ground sooner. Be ready to cover plants with a floating row cover or similar light fabric covering in case a frost warning pops up in the forecast. A

compromise is to watch the ten-day forecast for overnight lows before deciding whether to plant.

Use the same last-frost timing to determine when to move houseplants outside for the summer. Give these an extra week or two (or three) because many tropicals don't tolerate even sub-50-degree nights very well. Gradually acclimate them to the outside over seven to ten days. Don't just set them outside in full sun all day right off the bat.

To match annual flower color to your house trim, paint small strips of wood or plastic with the same paint you used for the doors, walls, railings, and/or shutters. Then take those to the garden center to hold up next to the flowers. An alternative is to get paint-sample strips from a home-improvement center, and match those to your trim.

Don't overlook annuals just because they aren't blooming yet. Growers manage to have almost everything in flower by early May so they're enticing for prime shopping time. However, some beauties just take longer to get going, such as blue salvia,

■ *This pot design uses the classic combination of a thriller, filler, and spiller.*

browallia, and gloriosa daisy. They might not look like much now, but they'll flourish in a few weeks.

BULBS

Get your tender bulbs out of storage. Discard any that have shriveled or rotted. Do you need to replace or expand any? How about new types? You'll be able to buy summer bulbs such as dahlias, callas, gladioli, and tuberous begonias now at the garden center or from mail-order vendors.

Continue to watch for spots where the yard could use more spring-blooming bulbs. The crocuses, hyacinths, and most of the daffodils are done, but May is when you could be getting color from tulips, alliums, fritillaria, camassia, and Spanish bluebells.

LAWNS

Your lawn should be at its best this month. Grass has had weeks to green and fill in, sunlight is increasing, and soil moisture is usually good. Brutal heat and drought haven't hit yet. If all isn't well in grassland, think about why:

- Are you cutting too short?
- Is the soil nutrition lacking?
- Is the lawn thin, allowing crabgrass and weeds to elbow in?
- Have you had outbreaks of grubs killing off whole patches?
- Are tree roots expanding, signaling it's time to switch to another more shade-tolerant groundcover?

PERENNIALS & GROUNDCOVERS

Garden centers have their best selection of perennials and groundcovers this time of year, often in a selection of sizes. Plants in 4- or 6-inch pots are least expensive but will require more patience. Larger plants in quart or 1-, 2-, or 3-gallon pots cost more but have immediate impact.

Look for healthy plants at purchase. Signs of setbacks include:

- Wilted foliage from lack of water.
- Yellow or limp foliage from insufficient light or fertilizer.
- Holes or a stippling of the leaves from insects.

- Blotches or gray coating on the leaves or stems from possible fungal disease.
- Thin, lanky stems from lack of light during early growth.
- Excessive flowers on an undersized plant from overfertilization.
- Roots emerging from the pot's drainage holes, which can signal circling roots or a plant that's been in the pot too long.
- Weeds in the container from lack of attention by the seller.

Not all of these are deal-killers. Some are temporary or cosmetic issues, ones that plants will grow through once in the ground. However, the closer you can get to perfection at buying time, the better your success odds.

Maximize your first-year enjoyment by picking perennials that have a lot of buds just about to open as opposed to plants already in full bloom.

SHRUBS

Five things to consider when you're shopping for a healthy shrub are:

- Good leaf color; no yellowing or dull color that might indicate poor soil nutrition or insect trouble.
- No spotting of the leaves or a grayish coating. Those are possible symptoms of disease.
- Good full shape without broken or missing branches.
- No wilting, which indicates the plant hasn't been watered often enough or has outgrown its pot.
- Roots that aren't tightly circling or matted when you gently slip the plant out of the pot.

Among the choices you'll encounter for May-flowering shrubs are azalea, rhododendron, roses, beautybush, cherry laurel, chokeberry, coralberry, deutzia, lilac, shrub dogwood, tree peony, sweetshrub, viburnum, and weigela.

Honeysuckle, ornamental kiwi vine, and spring-blooming clematis are three vines that add vertical color in May.

Install trellises several inches out from walls to allow air circulation. This will protect wall surfaces from mildew and marks from the vine. Building them so they're detachable is also convenient for painting or repairing the wall surface.

TREES

What size tree should you buy? Some gardeners use a "the-bigger-the-better" approach, but small to mid-sized trees—4 to 6 feet tall at purchase—offer several advantages. They're less expensive, easier to transport, easier to handle when planting, and quicker to establish once in the ground. Small trees often catch up size-wise with larger ones in a few years because their rootballs are more in balance with the canopy.

When tree-shopping, look for well-spaced, firmly attached branches, a trunk without wounds, and the same five traits as healthy shrubs (see Plan, Shrubs).

If your yard is weak in May-blooming trees, consider crabapple, Carolina silverbell, fringe tree, Japanese snowbell, Kousa dogwood, hawthorn, horse chestnut, and some magnolias.

PLANT

ALL

"Transplant shock" refers to the wilting that can happen to plants soon after they're moved to a new location. It can happen both to existing landscape plants that are dug and moved, and to newly bought potted plants going into the ground from a sheltered greenhouse. Minimize shock by planting on a cloudy day, or at least out of the hot, midday sun. Early morning and evening are two better times. Always soak a plant well with water immediately after it's planted or transplanted.

HERE'S HOW

TO PLANT ANNUALS

■ *Annual flowers used for mass-planting are typically sold in four- to six-plant cell packs.*

■ *Plant annuals at the same depth as they were growing in the pot or cell pack.*

1. Loosen the planting bed to 10 or 12 inches deep and work in 1 to 2 inches of compost, rotted manure, rotted leaves, or similar organic matter. Mix in a light scattering of granular organic flower fertilizer or a pelleted, gradual-release flower fertilizer.

2. Open a planting hole, deep enough so that the plant will end up at the same depth it was in the pot.

3. Squeeze the sides of the pot, invert, and gently slip the plant out into your hand. Set it in the hole.

4. Gently firm the soil so the rootball is covered. Water well.

5. Mulch isn't necessary if you stay on top of weeding and watering. Otherwise, 1 inch is fine. Keep mulch from touching the stems.

HERE'S HOW

TO PLANT AND CARE FOR CONTAINER PLANTS

1. Think big. Smaller pots dry out faster than larger ones. Also, terra-cotta dries out faster than plastic, foam, concrete, and metal.

2. Fill the pot about two-thirds full with lightweight potting mix, or so the soil line will end up an inch or two *below* the pot lip once the plants are planted.

3. Set your plants, spaced almost to touching, and cover the rootballs with additional potting mix.

4. Lightly scratch a scattering of granular, gradual-release flower fertilizer into the surface, and soak the pot well until water runs out the bottom.

5. Start your season-long care. Figure on daily soakings (except in cool, cloudy and rainy weather), and add a half-strength flower fertilizer to the water once a week throughout the growing season.

6. Snip back stems of plants that are overtaking neighbors or growing too long. Deadhead spent flowers.

■ *Add a dose of long-acting, gradual-release fertilizer to the flowerpot soil before planting.*

■ *Plant flowers closely in pots for a full effect.*

ANNUALS & TROPICALS

Once you're convinced frost is finished, get busy planting those petunias, salvia, angelonias, and other warm-season annuals. One foot apart is good spacing for most. A few, including geraniums, lantana, and most petunias, spread quicker and more vigorously and can go 15 to 24 inches apart. (See "Here's How to Plant Annuals.") If cool-season pansies and violas are going downhill, replace them with these warm-season annuals.

If you're using transplants that you started from seed, be sure to "harden them off" first. This means gradually getting them used to increasingly more light and outdoor exposure over a seven- to ten-day period before planting.

The end of frost means it's time to direct-seed annuals into the ground. Ones that start well this way include calendula, cleome (spider flower),

cosmos, marigold, nasturtium, nigella (love-in-a-mist), sunflower, and zinnia. Loosen the soil, scatter the seed, and cover with the soil to the depth listed on each variety's seed packet. Keep the bed watered until the seeds are up. Snip off excess seedlings with scissors.

Don't overlook direct-seeded annual vines as a good way to add vertical color to bare walls, arbors, trellises, and such. These include purple hyacinth bean, scarlet runner bean, black-eyed Susan vine, morning glory, moonflower, cypress vine, cardinal climber, cup-and-saucer vine, and climbing nasturtium.

It's also warm enough to plant annual vines normally grown from transplants, including mandevilla, dipladenia, bougainvillea, sweet potato vine, Rex begonia vine, and passion vine, which is perennial in Zones 7 and 8.

May is the time to put together containers of summer annuals. The classic design is an upright "thriller" as the centerpiece, several bushier bloomers as the "fillers," and one or more "spillers" to trail around the edges. You don't have to stick with that, though. A pot filled with a single type of showy flower, Dragon Wing® begonias, for example, can be simple but elegant. Or if you like a more action-packed cottage-garden look, go with a collection of "onesies."

BULBS

Tender bulbs, such as caladium, dahlia, calla, tuberose, and gladiola, can go in the ground once all danger of frost is gone. Clean the soil from ones you've dug and saved from last season, and discard any shriveled or rotted bulbs. Divide dahlia tubers, making sure each separate tuber has an "eye," or growing point. Separate begonias and gladiolas, and plant those separately, too.

Gradually acclimate tender bulbs you've started inside before transplanting into the ground. Ditto for that amaryllis you've been growing inside all winter. Amaryllis can be planted in the ground or left to grow in a pot outside over summer.

You'll find dahlias, gladiola, calla lilies, cannas, tuberous begonias, and more on sale now in bulb form at the garden center. These can be planted throughout May, once all danger of frost is past. Stagger plantings every two weeks into early June to spread out the bloom times.

One other plant you'll find in bulb form this time of year is the lily. Most lilies are winter-hardy and will come back year after year, as will some of the above other varieties in warmer parts of the mid-Atlantic region. Buying lilies as bulbs is less expensive than buying them in plant form. They can also be planted this month.

Spring-flowering bulbs that are done blooming can be dug, divided, and transplanted. Gently dig up masses, and shake away excess soil. Tease apart individual bulbs. Discard any bulbs that are damaged or diseased. Replant some of the bulbs in

HERE'S HOW

TO PLANT AND CARE FOR A HANGING BASKET

1. Lean toward larger baskets, which won't dry out as fast as smaller ones. Line the inside of your frame with sphagnum moss or with a ready-made moss or fiber liner. Reduce evaporation loss by lining the inside of that (but *not* the bottom) with a sheet of thick plastic.

2. Fill the basket with lightweight potting mix about two-thirds full.

3. Set your plants, spaced almost to touching, and cover the rootballs with additional potting mix. The mix should end up an inch or two *below* the lip.

4. Lightly scratch a scattering of granular, gradual-release flower fertilizer into the surface.

5. Install the hanger hooks and chain. Make sure the hangers are sturdy enough to hold the weight of the basket, potting mix, and water. Hang the basket.

6. Once in place, soak the basket until water drains out.

7. Start your season-long care regimen. Check regularly for water (daily watering is the norm in hot, dry weather), and add a half-strength flower fertilizer to the water once a week throughout the growing season.

8. Snip back stems of plants that are overtaking neighbors or growing too long. Deadhead spent flowers.

the original spot, and plant the rest where you'd like to spread the colony. Cut foliage once it yellows.

LAWNS

May is still okay to plant grass seed—the sooner the better. Grass can be planted all summer, but it's harder to germinate grass and keep it damp when it's boiling hot and bone dry.

■ *Laying sheets of sod is a quick way to establish a new lawn.*

An alternative to seeding bare lawn spots in the impending heat is to use sod. Sod is sections of already-growing grass, complete with roots and soil, which is sold like strips of carpet in garden centers. Sodding is more expensive than seeding, but sod sections can be laid right on top of loosened soil, tamped down, and watered to produce an instant lawn. (See September's "Here's How To Start a New Lawn from Sod.")

PERENNIALS & GROUNDCOVERS

May is still an excellent time to plant perennials and groundcovers. Just be vigilant with the water since we're heading into the hot season. (See April's "Here's How To Plant Perennials.")

Perennials aren't just for in the ground. Coral-bells, hosta, brunnera, Japanese forest grass, and others with colorful foliage are excellent additions to flowerpots. Mix them with color-coordinated annuals or create entire pots using long-blooming and/or colorful-leafed perennials.

SHRUBS

The vast majority of flowering and evergreen shrubs are sold as container-grown plants these days. May is one of the year's best months to plant them. (See March's "Here's How To Plant a Shrub.")

Azaleas and rhododendrons require special attention since plants in this family (*Ericaceae*) don't prefer the conditions many homeowners give them, which is compacted, clayish, alkaline soil in hot, dry sites. These and related shrubs such as pieris, mountain laurel, and heather appreciate very well-drained, acidic soil and a site out of direct afternoon sun.

TREES

May is a good month to plant both container-grown and balled-and-burlapped trees. (See April's "Here's How To Plant a Tree.")

Most nurseries and garden centers will plant trees that you purchase from them (at an extra fee) if you can't or would rather not plant your new tree.

Earlier advice to remove branches at planting to "balance the roots with the aboveground growth" has been found counterproductive. Remove only broken or torn branches at the time of planting. More wood means more leaves to grab the sun's energy and feed energy to the growing roots. Wait a year to start corrective pruning and training.

CARE

ALL

May is mulch month. The soil has warmed enough now that you don't have to worry about trapping cold or root-rotting excess moisture. May is ideal mulch timing for two reasons: mulch excels at stopping weeds, many of which germinate in May, and mulch conserves soil moisture, which is needed as summer heat, dryness, and peak sunlight arrive.

Don't overmulch. Use no more than 3 to 4 total inches around trees and shrubs. Two inches is ideal around perennials, and 1 inch is ideal around annuals. In all cases, keep mulch back away from trunks and stems to avoid encouraging rot.

If you already have the mulch totals noted in the previous paragraph, *don't add more.* Resist the urge to automatically top the beds with more and more mulch, just because you like the look of fresh mulch. If you have enough and want a fresh look, cultivate the existing mulch.

When working compost into new beds, you'll end up with slightly raised beds that are ideal for almost all plants. To keep mulch from sliding down the sides and onto the lawn or sidewalk, taper the bed edges down to 2 or 3 inches *below* grade. That'll create a "lip" to catch sliding mulch.

■ *Keep mulch pulled away from the stems of plants.*

ANNUALS & TROPICALS

Nurse newly planted annuals through a hot spell by erecting temporary shade over them for a few days. An inch of organic mulch (chopped leaves or pine needles are ideal) over the bare soil will discourage weeds and keep the soil moist and cooler.

Watch for new sprouts from last year's self-sowing annuals, such as cleome, nigella, and larkspur. These can thickly carpet a bed if you don't thin them early with scissors. Or dig and transplant "volunteer" seedlings.

BULBS

Some summer bulbs such as lilies, gladiolas, crocosmia, and dahlias can get tall enough to flop once they flower. Erect supports or install plant rings soon after the shoots are up. That'll corral them more neatly than trying to bring floppers back under control later. Be careful you don't ram stakes into the buried bulbs.

As the foliage of daffodils, tulips, and other bloomed-out spring bulbs yellows and starts to collapse, cut it off and compost it.

LAWNS

Let your grass clippings lay. They decay quickly and return nutrition and organic material to the soil. They don't cause thatch, which is a spongy layer composed mostly of dead roots at the soil surface. Mulching mowers cut blades multiple times before dropping them, but even ordinary mowers disperse clippings without matting if you're mowing often enough.

The lawn can be dethatched this month if a thatch layer has grown more than 1 inch thick.

Now that the grass is growing at peak rate, raise the blade on your mower to 2½ or 3 inches (except for zoysia grass; 2 inches maximum for that). Taller grass retains soil moisture, denies sunlight to weeds, and provides more chlorophyll for stronger grass-root growth.

Continue mowing often enough that you're never removing more than one-third of the grass blade at a time.

Control lawn weeds by spot-spraying scattered outbreaks with a liquid broadleaf weed-killer or by broadcasting a granular broadleaf weed-killer in widespread outbreaks. Hand-pick or dig larger weeds such as dandelions, hawkweed, plantain, and thistle.

If you're using a crabgrass product that both stops crabgrass from sprouting and kills it in its early stages, such as ones containing dithiopyr, May is a good time to apply it. A cue is when dandelions are blooming.

PERENNIALS & GROUNDCOVERS

May is still okay to dig and divide perennials that already have bloomed or that bloom in fall, although it's not as desirable as the cool of earlier spring. We're heading into hot, dry weather soon. That's more stressful on a newly moved plant. Be extra vigilant to keep May-divided perennials watered all summer. (See April's "Here's How To Divide Perennials.")

Taller perennials, such as peony, boltonia, goldenrod, and perennial sunflower, benefit from staking or similar supports to keep them from flopping later. Get your supports in place now so the plants grow within them. It's easier than trying to corral flopping plants later.

For supporting tall perennials, use plant rings or similar store-bought metal staking gizmos available at garden centers. Or build your own by hammering bamboo stakes around the clusters in need of support and tying jute tightly around the staking. The stakes should be slightly shorter than the plant's maximum height.

■ *Get stakes and other plant supports in place at the beginning of the season. It's easier than trying to corral sprawlers later.*

■ *Circular stakes help hold tall plants in place. You can also create your own do-it-yourself plant supports out of bamboo stakes and jute.*

Neaten perennials that have finished blooming by "deadheading" them; that is, snipping off their spent flowers and/or flower stalks. Use shears to speed the job of deadheading masses of perennials with clustered flowers, such as candytuft, dianthus, and creeping phlox.

Keep late-blooming perennials from flopping by shearing them back this month. Mums are the best example, but sedum, aster, goldenrod, beebalm, boltonia, and even coneflower and black-eyed Susan can be trimmed by one-third to one-half. The plants will look ragged for a few weeks and bloom slightly later, but they'll bloom more fully and be markedly more compact.

SHRUBS

Is it dead? That's a common question after a particularly cold winter that's caused a lot of branch dieback and brown leaves and needles. New buds should be poking out of most shrubs by the end of May to early June, so that's the surest way to tell what's alive and what's not. Be patient and watch for new growth.

Two tests to assess live versus dead wood are:

• Bend a branch in question, and see if it's flexible or brittle. Bending is good, snapping is bad.
• Scrape a sliver of bark off a stem or two with a fingernail or knife blade. If there's green or pale moist tissue beneath, it's probably still alive. If it's brown and dry underneath, that wood is dead.

Once you're sure branches are dead, prune them off. Occasionally, cold winters kill sensitive shrubs such as bigleaf hydrangeas, vitex, and crape myrtle the whole way back to the ground. If that happens, cut off all dead top growth to make way for new growth emerging from the base.

Prune spring-blooming shrubs right after they're done flowering, such as quince, azalea, daphne, fothergilla, deutzia, and weigela. (See April's "Here's When To Prune Which Trees and Shrubs.")

Snip off faded blossoms from large-flowered rhododendrons as they finish blooming. Go down to the next lower truss to control the shrub's size. Rhododendrons are best not sheared.

Fresh mulch under roses discourages weeds, retains soil moisture, and prevents last year's fallen disease spores from splashing up on the stems. Keep it to no more than 3 inches total. Top off what you have, or remove and replace the mulch if you're tackling disease problems. Remove fallen leaves from around the bushes before mulching, especially if the leaves were diseased last season.

Fasten the canes of climbing roses to their supports as they grow. These don't cling or twine on their own. Loop soft ties around the cane, then around the trellis to fasten. Don't tie too tightly and cut into the wood.

Check your roses for new stems growing from below the graft, the point where an attractive stem was attached to a durable root section at the nursery. Sometimes the roots send up different-looking and less desirable shoots. Cut these off at ground level.

TREES

Most trees should have leafed out by now. If you see bare branches or leafless tips, that wood is likely dead and will have to come off. Do the live-wood tests (see Care, Shrubs) or wait a few weeks to be sure.

Prune spring-flowering trees once they're done flowering, although it's a little harder to see the branching now than over winter. Examples include dogwood, redbud, flowering cherry, flowering pear, and early magnolias. (See February's "Here's How To Prune a Tree.")

Some trees "bleed" sap profusely when you prune them this time of year. Maples, yellowwood, snowbell, birch, and elm have this tendency. This sap loss isn't harmful, but it can make the job needlessly messy. Avoid this leaking by pruning during the winter dormant season.

Do not pile excess soil on top of tree roots. Gardeners sometimes do that to cover exposed roots or to help keep grass growing in the losing competition with bigger tree roots. You can get away with 3 or 4 inches, but covering tree beds more than that starts to deprive the roots of oxygen.

WATER

ALL

Even if it's rained recently, soak a plant immediately after planting. This settles the soil around the roots and makes sure there's plenty of moisture to encourage root penetration. Don't count on that sure-fire soaking rain that's being forecast.

■ *Tie climbing roses to their supports to help them grow upright.*

ANNUALS & TROPICALS

Annuals are shallow-rooted and benefit from frequent watering, especially in the first four to six weeks after planting. Water every other day when rain doesn't happen—or whenever the top few inches of soil is dry.

For annuals you're starting by seed directly in the ground, sprinkle the surface daily until the seeds are up. Then give them slightly deeper waterings every two or three days for the next four to six weeks.

Annuals and tropicals in containers typically need water daily, especially ones displayed in a sunny location. Soak them until water comes out the bottom drainage holes.

BULBS

Avoid watering summer-bulb beds so much that the soil becomes soggy and rots the bulbs. However, keep the soil consistently damp until the shoots of newly planted summer bulbs are up. You'll likely need to water two or three times a week until that happens. Then cut back to a weekly soaking when it's hot and dry. These need a little less water than new annuals.

Bulbs growing in pots need more water more often than in-ground ones, though. Check the pot daily and soak until water runs out the drainage holes if the pot is noticeably lighter in weight and the soil is dry when you insert your finger.

LAWNS

Keep the soil under newly seeded or sodded areas consistently damp. Otherwise, established lawns seldom need much, if any, irrigation in May. The exception is an unusually early drought.

PERENNIALS & GROUNDCOVERS

Soak new perennials and groundcovers twice a week for the first four to six weeks after planting. Then a weekly soaking is usually sufficient the rest of the first year when rain doesn't happen.

Most established perennials need little to no water in May, unless the month is unusually hot and dry, in which case a weekly soaking is helpful.

SHRUBS & TREES

When rain doesn't happen, soak new shrubs and trees two to three times a week for the first two months, close to the rootball where the roots are. Then soak once or twice a week for the rest of the first season.

A rough guide for the water needs of a new tree is 1 to 2 gallons for every inch of trunk diameter at shoulder height. For new shrubs, apply 3 to 5 gallons of water per watering. As roots spread, widen your watering area and increase amounts to 1 gallon of water for every square foot of soil surface.

Trees and shrubs that have been in the ground for at least three or four years usually won't need water in May, and most times only in extended hot, dry summer spells.

Trees and shrubs growing in containers need water more often—usually daily. Water until it drains out the bottom.

Roses survive well with little water, but they perform and flower better in consistently damp soil. Your goal can be your guide here. If you're growing shrub roses and/or trying to minimize maintenance, soak them occasionally when it's hot and dry. If you're trying to maximize performance, soak the ground around your roses two to three times a week whenever it's not raining.

ALL

Now that your plants are actively growing, watch their leaf color. Yellowing, paleness, or light tissues between dark veins are signs of possible nutrient deficiencies. Before you guess and take the wrong action or buy the wrong product, test your soil if you haven't done that lately.

■ *Yellow leaf tissue surrounding green veins is a typical sign of chlorosis, or lack of iron.*

ANNUALS & TROPICALS

If you added compost and/or granular slow-acting fertilizer to the soil when preparing your beds, you don't need more fertilizer now. If you prefer water-soluble flower fertilizer, apply your first dose as you water your new plants after planting. Then follow the timing on your product's label, which is typically once a month.

Annuals in pots and baskets need more fertilizer more often since frequent watering carries many nutrients out with the drainage. In addition to slow-acting fertilizer at planting, use a water-soluble flower fertilizer at half-strength weekly. Some gardeners use a quarter-strength dose each watering.

BULBS

Although summer bulbs, corms, tubers, and rhizomes store energy for the plant to use, high performers such as dahlias and begonias flower all summer and welcome some extra nutrition. Use a product formulated for bulbs. One option is to scatter a dose of slow-acting, granular bulb fertilizer over the soil within a month of planting. Another is to apply a water-soluble bulb fertilizer in that same timeframe and another dose in June or early July. Don't overdo it by applying too much nitrogen.

LAWNS

If you're using an organic program and fertilizing twice a year, make the season's first application. (Late September through October is the other option.)

If you're using a three-times-a-year program—whether organic or with a chemical lawn fertilizer that's high in slow-release nitrogen—May is a good time for the season's first application. (Products that are high in slow-release nitrogen are coated in order to release the greening effects of nitrogen more slowly and over a longer period of time. Fertilizer bags list the percentage of their nitrogen that is slow-release.)

If you're using a commercial "four-step" lawn-fertilizer program, you should've put down the first application in March to early April. Wait until mid-May through mid-June to put down the second application.

Good timing to apply lawn fertilizer is right before a gentle, soaking rain. The water starts to dissolve the fertilizer and carry it down into the root zone. However, Maryland bans applying fertilizer right before a *heavy* rain that could cause it to wash off instead of dissolve in.

Maryland has other lawn-fertilizer rules that still apply this month, including no phosphorus unless a soil test indicates it's needed, limits on nitrogen, and a requirement to sweep any spills from hard surfaces. See March, Fertilize, Lawns for more details or check the website www.mda.maryland.gov/Pages/fertilizer.aspx for current rules and additional details.

PERENNIALS & GROUNDCOVERS

If you worked compost and/or slow-acting granular fertilizer into your soil at planting, there's no need to add more fertilizer now to new perennials.

Established perennials also don't need additional fertilizer now, especially if you did a scattering of a slow-acting granular fertilizer over the beds last month. Just watch for signs of poor growth or nutrient deficiencies, and act on those accordingly. Otherwise, you're off the fertilizer hook here.

■ *Booster doses of a liquid flower fertilizer throughout the summer help annual flowers, particularly potted ones, bloom at peak performance.*

■ *A drop spreader is calibrated to dispense the amount of fertilizer needed.*

Established groundcovers and ornamental grasses also hardly ever need supplemental fertilizer. The exception is if poor growth and a soil test indicate a deficiency.

SHRUBS, TREES & VINES

Routinely fertilizing established trees, shrubs, and woody vines is not necessary. Skip fertilizer unless poor growth or a soil test indicates a nutrient deficiency, then address it specifically. Adding more fertilizer where it isn't needed wastes time and money, may pollute waterways, and can be counterproductive to plant health.

Fertilizing roses can be linked to your expectations. Most roses (shrub and antique types in particular) perform adequately with no fertilizer or with an annual springtime scattering of a granular, slow-acting fertilizer formulated for roses. But for peak performance, roses benefit from a scattering of rose fertilizer this month, as well as another in June, another in July and another in early August.

HOMEMADE ROSE FERTILIZER

Here's a recipe for making your own homemade rose fertilizer using organic ingredients. It's one that many amateur rosarians use:

8 parts alfalfa meal
2 parts cottonseed meal
2 parts rock phosphate (not super phosphate)
2 parts bone meal
1 part blood meal
1 part Epsom salts (magnesium sulfate)

Combine all of the above and scratch the mix around each rose bush. Use 1 cup for each foot of bush height (i.e. 3 cups around a bush that's 3 feet tall). Water well after applying.

PROBLEM-SOLVE

ALL

Lots of bugs become active now. Monitor your plants regularly and learn the difference between ones that do no, little, or only cosmetic damage versus the relative few that are more serious plant-health threats.

Insects fall into three main types so far as plant damage goes:

Chewing insects. They eat plant tissue such as leaves, flowers, buds, roots, and twigs. Damage is often seen as holes or missing tissue around the leaf edges or between the leaf veins. Key plant-chewers are beetles and caterpillars.

Sucking insects. These insects insert their beak (proboscis) into leaves, twigs, flowers, or fruits to feed on the plant's juices. Damage shows up in discolored tissue, drooping leaves, and tiny spots in the leaves ("stippling"). Suckers include aphids, mealybugs, thrips, and leafhoppers.

■ *Caterpillars are leaf-chewing insects that do their damage primarily in spring and early summer.*

Boring insects. These are the most destructive and hardest to detect because they feed inside stems or beneath bark. Damage includes dead branch tips, wilting, and even death of the whole plant. This family includes the dreaded new emerald ash borer and Asian long-horned beetle as well as the oldie-but-baddie dogwood borer and assorted bark beetles.

■ *A lady beetle is about to have a lunch of aphids.*

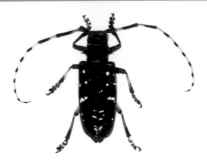

■ *The Asian longhorned beetle is a fairly new bug that threatens many tree species.*

One common May bug in the mid-Atlantic region is the aphid. Aphids are small, green or black, pear-shaped insects that suck chlorophyll out of leaves and can be seen on a wide variety of plants from sedum to roses. They can be blasted off with a stiff spray of water, killed with insecticidal soap or chemical insecticides, or left for the lady beetles to clean up.

A second common bug is the tent caterpillar. Moths lay eggs in a variety of trees and some shrubs, resulting in masses of caterpillars that feed inside of weblike bags (their "tents"). The bags are usually seen in branch crotches, at the base of where two branches meet. Insecticides control them, but just as effective is whacking open the bags to let birds have a feast.

ANNUALS & TROPICALS

Deer, rabbits, voles, chipmunks, and groundhogs are all fond of many of the tender new annuals you've just planted. Your plants will become less attractive as they grow, but in the short term, think about repellents or a protective fence.

Slugs occasionally chew on young annuals and tropicals, especially those planted in shadier spots. (See April, Problem-Solve, Perennials.)

BULBS

Deer and rabbits are still on the lookout for the last of your tulips, so keep the repellent handy.

Rabbits are especially fond of lilies, and they nibble the young shoots as they're emerging. If you see this, spray the new plants with a rabbit repellent, or scatter granular rabbit repellent over the bed.

Watch for early mildew or leaf spot problems with your young tuberous begonias. The best defense

is a good offense. Make sure they have good air circulation, don't water over the top of the foliage, pick off infected leaves, and clean up fallen diseased leaves.

LAWNS

You may see tearing-type holes in the lawn. The culprit is usually skunks (sometimes birds) in search of grubs, which are nearing the surface and about to pupate into adult beetles next month. It's annoyingly helpful. Scatter new seed and water to patch the damage. Grubs are very hard to kill at this stage and will turn into adults soon anyway, so there's no sense trying to kill them.

You might also notice volcano-like mounds popping up here and there. Those are the work of moles, which are different from the mouselike voles that surreptitiously feed on roots and low-to-the-ground stems. Moles are primarily meat-eaters. Earthworms and grubs are favorite snacks. Solutions include trapping, baiting active burrows, and spraying the area with castor oil repellents.

Ants often swarm in the lawn and construct small mounds. These are more of a minor nuisance, not nearly as troublesome as the fire ants of the South. Our cool-season ants feed on pest insect eggs and can actually help a lawn.

The arrival of warm, humid air can lead to several lawn diseases, one of which is "dollar spot," named for the half-dollar-sized yellowish blotches that turn straw brown. In severe cases, the blotches merge into bigger dead patches. Lawns that are low in nitrogen are more prone to dollar spot, so fertilizing can help. Granular fungicides are options in bad outbreaks.

PERENNIALS & GROUNDCOVERS

You'll likely see ants swarming over your peony buds this month. They're not hurting the plants; they're interested in a drink of the sugars the buds are secreting. And no, ants aren't needed to make peony buds open.

Don't be surprised if some perennials start to disappear late this month and next. Some bloom in spring and go dormant until the following year. Three common examples are bleeding heart,

Virginia bluebells, and Oriental poppies. Just cut off the foliage as it yellows and collapses. They'll be back next spring.

SHRUBS

De-icing salt problems may show up now as scorched lower leaves or twig dieback on shrubs near the street or sidewalk. If you suspect this problem, drench the soil with copious amounts of water to leach out remaining salts.

Sawfly larvae are brownish-black caterpillars that chew the needles on pine, spruce, and other needled evergreens. Early infestations can be squished or hand-picked. Insecticides control bad outbreaks.

Thrips are an early-season bug threat to roses and several other flowering shrubs. These are tiny, winged, sucking insects that cause discoloration of the flower petals. A variety of insecticides control them if they're getting out of control.

Dog urine may be the culprit if foliage yellows only on contained patches low on the plants. Erect a small wire fence, or plant prickly groundcover plants around the targeted shrubs to deter the dogs.

Wilting is somewhat common in newly planted shrubs and roses, especially if a hot, dry, sunny spell follows planting. Be sure new plants get enough water. Consider erecting a temporary shade structure over the plants until the roots begin to take hold.

Lilacs not blooming? Issues to consider are not enough sunlight and pruning at the wrong time (fall, winter, or early spring when the formed flower buds are being cut off). Old lilacs often bloom poorly and benefit from rejuvenation pruning. Late this month or in June, cut one-third of the biggest, oldest shoots to the ground. Shorten the remaining shoots by one-third. Repeat each year, and you'll eventually end up with all younger wood that flowers best. Infections of powdery mildew in summer weaken but seldom kill lilacs.

Blackspot is the bane of roses, especially hybrid teas. Watch for black rings and then yellowing on the lower leaves. Limit its spread by spraying foliage with organic or chemical fungicides at the first sign of infection (and beyond, if spots continue to form). Infected leaves can be picked off to slow the early spread.

Raspberry cane borer is a rose pest that can cause unopened buds to droop. Look carefully for a tiny, discolored entrance hole just below the affected bud or at the tops of pruning cuts. Prune off the rose cane below the hole. Seal cuts with a dab of white glue.

The roseslug is another early-summer rose pest. It's a type of sawfly whose larval stage looks like a ½-inch-long caterpillar. Roseslugs chew on rose leaves. The damage won't kill plants and will stop in a few weeks as the insect graduates into adulthood. Sprays kill them if you're impatient.

TREES

Anthracnose is a common fungal disease of American dogwood. If you see brown splotches with purplish "halos" on dogwood leaves this month, that's probably it. Anthracnose can kill twigs and branches and generally weaken the tree over time. Prune off dead wood, get rid of fallen diseased leaves, and in severe, ongoing cases, treat with a fungicide as soon as the leaf buds open in spring.

Protect tree trunks from getting whacked by string trimmers and lawn mowers by surrounding them with mulched beds instead of allowing grass to grow up to the trunks.

Bacterial leaf scorch is an increasing early-season threat to red and pin oaks. It's caused by a bacterium spread by insects. The disease clogs the channels that carry nutrients from the tree's roots to its leaves. Watch for browning and withering leaves, then dying limbs. There's no easy homeowner cure for this one.

Vining euonymus isn't as prone to scale insects as some of the variegated-leaf bushy types, but check anyway for what look like white flecks on stems and leaves. These are the shells giving protection to sucking insects underneath. Plants often survive minor outbreaks, but severe and repeated infestations can kill euonymus. Horticultural oil or an insecticide might be warranted.

June is a bridge month. It's a time when spring hands off to summer, and May's flurry of gardening activity settles into a more maintain-and-monitor pace.

That's a good thing, because June is when the year's first oppressive, *really* hot and humid spells begin showing up, especially in the southern and coastal fringes of our region. Some fairly pleasant daytime highs in the 70s and 80s can still happen, but so can those days when it seems both the thermometer and the humidity gauge are pushing 100. Rain can start to get iffy this month, too. Some years enough storms occur to keep plants watered without constant hose duty, but others mark the beginning of extended heat waves in which weeks go by without so much as a shower. Most years, June brings a little of all of these.

The majority of woody landscape plants finish blooming in June, especially with the month's prolific peaking and waning of roses and hydrangeas. Perennial flowers pick up the slack, with daylilies, coreopsis, astilbe, and hardy geraniums being some of the more common. May-planted annuals also bulk up enough by June to impress.

Depending on how the weather leans, plant disease can become a June issue. Problems such as blackspot on roses, rust on crabapple leaves, and mildew on hydrangeas can pop up along with the humidity readings. Bugs arrive in full force, too, from pesky, in-your-eye blackflies to biting mosquitoes to our infamous, leaf-chomping, lawn-killing Japanese beetle that's pretty much everywhere by June into July.

Keep an eye out for four-legged garden pests, in particular rabbits, groundhogs, chipmunks, voles, and deer. These vegetarians appreciate the buffet you've set out for them. It's all so nice, tender, and tasty this time of year. Weed germination tapers off ever so slightly in June, but enough species continue to sprout in summer that you'll still need to be on alert. Patrol your garden beds regularly, and keep yanking so that no weeds go to seed.

Now if only you could train those groundhogs to switch to an all-weed diet . . .

PLAN

ALL

If your cheapie plastic plant labels keep blowing away or breaking, switch to something lasting. Metal, ceramic, or sturdier plastic ones are available at garden and home-improvement centers. Cut-up vinyl window blinds make a free homemade alternative. Use a china marker or wax pencil to write names on the labels. And insert them in the same place at every plant so you always know where to look.

If you've planned well for wildlife, you should see a variety of birds, pollinators, and butterflies in the yard this month. If not, evaluate what's missing. (See "Here's How To Attract Birds and Butterflies to Your Landscape.")

ANNUALS & TROPICALS

Fill in gaps in the landscape with a few last annual flowers. Or put together another flowerpot or three for the patio. Plant sizes generally increase at the garden center, from May's four-packs and six-packs to larger, individual plants in 4- and 6-inch pots.

Don't overlook the houseplant section for seasonal color. Most tropicals are happy growing both in pots and beds during our hot, humid summers. It reminds them of home. Dracaena, cordyline, ornamental bananas, and palms make especially nice pot centerpieces. Aluminum plant, wandering Jew, and Moses-in-a-boat make colorful summer groundcovers in the shade. Move them back inside to overwinter as houseplants before fall frost.

HERE'S HOW

TO ATTRACT BIRDS AND BUTTERFLIES TO YOUR LANDSCAPE

1. Avoid spraying insecticides whenever possible. Those caterpillars you're killing might turn into beautiful butterflies, while birds could be dying from eating pesticide-laced bugs.

2. Plant a diverse variety of plants, especially natives and ones that bloom at various times throughout the season.

3. For butterflies, include host plants on which to lay eggs and nectar plants to provide food as adults. Good host plants include fennel, dill, parsley, marigold, snapdragon, turtlehead, milkweed, clover, and many native trees. For nectar, favorites are ones with clustered flowers and bright colors, especially purple, red, yellow, orange, and hot pink. Good nectar plants include cosmos, pentas, salvia, catmint, coreopsis, goldenrod, Joe-pye weed, mountain mint, and beebalm.

■ *You won't have butterflies if you don't also provide host plants, like this fennel, to feed their caterpillars.*

4. Set out a mix of different feeders in protected areas in late winter and early spring to lure hungry birds to your yard.

5. Include shrubs and trees in the landscape that provide fruits in fall and winter, such as winterberry holly, crabapple, and native honeysuckle.

6. Don't forget shelter and nesting plants, such as a few taller trees, some dense evergreens, and grasses for nest-building.

7. Add a water source, such as a water garden, birdbaths, and a mud puddle or two that butterflies use for extracting salt and dietary minerals.

8. Add a few rocks for butterflies to sun themselves and set out a mash of overripe fruit as an attractant.

BULBS

This year's spring bulbs are barely finished, and already you're getting catalogs to pre-order new ones for fall planting. Advantages to ordering this early: the bulbs you need are fresh in your mind, you'll have first choice of varieties in limited supply, and suppliers often offer a discount for early orders. Pre-ordered bulbs are shipped at the appropriate planting time in fall.

LAWNS

Decide whether you're going to allow the lawn to go brown in a dry spell this year or try to keep it green and growing by irrigating. A healthy lawn can stay brown for four to six weeks in summer and quickly green up when rain returns. Summer dormancy is a survival skill of cool-season grasses. Keeping it green all summer despite a drought is more of cosmetic decision by the lawn-owner. It's doable but it requires a lot of water.

PERENNIALS & GROUNDCOVERS

Tired of cutting grass already? Think about whether too much space is tied up in turfgrass. Trees underplanted with shady groundcovers will gradually convert sunny open areas into shade, while mixed beds of shrubs, perennials, and groundcovers offer a colorful and more pollinator-attractive sunny yard than an ocean of grass.

Keep track of when your different perennials start and finish blooming to help with selecting new varieties to plug those bloomless gaps.

SHRUBS

Fewer shrubs flower from here on out, but June isn't colorless. Among flowering shrubs that bloom in June are abelia, elderberry, hydrangea, Japanese spirea, mock orange, nandina, ninebark, potentilla, smooth hydrangea, St. John's wort, and Virginia sweetspire.

With spring shrub performance still fresh in your mind, assess the troops by asking these questions:

- Are you happy with the color, the bloom length, and other performance issues?
- Any shrubs running into health issues that are either unacceptably ugly or threatening the plant's survival?

- Are the maintenance levels acceptable, or are some plants taking up more than their fair share of your workload?
- How are the sizes? Is anything crowding out neighbors, blocking windows, or generally overpowering the assigned space?
- Are the shrubs still getting adequate light, or has tree growth allowed shade to creep in and limit flowering?
- Has something new come along that you think will look and grow better than your struggling shrub?

Answers to these questions will help you decide what changes to make with your current shrub lineup. Options include renovation via pruning, transplanting (see May's "Here's How To Transplant a Tree or Shrub"), or removal.

Get rose-variety ideas by visiting some of our region's many public gardens that have outstanding rose displays. Among them are Delaware's Winterthur Museum, Garden and Library (Winterthur); West Virginia's Ritter Park Rose Garden (Huntington); Virginia's Lewis Ginter Botanical Garden, (Richmond), Huntington Park Rose Garden (Newport News), and Norfolk Botanical Garden (Norfolk); Maryland's Brookside Gardens (Wheaton); and D.C.'s Dumbarton Oaks, Hillwood Estate, and of course, the National Rose Garden at the U.S. Botanic Garden.

Without a support, vines will ramble across the ground and/or spill over wall edges, making them good options for adding color to stonework or even as groundcovers.

Japanese hydrangea vine and climbing hydrangea are two woody vines hitting peak bloom in June. Many clematis also flower well through June, and some honeysuckles remain in color, too.

TREES

June is a good month to assess trees as you did shrubs (see Plan, Shrubs). As temperatures rise during the next couple of months, the lack of shade—and the need for more trees—will be most apparent.

A few trees bloom in June, including Japanese tree lilac, goldenrain, smoketree, and sweetbay magnolia.

■ *Sweetbay magnolia* (Magnolia virginiana) *is one of the relatively few trees that bloom in summer.*

PLANT

ALL

Container-grown perennials, groundcovers, shrubs, evergreens, trees, and vines can be planted during June, but it's more stressful than spring. Plant on a cloudy day or in the evening, if possible, to minimize the wilting effect of bright, hot sun on new plantings. Keep new plants well watered throughout summer.

ANNUALS & TROPICALS

Pansies, violas, and other cool-season annuals usually shut down flowering as heat shows up. Some people milk extra life out of these by transplanting them to shadier spots. Or just replace them with heat-loving summer annuals.

It's plenty warm enough now for houseplants to go outside for the summer. These plants can stay in their pots for use on a deck or patio outside, but most do fine planted in the ground, too. If your houseplants are in pots without holes, either transfer them to pots *with* holes or keep them under cover so you can control water. A heavy rain will quickly saturate the soil in a hole-less pot.

BULBS

Last call for planting those tender summer bulbs that you started inside in pots.

Time is running out to dig and divide crowded clusters of spring bulbs while the withering foliage is still attached and you can see where to dig.

Replant where you want them now. There's no need to wait until fall.

Continue to plant summer bulbs such as dahlias, calla lilies, and gladiolas every two or three weeks through June to extend the bloom times.

LAWNS

June gets harder to plant new grass from seed because it's now hotter and drier. Cover new seed with a light layer of straw, and sprinkle the planting daily; even twice a day isn't too often. The surface dries quickly this time of year. Water frequently and *lightly*, not so much that water runs off.

Sod is more expensive for patching or installing new lawns, but it usually yields better results in summer because it comes with established grass roots. Sod has to be kept well watered all summer.

■ *Cover newly planted seed lightly with straw and water daily.*

PERENNIALS, GROUNDCOVERS, SHRUBS & TREES

It's still okay to plant these, but the sooner the better. Remember, lean toward cloudy days, and keep the plants well watered, especially the first four to six weeks but all through summer.

Early morning and evening plantings are options if you can't avoid planting during a hot, sunny spell. Another anti-wilt aid is erecting a temporary shade structure for the first few weeks.

You might see shoots coming up from the around the base of some woody vines. These can be dug or severed, and so long as they've got roots attached, they can be transplanted to create new plants. Keep these transplanted "babies" well watered and ideally out of direct sun at first (one of those shade structures above can help).

CARE

ALL

If you're down to bare soil over your garden beds (or close to it), it's not too late to lay new mulch. It's a little harder now working around growing plants, but mulch will slow the summer sun from heating and drying the soil surface and discourage the sprouting of purslane, prostrate knotweed, pigweed, and other summer-germinating weeds.

Poison ivy is clambering full speed up trees, but it'll romp across the ground If it can't find anything to grab onto. This native vining weed has fall berries; glossy, burnt-red fall color; and three-lobed leaves that grow in clusters of three. Remember, "leaves of three, let it be."

■ *Deadhead flowers in summer by snipping off the browned, spent flower tips.*

This "deadheading" neatens the plant, encourages continuing bloom, and sometimes lessens the odds of mildew disease.

If your cool-preferring pansies, viola, lobelia, dianthus, nemesia, osteospermum, ageratum, and snapdragon are shutting down bloom in the heat, try cutting them back to a low set of leaves rather than yanking them out. Keep them watered throughout summer, and often these will resume flowering when the weather cools.

Get stakes in place if tall annuals such as zinnias, cosmos, and larkspur start flopping.

Snip a few flowers to use in bouquets. You might have a few fewer flowers outside, but clipping encourages bushier branching and more flowers later.

BULBS

Continue staking plants that need support. Some dahlias grow very tall by midseason, and their brittle stems break easily. Stake gladiolus stems individually to prevent their heavy blossoms from flopping in heavy rains.

Remove shabby leaves and faded flowers of begonias and alliums.

■ *Lay down more mulch if you can see bare soil.*

ANNUALS & TROPICALS

Pinch off faded blooms of any flowers as they need it. Some are better at self-cleaning than others.

LAWNS

Mow often enough that you're never removing more than one-third of the grass blade. Cut high: 2½ to 3 inches for cool-season grasses, 1½ to 2 inches for zoysia. Let the clippings remain.

Alter your mowing pattern to minimize wear on the turf. Mow in horizontal rows one week, in vertical rows the next, and diagonally the next.

PERENNIALS & GROUNDCOVERS

Deadhead the spent flowers of perennials as they finish blooming, including cutting off the entire flower stalks of plants that bloom on separate flowering stems. A prime example is the daylily, which hits peak bloom this month. Once all of the flowers on a daylily stem open and brown, cut the stalk off at the base.

Trim mums in half a second time (May was the first) to encourage denser branching, more flowers, and less flopping in the fall.

Cut back the stems and/or dig out runners of groundcovers trying to creep into the lawn.

Don't let English ivy grow up your trees—at least not very far. The stems don't suck the life out of trees, but if the vines grow up and out tree branches, the ivy leaves block sunlight getting to the tree leaves.

SHRUBS

Spruce, fir, and pine have finished most spring growth, so this is a good month to clip off most of this season's growth to maintain size. The new growth is lighter or different in color than older needles. Avoid cutting spruce, fir, and pine shrubs back so far that you're into older growth and *definitely* not back into where the branches are needleless. They won't push new growth from it.

Add a layer of chopped leaves or bark mulch to the soil surface of shrubs growing in pots. These dry out quicker than shrubs planted in the ground. Mulch slows moisture loss.

Continue to prune spring-blooming shrubs as they finish flowering, such as rhododendron, lilac, weigela, pieris, daphne, heath, and mountain laurel.

■ *Roses can be snipped continually throughout summer as flowers come and go.*

Watch that clinging vines such as climbing hydrangea and Japanese hydrangea vine aren't creeping onto surfaces where you don't want them. If these vines adhere and are pulled off later, they'll leave behind hard-to-remove rootlets.

After wisteria finishes blooming, cut back all side branches to about 6 inches to control size and encourage the next round of flower buds. If there's also a tangle of excess branches, remove up to one-third of those back to the main stem.

TREES

Tree varieties such as honey locust, crabapple, cherry, and pear regularly send up straight branches from around the base. These skinny, upright "suckers" serve no useful purpose. Cut them off at the base as soon as and as often as you see them.

If necessary for size control, prune spruce, fir, and pine trees. The idea is to let new growth occur, then trim most of it back off. Avoid cutting back into branches that no longer have needles.

WATER

ALL

Since rain can shut off this month, be ready with the hose, watering can, and/or sprinklers. Plants' water demands also go up due to a combination of high growth and rising heat and light.

Pay particular watering attention to anything new you've planted this spring. The young roots haven't yet spread enough to "mine" much water, so they'll need more help from you and your hose. Focus close to the plant since that's where all of the roots are for now, but apply enough water so the soil all around and just below the roots is consistently damp. That encourages rooting.

Two guiding principles for all plant watering are:

1. Apply water to the *soil*, not over the tops of the plants. Wet leaves are more prone to leaf disease.

2. The two best times to water are early in the morning and early in the evening. Wet leaves dry quickly as the sun rises after a morning watering (if you ignored Rule No. 1), while an early-evening watering allows time for wet leaves to dry before dark. Avoid midday waterings, the time of maximum evaporation loss.

Humans have built-in soil moisture meters. They're called index fingers. Insert a finger in the soil a few inches, and if the soil is damp, that's good. If it's dry, it's time to water. If you prefer something more high-tech, soil-moisture meters are sold at garden centers, home-improvement stores, and in catalogs. Digital devices with software applications are now available that send soil-moisture readings wirelessly to your smartphone or computer.

ANNUALS & TROPICALS

New weeds keep popping up, thanks largely to the regular watering you're doing to get your annuals off to a good start. Pick weeds regularly and when young. Their sprouting will taper off as the annuals fill in and start to shade space between plants. In the short term, don't let weeds overgrow your annuals and steal sunlight, nutrition, and water.

Annuals are shallow-rooted and dry out quickly when there's no rain. If you see annuals wilting, the best time to water was yesterday. Shallow but frequent watering is the strategy, usually every other day for the first four to six weeks, then slightly deeper waterings once or twice a week as the roots establish.

Annuals in pots and baskets likely will need water every day. At least check them daily. Soak until water comes out the drainage holes.

■ *A soil moisture meter is one way to determine whether it's time to water the plants.*

If you have a lot of pots and baskets, consider rigging up a drip-irrigation system. Small, plastic tubes run water to the area, then side tubing with emitters can be installed to spot-water each pot. Attach a timer at the hose to make the whole thing automatic.

A 1-inch layer of rotted leaves, pine needles, or bark mulch helps retain moisture in annual beds.

BULBS

Hardy summer bulbs such as lilies and crocosmia (ones that you're not lifting each fall for winter

■ *Water at the base of plants, not overhead, whenever possible.*

storage) usually don't need water, unless it's exceptionally hot and dry. These function more like perennials.

Tender summer bulbs that you've just planted/replanted in spring are a different story. Their roots are still developing and appreciate a soaking about twice a week, similar to what you'd give a newly planted perennial.

Avoid watering spring bulb beds. Once tulips, daffodils, hyacinths, and such go dormant for the summer, they don't need or want water.

LAWNS

Most crabgrass preventers work for eight to ten weeks. That means early-spring applications can run out of steam before crabgrass seeds are done sprouting for the year. If you've had a crabgrass problem in the past, and it's been a cool, damp spring, a second application of crabgrass preventer might be warranted early this month.

Continue to pull or spot-spray weeds.

Cool-season grasses can brown this month if June turns hot and dry early. This is when your green versus dormancy decision comes into play. Let the lawn go brown and dormant if you can live without summer-long green grass; start irrigating if you can't. Established lawns can go four to six weeks in a summer-dormant state before needing water.

To keep grass green when nature wants to turn it brown, apply 1 to 1½ inches of water per week. Apply the full amount with a once-a-week soaking or break it up into ½-inch waterings twice a week. Set out a rain gauge or empty tuna cans to determine the amount.

Avoid shallow daily waterings to established lawns. This wets the grass blades frequently and encourages lawn disease. Worse, wetting only the soil surface is counterproductive to deep rooting.

Three other lawn-watering principles:

- Set your sprinklers or irrigation system so that you're watering as evenly as possible. Avoid missed spots and areas that are getting double coverage.
- Keep water confined to the lawn. Sidewalks, driveways, and streets don't need water.
- Don't apply water so fast that it runs off. Tinker until you get it right because saturation points vary depending on water pressure, equipment you're using, and how fast the soil drains.

Water newly planted grass seed beds lightly at least once a day until the seed germinates, then keep the soil consistently damp in the top 2 inches by sprinkling it every other day. New grass has shallow roots and needs regular moisture near the surface. Water deeper as the grass grows. Established grass needs moisture down about 6 inches deep.

PERENNIALS & GROUNDCOVERS

Established perennials and groundcovers, especially drought-tough species such as salvia, gaillardia, and goldenrod seldom need supplemental water. However, even those perform best when supplied with about 1 inch of water per week, whether it comes from rain or from your hose.

Newly planted perennials are still establishing their root systems, so give them a good soaking (1 inch) once or twice a week.

SHRUBS & TREES

Shrubs and trees are deeper rooted and prefer deep soakings once or twice a week instead of the shallow, frequent watering preference of new annuals and new lawns. Be particularly vigilant about keeping the soil damp around shrubs and trees planted within the past two or three years. Apply water regularly enough that the soil is consistently damp all around the rootball and to just below it. (See July's "Here's How To Tell If You're Watering Enough.")

Most established shrubs and trees usually need no water, except for an occasional deep soaking during a drought or unusually hot, dry spell.

Whether you're holding a hose, using a sprinkler, or setting the hose down on trickle, apply water evenly. Wet the *whole* root zone, not just one side.

Trees and shrubs growing in containers likely will need daily soakings throughout the summer. These dry out much faster than in-ground plants.

For peak performance, give roses a deep soaking two to three times a week (over the ground, not the leaves, to limit black spot disease). Most perform well with a single, once-a-week, 1-inch soaking, and most at least survive with as little as an occasional soaking during long, hot, dry spells.

FERTILIZE

ALL

Only a few types of plants benefit from booster doses of fertilizer over summer. If you've topped the soil with compost or organic mulch and/or scratched in granular, gradual-release fertilizer in the spring, you're fine now in most of the garden.

ANNUALS & TROPICALS

Annuals are heavy feeders and usually benefit from water-soluble flower fertilizer, applied during watering according to the package directions (typically once a month). If your soil is compost-rich, or if you worked in gradual-release fertilizer at planting, that's probably sufficient.

Annuals in pots and baskets need more regular fertilizer. These perform best by adding a water-soluble flower fertilizer at half-strength once a week.

BULBS

No additional fertilizer is needed if you've already worked a gradual-release fertilizer into the soil around your summer bulbs. If you're going the liquid-fertilizer route and applied a dose in May, apply a second dose this month or in early July. A nutrition breakdown of 5-10-10 is good.

Don't fertilize your spring bulb beds. Those bulbs are dormant and don't need fertilizer in summer.

LAWNS

If you're using an organic program and fertilizing twice a year, you should have done the first application in May. There's no need for more now. If you forgot, it's still okay to apply it early this month.

If you're using a three-times-a-year program, the first application also should have been in May.

Early June is still okay if you didn't get to it then. Otherwise, the next application is late summer.

If you're using a commercial "four-step" lawn-fertilizer program, you should have applied the first part in March to early April. Late May to mid-June is good timing for the second application.

For a zoysia grass lawn being fertilized twice a year, June is prime time for the second treatment (April was the first).

One rule that trumps all: Never fertilize lawns stressed by drought or heat. If the lawn already is browning in an early hot, dry spell, don't add fertilizer—especially high-nitrogen chemical ones. Salts in these can compound the moisture-sapping effects of dry soil. Wait until the grass is green and rain has returned to apply either a full or half-dose fertilizer.

Marylanders have additional rules, including no phosphorus and limited amounts of nitrogen in lawn fertilizer. See March, Fertilize, Lawns for more details or check the Maryland Department of Agriculture's website at www.mda.maryland.gov/Pages/fertilizer.aspx.

PERENNIALS & GROUNDCOVERS

The granular, slow-acting fertilizer you added to the soil when preparing the garden bed or at planting is still at work. There's no need to add more now.

Perennials in pots benefit from more regular nutrition, since the frequent watering leaches nutrients out the bottom with the drainage. Add water-soluble flower fertilizer to the water, similar to how you're fertilizing annuals (half-strength once a week).

SHRUBS & TREES

Skip fertilizer unless poor growth or a soil test indicates a nutrient deficiency, then address it specifically. Routine fertilizing of established trees, shrubs, and woody vines is not necessary.

Do not fertilize shrubs, trees, and vines when they're stressed by heat, drought, or bug problems. Salts in chemical fertilizers can compound the effects of dry soil, while bugs are often *more* attracted to fertilizer-rich plants.

Scratch in another dose of granular rose fertilizer around your rose bushes this month if you're shooting for peak performance. If you're not, that springtime scattering of a granular, slow-acting fertilizer is sufficient.

PROBLEM-SOLVE

ALL

The dreaded Japanese beetle appears this month. This bug feeds on lawn roots in its larval grub stage and then pupates into shiny, hard-shelled, fingernail-sized, green-and-copper-colored adults in early summer. Japanese beetle adults feed on some 300 species of plants. (See July, Problem-Solve, All for ways to control them during peak feeding season.)

■ *Japanese beetles are out in force, and they especially love roses.*

For now, a more immediate issue is heading off future grub trouble in the lawn. If you've had regular grub damage or don't want to deal with that prospect this fall, June is prime time to apply a grub preventer. These granular products are spread on the lawn so that when this year's adults lay eggs, the young grubs are killed as they feed on the treated roots. Ideally, spread grub preventer before a rain. Otherwise, water it in well after applying.

Continue to watch for slugs, especially in the moist, shady parts of your yard. They chew leaves (usually at night), and leave behind shiny trails of dried slime. (See April, Problem-Solve, Perennials for slug-control ideas.)

ANNUALS, TROPICALS & BULBS

Pest insects arrive in the garden before beneficial ones, which is why you may see more pest problems early in the season. An example is aphids, which cluster at the new tips of stems and suck the juices out of young plants. Often, lady beetles and other predators swoop in to clean up the infestation. Otherwise, a stiff spray of water or a spray of light horticultural oil or insecticidal soap will control them.

Maturing plants with tougher stems and leaves are less attractive to the bunnies and chipmunks, but you still may find some of your petunias buzzed off at the base any fine morning. Keep the repellents handy.

LAWNS

Besides Japanese beetles, you might notice a much bigger, thumbnail-sized, shiny green bug flying out of and over the lawn. These are June beetles. They "buzz" but don't sting and don't do as much plant damage as Japanese beetles (in part because of fewer numbers). But their larval grub stage causes lawn damage. The same chemical grub preventer that you apply this month for Japanese beetles will control June beetle grubs. Swat the adults with a tennis racket in the meantime. It's good exercise.

The lawn disease "brown patch" can thin lawns or cause brown, blotchy patches in hot, humid weather. It's caused by a fungus and is encouraged by overfertilizing and by too-frequent watering. Solutions include cooler, drier weather and knocking off the excess fertilizing. Granular fungicides are an option in severe outbreaks.

Moss does best in shade, dampness, and acidic soil, although it can do reasonably well without any of those. If you don't want it in your lawn, create less favorable conditions by limbing up and thinning out nearby trees to improve air circulation, aerating the soil in fall to improve drainage, and applying lime to make the soil more alkaline.

PERENNIALS & GROUNDCOVERS

Watch for leafminers, which are bugs that feed between the upper and lower surface of leaves,

HERE'S HOW

TO SCOUT FOR PESTS AND PROBLEMS

1. Start by knowing what's normal and what's not for your plant. For example, some species naturally slough off bark or drop inner needles each fall.

2. Regularly inspect your plants. You'll notice changes or potential problems sooner. Corrective actions are usually most effective at the beginning of a problem.

3. If something's amiss, look closely both for direct clues (such as dot-sized black fungal spores on the underside of plant leaves or tiny bugs crawling on stems) and for symptoms (how plants have reacted to a problem).

■ *Learn to recognize what is really a problem; a river birch's peeling bark, for example, is normal.*

4. Evaluate whether what you're seeing is causing life-threatening or unacceptable damage to the plant or whether it's something that's temporary and cosmetic. Most leaf damage, for example, is non-life-threatening, but sap leaking from a trunk could be serious.

5. County Extension offices, garden centers, and a host of university- and botanic-garden websites are good sources for identifying specific problems and their solutions.

6. A few common plant problems and their possible causes:

   - **Plant is yellowing all over:** Poor soil fertility; extreme heat; light is too intense or lacking; plant is potbound.
   - **Young leaves are yellow:** Not enough light; iron or manganese deficiency in the soil; excessive fertilizer.
   - **Old leaves are yellow:** Nitrogen, magnesium, or potassium deficiency in the soil; overwatering; natural aging of leaves; plant is potbound; roots are rotting.
   - **Random leaves or needles yellowing or browning:** Mite damage; herbicide spray drift; root or stem injury; stem galls.
   - **Dead or yellow spots on leaves:** Fungal, bacterial, or viral infection; excessive fluoride in the soil; pesticide damage.
   - **Holes in leaves:** Caterpillar, slug, or other bug damage; fungal leaf spot disease; hail or wind damage.
   - **Leaves brown around the edges:** Wind damage; excessive salt in the soil; lack of water; excessive fertilizer; pesticide damage; air pollution.
   - **Leaves falling off:** Excessive fertilizer; lack of water; reaction to move or transplanting; cold damage; pesticide damage; lack of light; rotting roots; natural life cycle of plant.
   - **Leaves wilted:** Under- or overwatering; excessive fertilizer; roots or stems rotting; rodent damage to roots; pesticide damage; frost damage; excessive heat.
   - **Weak growth and/or gradual dieback of branches:** Lack of water; root injury or girdling roots; compacted soil; plant was planted too deeply; excessive mulch; poor soil nutrition; lack of light.

leaving behind tunnels through the foliage. Columbine is a favorite. Clip off infested leaves to remove the bugs along with the leaves.

Elongated brown spots on iris leaves usually mean a fungal leaf spot disease. It's more prevalent after cool, damp springs. Cut off infected foliage, and add a fresh topping of mulch around the plants to discourage spores from splashing up. Divide your irises (now is a good time) if you haven't done that in the last three years. Too-thick patches are more prone to disease because air can't dry out the leaves as quickly.

Caterpillars often chew around the edges of many perennial leaves in early summer. Keep in mind that most of those will turn into the butterflies and moths you've been trying to attract. Tolerate this temporary leaf damage. It won't kill your plants.

SHRUBS

Pale or yellowing leaves with dark green veins is likely "chlorosis," which is a lack of iron in the plant tissue. Acid-preferring species such as rhododendron, mountain laurel, and blueberries are particularly prone to it. Usually, there's sufficient iron in the soil; the plants just aren't taking it up because the soil isn't acidic enough to dissolve enough of it. A soil pH test will confirm

this. Add sulfur to lower the pH (make the soil more acidic). Adding iron or an iron-and-sulfur product may correct chlorosis, too.

Bigleaf hydrangeas, shrub dogwoods, and other flowering shrubs may develop leaf spots or a whitish cast to the leaves, especially if it's been damp. These are fungal diseases. Damage is seldom bad enough to warrant spraying. Pick off ratty, infected leaves, then clean up any infected leaves in fall to reduce spores on the ground that can reinfect future growth. Plants usually grow through these setbacks when drier weather arrives.

Bagworms start to do damage this month on a variety of evergreens. These are caterpillars that feed inside cone-like sacs constructed from the needles of the plant the bagworms are inhabiting. Bagworms are hard to detect now because they're small, and the sacs are the same color as the plant's needles. They're much more noticeable later in summer when the sacs enlarge and turn brown. By then, the caterpillars are harder to kill. Check now for little sacs, and either handpick them or spray with Bt, a caterpillar-targeted organic spray.

Scale insects may turn up on evergreen euonymus, holly, and other shrubs. Some types are evident as powdery white spots; others are waxy white bumps

■ *Blackspot is a fungal disease that's the bane of most roses.*

that dot leaf and stem surfaces. If plants are losing color or dropping leaves, treat with a spray or two of light horticultural oil as directed on the product label.

Wilted or dead shoots on your rhododendrons could be phytophthora root rot, a common soilborne fungal disease that kills roots and shoots. Poor drainage is a leading cause, and fungicides may be needed to keep the disease from progressing. Another possibility is the rhododendron borer, a bug whose larvae tunnels into stems and feeds on the wood, often killing tissue above the feeding area. Check the branches for entry slits, and either prune off the bug-containing wood or consider an insecticide labeled for borer control.

Mites often attack heat- and drought-stressed roses. Look for fine webbing on twigs and leaves. Disrupt light infestations with a stiff spray of hose water to leaf undersides every day or two for a week. Stubborn infestations of these tiny sucking insects can be controlled by insecticidal soap or Neem oil.

Pick up and discard fallen, diseased leaves from around your roses. This removes disease spores that can reinfect the plants.

The rose midge becomes active as the weather warms. The damaging stage is a larval maggot that feeds at the tip of new shoots, causing buds to wilt and die. Multiple generations can occur throughout summer. Cutting off the stem tips along with the bugs may help. Or spray the maggots while they're feeding, or apply an insecticide to the soil to interrupt the next generation after the maggots drop to pupate.

Neat, C-shaped cutouts from the edges of rose leaves are the work of leaf-cutter bees. It looks as if someone has carefully cut the leaves with scissors. Damage is temporary and cosmetic.

Continue to watch for and treat, if needed, blackspot disease on roses. (See May, Problem-Solve, Roses.)

Pyracantha berries sometimes turn black and fall off. That's usually pyracantha scab, a fungal disease that's also characterized by leaves and stems that have velvety, sooty spots. Rake fallen infected

leaves and fruits to head off future infections. In bad or ongoing infections, you might need to intervene with fungicide sprays, ideally every seven to ten days starting when the buds first open in spring to two weeks after the flower petals drop.

TREES

Watch for signs of rust disease on crabapples and hawthorns. The telltale sign is rusty-orange spots on the leaves. Leaves drop prematurely, and twigs and branches die if the infestation is bad enough. Fungicides may be needed. The best solution is choosing disease-resistant varieties in the first place. Also, avoid planting junipers near crabapple and hawthorn because rust jumps back and forth between these two host families.

Gypsy moth caterpillars can cause significant chewing damage to many tree species, especially oak. Trees can grow through limited and occasional attacks, but repeated heavy infestations can kill them. Spraying insecticides and setting out baited traps are options. Egg masses can be scraped off trees, and burlap wraps near the base of trees will trap females as they search for a place to lay eggs.

Anthracnose and similar wilt diseases can cause an early leaf drop of sycamore and their plane tree cousins. Some will drop almost their entire first set of leaves in early summer. Treatment is difficult, but trees usually cope by growing a second flush of foliage.

Trees run into many of the same issues as shrubs, including chlorosis, leaf spot, mildew, bagworms, and scale. (See Problem-Solve, Shrubs.)

■ *Gypsy moth caterpillars can be destructive when their populations swell.*

July

There's no mistaking it. Summer is here now.

July is the hottest month in the mid-Atlantic region, a time when the mercury can hit 100 degrees Fahrenheit, and the humidity can give Dallas a run for its money.

Sometimes the rain shuts off, and gardeners end up spending more time with their hoses than their significant others. Other times, the broiling humidity is enough to make gardeners sweat just *thinking* about weeding the flowerbed. But in a merciful July, warm days and well-placed summer thunderstorms can add up to a verdant month in the landscape.

Enjoy the summer-blooming perennials, the colorful flowerpots and hanging baskets (which should be hitting peak lushness by now), and especially that water feature you added with its cooling cascade or waterfall. If you've been keeping up with the to-do list in May and June, July should be a month to kick back a bit and enjoy what you've created.

Garden time this month is mainly about monitoring pests and diseases, patrolling for weeds, keeping the soil damp for new and water-wimpy plants, and generally puttering about. July gardening can be done mostly in first gear instead of spring's more harried third gear. While you're out there, assess how well you've done with plant planning. July can be a dead time in gardens if the gardener did all of his/her plant shopping in May and therefore loaded up on spring bloomers. That can lead to a no-color, game-over look from July on.

The solution is to scope out July-interest plants that grab your eye. Go back to the garden centers now. Visit a public garden or two. They're great for plant-picking ideas, and the Mid-Atlantic is loaded with dozens of them within day-trip range. Closer to home, notice plantings that your neighbors have that are looking good this month. Then make it a point to add some to your yard—even if they're out of bloom at planting time.

Container-grown plants can be added in summer. You'll just have to pay close attention to keeping them—and yourself—well watered.

PLAN

ALL

Most people with water features say their favorite trait is the sound of moving water. But water also adds a cooling "feel" in summer and provides a drink for wildlife. Options range from patio-top container water gardens to traditional in-ground ponds to "pondless water features" that consist of falls draining into buried vaults that recirculate the water (no open water).

Garden centers get fresh shipments for fall planting and usually are willing to add any special plant requests you have for fall planting at no extra charge.

ANNUALS & TROPICALS

Flowers for drying can be cut now. They're best taken around midday and chosen at peak bloom. Most flowers air-dry, but some dry better in silica gel and/or borax and sand.

BULBS

Now that the spring bulb season is done, note what worked, what didn't, and why. The information will help you plan for bulb planting this fall.

LAWNS

Will someone cut your grass while you're away on vacation? Long grass is a sign to burglars that no one is home. Grass won't get out of control in a week, but if you're gone two weeks or more, it might need a trim.

Double-check the automatic lawn-sprinkler system before you leave on that vacation. This is when these systems pay for their keep. But if a malfunction or leak is brewing, you won't be home to catch it.

PERENNIALS & GROUNDCOVERS

Growing grass under trees is an uphill battle, especially in summer's heat and dry soil. Groundcovers that tolerate dry shade and tree-root competition are better options. Among them are liriope, barrenwort, pachysandra, hosta, barren strawberry, sweet woodruff, leadwort, hardy ginger, and foamflower.

Bloomless gaps in the perennial garden can happen as spring bloomers finish but the later ones aren't

■ *Substituting a groundcover where grass is struggling makes good sense and saves work. Leadwort is an example of a groundcover that also flowers.*

yet peaking. Ways to plug this gap include: add July bloomers such as butterfly weed, coreopsis, black-eyed Susan, and liatris; add more perennials with colorful foliage; and spot more season-long annuals to bridge the gap among perennial bloom times.

SHRUBS

The first round of shrubs that bloom on "new wood" (branches that have grown this season) kick into flower in July. Ones that give summer color include abelia, butterfly bush, compact crape myrtles, rose-of-Sharon, smooth hydrangea, panicle hydrangea, St. John's wort, and summersweet.

That Fourth of July cookout hammered home the realization that you need more privacy around the patio, eh? Other than a fence, consider a shrub hedge. Flowering ones give you privacy during the growing season, while evergreen ones give you privacy year-round. In most cases, plants that mature at 6 feet are tall enough to do the job.

Good flowering hedge choices include viburnum, elderberry, winterberry holly, shrub dogwood, lilac, ninebark, photinia, fringe flower, and the panicle, oakleaf, and smooth hydrangeas.

Good evergreen hedge choices include upright juniper, assorted hollies, upright yew, upright Japanese plum yew, cherry and schip laurels, privet, upright boxwoods ('Dee Runk' is excellent),

Hinoki cypress, and the green- or gold-thread false cypresses.

Vine-covered trellises are a patio-privacy option where space is limited. Build a lattice support or use multiple trellises—bumped side by side—to screen the patio length desired.

Choose vine supports based on what kind of vine you use. Small trellises and lattice supports are fine for clematis, honeysuckle, and all of the annual vines. But you'll need more muscular support (think 4 × 4 posts and bolted lumber) for larger vines such as wisteria, climbing hydrangea, Japanese hydrangea vine, trumpet vine, and kiwi vine.

TREES

Crape myrtle, goldenrain, and stewartia are among the few trees that put on a July show.

Inventory and photograph trees every few years in case something happens to them. Some can be very valuable. Store the information in a safe place in case you need it for the insurance adjustor.

PLANT

ANNUALS & TROPICALS

Last call to get a few final summer annuals in the ground or in pots. You'll find sale prices as demand plummets and the compost pile beckons unsold annuals.

■ *Size the support to the needs of the vine. This wisteria, which can be very heavy, needs timbers, not a wimpy trellis support.*

Grow annuals in the dry shade under trees by planting them in sunken, wide, shallow plastic pots. The pots shield tree roots from encroaching into the annuals' territory. Cover the pot edges with mulch to disguise them. You'll need to regularly water these sunken-pot annuals, but at least not as often as aboveground pots. Be sure the pot bottoms have drainage holes.

Inside, start the seeds of cool-season annuals that you plan to plant in fall, such as pansy, viola, calendula, and sweet alyssum.

BULBS

The last round of gladiolus corms can be planted this month for late-summer flowers.

■ *Adding an evergreen hedge around your patio or deck will provide year-round privacy.*

■ *It's not too late to plant a second round of gladiolus corms.*

LAWNS

Patching a few bare spots with seed or sod is possible despite July's heat, so long as you keep the water coming. If you're looking at a new lawn or thinking about revamping a poor one, wait until after Labor Day.

PERENNIALS, GROUNDCOVERS, SHRUBS & TREES

It's not the ideal month to plant because of the heat and potentially dry conditions, but container-grown perennials, groundcovers, shrubs, evergreens, trees, and vines can be planted throughout summer. Plant on a cloudy day or in the evening to minimize transplant shock, and stay on top of watering.

CARE

ALL

If you're taking an extended vacation, recruit someone to keep a lid on weeds and aggressive growers. It's disheartening to return to a jungle.

How's the mulch? If it's thin and you're getting lots of weeds, add a fresh topping. A total of 3 to 4 inches is plenty around trees and shrubs. Two inches is fine around perennials.

Weedy vines such as wild grape, poison ivy, Oriental bittersweet, Japanese honeysuckle, kudzu, and mile-a-minute vine don't mind heat at all. Don't let these invaders spread over tree foliage, blocking the leaves' access to the sun. Cut off woody vining weeds at their base, and the top growth will die. Then pull down the foliage, or let it eventually fall and/or decay. Dig out the weed's roots if you can. Otherwise, paint the stems and lower foliage with a root-killing herbicide such as glyphosate.

ANNUALS & TROPICALS

Revive wilted annuals by soaking them well and adding an inch of chopped leaves or dried grass clippings (which have not been treated with weed-killer) to keep the soil cool and to better retain moisture.

Stake tall plants that are flopping (sunflower, larkspur, and cosmos), patrol for weeds, and pinch

spent flowers to keep the flower display chugging along neatly.

Clip annuals if they're long or leggy. This is especially true in pots where bold growers such as lantana, petunias, and coleus may need July "haircuts" to keep them from dominating. Hand-pruners do the deed nicely. Often, these cuts stimulate bushier growth and more flowering.

To limit unwanted seeding of reseeding annuals such as cleome, larkspur, and nigella, snip off the flower heads before seeds mature.

BULBS

Deadhead spent flowers as dahlias, cannas, lilies, gladiolas, and other summer-blooming bulbs finish their show.

Stake tall dahlias, lilies, gladiolas, and others that are flopping if you didn't do that last month. Be careful not to poke any buried bulbs with the stakes.

LAWNS

Mow if the grass is still green and growing; skip it if it's not. This is when it pays to let the grass stand taller, say, 3 inches instead of 1 or 2. Long blades shade the soil, keeping it cooler and damper. That means grass stays greener longer as the weather gets hotter and drier.

■ *Kudzu can take over, swallowing everything in its path, including trees and shrubs.*

Stay off the grass as much as possible if it's browning from dryness. Early signs of drought stress are wilting blades and noticeable footprints left behind when you walk on the lawn. Grass gets brittle as it dries, and walking on it then can crush the crowns (the point where the blades emerge).

Dig or spot-spray weeds with a liquid broadleaf herbicide for lawns. Summer is a good time to eliminate weeds, clearing the way to fill the openings with grass seed right after Labor Day.

PERENNIALS & GROUNDCOVERS

Continue to deadhead spent flowers, cut off ratty or diseased foliage, and regularly patrol the perennial and groundcover beds for weeds.

Stake tall perennials if you didn't already do that last month. All it takes is one brief summer storm to blow those 3- or 4-footers over.

The first week of July is the end of the line for a last cutback to keep mums compact.

SHRUBS

You should be finished pruning spring-blooming shrubs by now (azalea, weigela, and lilac). Let them alone to form next year's flower buds. Bigleaf hydrangeas can still be pruned, ideally early in the month.

■ *Early summer is a good time to trim evergreens.*

As they brown, spent flower heads can be pruned off summer-flowering shrubs, such as ninebark and the oakleaf, panicle, and smooth hydrangeas. Browned flowers really *should* be regularly pruned off butterfly bushes to prevent unwanted and invasive seeding.

Finish pruning yew, arborvitae, boxwood, holly, laurel, and other hedge evergreens this month.

Continue pruning roses as repeat bloomers open and then brown. Clip lower on each stem than just the tips where the flowers were to keep the bushes more compact.

Shorten the ends of large woody vines such as trumpet vines, kiwi vines, climbing hydrangea, and Japanese hydrangea that are outgrowing their supports or growing beyond where you want.

Prune back and thin out large-flowered clematis varieties that bloomed in June. Cut back stems at least halfway to stimulate possible repeat bloom later in the summer.

TREES

Limit tree pruning to removing broken or diseased branches, clipping off useless "suckers" growing up from around the base, and removing the stray branch that's whacking you on the head as you mow. Winter and spring through early summer are better times for more widespread shaping, thinning, and size-reduction cuts.

Watch for cracked-off but hanging limbs following summer storms so none drop on unsuspecting passersby below. Prune off ones you can safely reach. Hire a pro to remove ones you can't.

Near the shore, hose off plants with fresh water if they've been hit with salty wind and spray.

WATER

ALL

Don't try to water your entire garden in one fell swoop, unless it's small. Break up the job with a thorough soaking in one area one day, then other areas on other days.

When you water, apply enough to moisten the roots. It doesn't help to wet just the mulch or the top ½-inch of the soil.

Apply water to the soil, not over the tops of plants. Try to water early in the morning or early in the evening when evaporation losses are less, but wet leaves will dry quickly.

Divide dry-season watering into priorities so that if you can't keep everything watered, at least you'll get to the most important things first.

HIGH PRIORITY
- Newly planted trees and shrubs that are the most expensive investments and ones at risk if their young root systems aren't kept damp.
- Hanging baskets and container plants that will die in a matter of days without water.
- Any sentimental favorites or expensive specimen plants in the yard that you really don't want to lose.
- Newly planted lawns.

MEDIUM PRIORITY
- Established but shallow-rooted trees and shrubs, such as azaleas, rhododendrons, dogwoods, hollies, and blueberries, especially if they're wilting or showing signs of drought stress.
- Newly planted perennials (more at risk than established ones).
- Annual flowers and vegetables.

LOW PRIORITY
- Established perennials and established trees, shrubs, evergreens, and roses, especially ones that are adapted to cope with dry soil.
- Groundcovers unless they're starting to badly wilt and turn brown.

BOTTOM PRIORITY
- An established lawn. Lawns are "smart" enough to go dormant in droughts. They can go four to six weeks in this straw-brown state with no lasting damage. One good rain and otherwise healthy grass will green up again.

ANNUALS & TROPICALS
In-ground annuals now have bigger, deeper root systems than when first planted (hopefully), so they'll benefit from deeper waterings once or twice a week instead of the more frequent, shallow waterings of the first four to six weeks.

Annuals and tropicals in pots and baskets will need daily soakings. If you're leaving on vacation, arrange for someone to take over this duty. Or rig up an automatic drip-irrigation system if you have a lot of pots. Or group pots together so one sprinkler hooked up to a timer can water them all at once.

BULBS
Summer bulbs growing in pots usually need daily soakings, the same as with annual flowers.

Summer bulbs growing in the ground can get by with a 1-inch soaking per week when it doesn't rain, similar to perennial flowers.

LAWNS
Cool-season lawns often turn straw-brown this month when it's hot and dry. They're not dead. They're just employing the survival skill of going dormant in unfavorable conditions. By shutting down growth, grass can conserve enough moisture in the crowns (where grass blades emerge) to go four to six weeks in this state.

If a drought drags on, and the lawn is straw-brown for six weeks and counting, water about ¼ of an inch per week. That's enough to replenish moisture in the crowns without stimulating the grass to resume growing.

Good reasons why *not* to try to keep grass green when it wants to go brown:

- You'll use a lot of precious (and expensive) water.
- If you don't water deeply enough, grass roots will develop near the soil surface, where the moisture is. That makes the lawn *less* drought-resistant in the long run, more at risk of heat injury, and more likely to develop excess thatch (that spongy layer mostly of dead roots between the growing grass and the soil).
- Beetle grubs proliferate best when the soil is moist during egg hatch in July and August. They'll thank you for irrigating.
- Grass that's frequently wet is more prone to disease.

■ *This glass set out in the lawn shows that a sprinkler has applied 1 inch of water.*

If you're dead set on a summer-long green lawn, figure on applying 1 to 1½ inches of water weekly. Apply the full amount once a week or ½-inch waterings twice a week rather than daily, shallower waterings. Set out a rain gauge or empty tuna cans to determine amounts.

A lawn planted just this spring isn't deeply rooted enough yet to tolerate brutal heat and dryness the first summer. Help it along with the same watering plan as noted, 1 to 1½ inches per week, either all at once or, better yet, broken into half, twice a week.

■ *An inch of water per week is enough to keep a lawn green in all but the hottest, driest weather.*

PERENNIALS & GROUNDCOVERS

Perennials and groundcovers planted earlier this spring benefit from twice-weekly soakings. Do the finger-insertion test to be sure, and water whenever the soil is dry in the root zone.

Established perennials and groundcovers can get by with a once-a-week soaking or less. Some of the most drought-tough ones (sedum, salvia, catmint, and most ornamental grasses, for example), almost never need supplemental water.

Some perennials and groundcovers are heat-sensitive and may wilt, brown, or die back even with plenty of water. These include lily-of-the-valley, lady's mantle, delphinium, lupine, lamium, sweet woodruff, and foamflower. Clip off any dead or diseased foliage, but otherwise let these alone to perk up when the temperatures drop.

SHRUBS & TREES

For recent plantings or transplantings (within the past three years), figure on deep soakings once a week if there's no rain. Apply enough that you're wetting all around and to the bottom of the rootballs. (See "Here's How To Tell If You're Watering Enough.")

After three to four years, most shrubs and trees can be considered "established." Their root systems have grown enough to mine sufficient moisture from the soil that they don't need supplemental water from you except in unusually long, hot, dry spells. If you're in doubt, a weekly soaking won't hurt.

Bigleaf hydrangeas are some of the first plants to wilt on a hot July day. Heat alone can cause that, although heat and dry soil can tag-team to create a hydrangea double-whammy. One way to tell the difference is to check your plants first thing in the morning. Heat-stressed hydrangeas won't be wilted; drought-stressed ones will.

For roses planted earlier this spring and for established ones that you're growing for peak performance, soak them two to three times a week (over the ground, not over the leaves, to limit disease). Established roses are fine with a single, once-a-week, 1-inch soaking, and most will survive with less than that.

FERTILIZE

ALL
By and large, this is a no-feed month in the landscape. That mulch, compost, and/or annual scattering of granular, gradual-release fertilizer that you applied in spring is enough for most perennials, groundcovers, evergreens, shrubs, trees, and vines.

Summer fertilizer, especially fast-acting synthetic-chemical types, can be counterproductive in two ways. One is that synthetic fertilizers contain salts that can compound the dry-soil stress that threatens plants in summer. The second is that even if fertilizers are watered well into the soil, they can stimulate growth at a time when plants are trying to conserve energy to survive the heat and dry soil.

A good rule of thumb is to never fertilize a plant under stress from drought or extreme heat.

ANNUALS, TROPICALS, BULBS & PERENNIALS
One exception to the no-fertilizer rule is plants growing in pots. These are being watered so often and using/losing nutrients so fast that a continuous supply of nutrition is needed. To maximize

performance, add a water-soluble flower fertilizer at half-strength once a week.

LAWNS
Do not fertilize the lawn if it's dormant. The salts in chemical fertilizers can worsen the effects of dry soil, possibly to the point of killing an already-stressed lawn. More than a few people have had lawns "burned" by fertilizer treatments in summer-dormant conditions.

Three of the four main lawn-fertilizer regimens consider July to be a no-fertilizer month. The exception is the four-step program, and only then in *early* July if the second application wasn't applied in June and only if the grass is still green and growing.

SHRUBS & TREES
No fertilizer is needed this month, except that rosarians shooting for peak rose performance usually scratch in another dose of granular, slow-acting rose fertilizer around their bushes in July, so long as they're also watering regularly.

PROBLEM-SOLVE

ALL
Heat stress is an underrated plant menace, not as well known as the obvious freezing damage at the opposite end of the temperature spectrum. Heat causes more insidious trouble, starting at around 86 degrees Fahrenheit, including:

- Flower buds may wither.
- Chlorophyll production goes down, robbing leaves of their healthy green color.
- Pollen can become non-viable, preventing fruiting plants from producing their fruits and berries.
- Chemical makeup changes in plant leaves, rendering them more vulnerable to bug attacks.
- Soil temperatures heat to the point where root activity slows and plant growth is stunted, especially on unmulched soil.
- And most noticeable, moisture loss from plant leaves increases, making plants more susceptible to dry-soil injury.

You can't air-condition your yard, but heat-busting measures include mulching bare soil; watering regularly (which cools the soil besides adding moisture); choosing heat-tough plants for your yard's hot spots; and moving heat-wimpy existing plants to cooler spots come fall.

The American Horticultural Society has a Heat Zone Map that's similar to its Cold Hardiness Map. Heat-zone ratings are listed on some plant labels. A copy of the map and more details on heat zones are on the AHS website at www.ahs. org/gardening-resources/gardening-maps/heat-zone-map.

The Japanese beetle is a double-trouble bug that chews the foliage of some 300 plant species. It is a shiny, brown-and-green adult, which kills off lawn patches in its larval grub form. Adults swarm and eat plant leaves in July. Then they mate and lay eggs, usually in sunny turf near favored plants. The eggs hatch in August into fat, white, C-shaped wormy-looking critters that feed on grass and plant roots in fall and spring. (See June and September, Problem-Solve, for tips on dealing with beetle grubs.)

Japanese beetles particularly like roses, grapes, cherry, crabapple, hydrangea, and a range of flowers and vegetables. While their chewing damage is chiefly cosmetic (plants typically recover), massed attacks can leave behind a bloomless, tattered garden. Damage is worse some years than others. If the damage exceeds your tolerance level, controls are hand-picking and either squishing beetles or dropping them in a container of soapy water; protecting targeted plants with cheesecloth or lightweight row cover; and spraying with Neem oil or one of several insecticides labeled for beetle control.

Japanese beetle traps attract beetles, and if they were everywhere, they might make a dent in the population. The problem is, if you're the only one using them, you'll draw beetles *to* your yard. A better situation would be if everyone *around* you had them, and you didn't. That's why there's merit to the advice, "Give beetle traps to your neighbors." If you use traps, set them as far away from your attacked plants as possible.

Spider mites are tiny bugs that thrive in this hot, dry month. They suck chlorophyll out of the foliage of many plants, including hemlock, azalea, many annual and perennial flowers, and their landscape favorite, the dwarf Alberta spruce. Look for stippling damage on foliage and fine webbing among the twigs and branches. Repeated stiff bursts of hose water over several days can control them. Or spray with insecticidal soap or a pesticide labeled for mite control.

■ *The two-spotted spider mite sucks chlorophyll out of plant leaves, creating a stippled appearance.*

ANNUALS & TROPICALS

Impatiens used to be easy to grow. Then came a disease called downy mildew that's deadly, widespread, and able to survive our winters. Symptoms are a grayish cast to the leaf undersides, stunted growth, then a fairly fast melting-out death. There's no good control once your plants have it. The recommended solution is to switch to mildew-resistant New Guinea impatiens, new mildew-resistant hybrids, or other shade-tolerant annuals, such as coleus, begonia, or browallia.

Powdery mildew is another damaging but less destructive fungal disease that causes a white coating on some annuals, particularly zinnias. Pick off infected leaves in an early infection, or use a fungicide labeled for powdery mildew for out-of-control cases.

■ *A plant that's under heat or water stress will respond by wilting.*

BULBS

Gladiolas sometimes get botrytis, a fungal disease that causes brownish-gray patches on the leaves and flowers that turn brown and slimy. It's most prevalent in rainy summers. Fungicides can head it off if applied early, but once botrytis hits, the best solution is to yank the bulbs and try fresh ones next year.

LAWNS

Triple-digit heat can kill some grass species and lead to a thin lawn by summer's end. Perennial ryegrass is among the most heat-sensitive. Plan to overseed a heat-thinned lawn in September or October.

If you're using grub preventers to head off a repeat of past lawn-grub damage, get this year's application down immediately if you didn't do it in June. Eggs will hatch into new grubs shortly.

Small white moths flitting above the turf is a sign of webworm activity. The moths are laying eggs that will hatch into light-brown caterpillars that chew grass blades, mostly after dark. A second generation feeds in late summer. Brown lawn patches result. Nematodes and insecticides are control options in bad outbreaks.

PERENNIALS & GROUNDCOVERS

Powdery mildew, that white coating on leaves, can do significant damage to some perennials this month, especially tall garden phlox, beebalm, and some coreopsis and Veronica. Fortunately, it usually happens after peak bloom. Fungicides can be used at the first sign of infection, or just cut off and remove foliage when it looks bad. Plants usually survive.

An increasing daylily problem is leaf streak, a fungal disease that starts with small brown splotches on leaves that coalesce into longer streaks and finally into widespread leaf browning. Daylilies are tough enough to grow through it. Cut off and remove diseased foliage, including cutting whole plants back to the ground, if necessary, and plants will grow fresh foliage.

Hollyhocks often suffer from rust, a fungal disease that causes brown-orange spots over the leaves and then widespread browning. Pick off and remove diseased leaves, then spray fungicides to protect the rest. Preventive fungicides are often needed to grow rust-free hollyhocks.

SHRUBS

If the leaves of your azaleas, pieris, rhododendrons, and mountain laurel are looking pale, check for lace bugs, a small flying insect with clear wings that feeds on the leaf undersides. Lace bugs suck plant juices as opposed to chewing and can produce three generations per year, from late April through September. Insecticidal soap, horticultural oil, and several chemical insecticides control them. Sprays are most effective early (late April to early June) and when sprayed underneath the leaves.

Pick off diseased leaves, remove fallen diseased ones, and remove weed competition from around the base of shrubs.

Bagworms become more noticeable this month on needled evergreen shrubs. Pick as many dangling "bags" as possible from shrub branches. Or spray with Bt (*Bacillus thuringiensis*) or other insecticides labeled for bagworm control.

Clematis wilt is a fungal disease that can brown out whole stems of clematis vines and even whole plants.

HERE'S HOW

TO TELL IF YOU'RE WATERING ENOUGH

1. Your goal is to keep the soil consistently damp (but not soggy) all around and just below a plant's root system.

2. Frequency and amount varies by plant size and age. Newly planted annual flowers, for example, benefit from shallow waterings every day or two. New trees and shrubs have much bigger roots and benefit more from deeper soakings two or three times a week.

3. A rough guide for the water need of a new tree is 1 to 2 gallons for every inch of trunk diameter at shoulder height. For new shrubs, water 3 to 5 gallons per watering. As roots spread, widen the watering area and increase amounts to 1 gallon of water for every square foot of soil surface.

4. A good check is to give the water fifteen minutes to soak and then use your finger, a stick, a probe, or a soil moisture meter to determine if the soil is damp to the edges of the roots. If so, you're done. Do the same thing next time. If it's not damp, apply more water and note to increase the amount the next time.

5. Never apply water so heavily that it runs off instead of soaks in. The moisture needs to go to the roots, not the sidewalk.

6. Supply water evenly all around the plant. Don't sit a hose down in one area and never move it.

7. Water often enough that your plants aren't wilting, losing vibrant color, or showing other signs of water stress. Sandy soil needs water more frequently than clay or loam soils. If plants wilt, the time to water was yesterday.

8. Pay attention to the weather. Plants use more water in hot, dry, windy conditions than in cool, cloudy weather.

■ *Use a rain gauge to determine how much rain or irrigation water has been delivered to your bed or lawn.*

Big-leafed and big-flowered clematis varieties are especially prone. Choose wilt-resistant varieties up front (*viticella* types, for example). If existing ones are infected, prune out wilted stems, remove dropped and diseased leaves, keep plants watered in dry weather, and consider preventive fungicides if wilt becomes an annual, unacceptable problem. Plants usually survive the setback.

TREES

The lace bug family has members that prefer hawthorn, sycamore, and some species of oak trees in summer. These discolor leaves but usually don't cause enough trouble to warrant treatment.

Japanese beetles love fruit tree species, including their more ornamental cousins the crabapple and

flowering cherry. Linden is a favorite, too. But surprisingly, beetles also sometimes feed on needled evergreens. The damage might look bad, but large, healthy plants such as trees almost invariably grow through this chewing without treatment.

If the tips of your pine and spruce trees are dying, be suspicious of the white pine weevil. The larvae of this insect feed just under the bark of branch tips high on trees, especially at the top of the main leader. Most of the damage is done in late spring, but it's typically July until the needles brown enough that people notice. Controls include cutting off infested tips, monitoring in April for brewing trouble, and spraying outbreaks with insecticides labeled for pine weevils.

August

One more muggy month to go before things start cooling off, and gardens (as well as gardeners) begin to look fresh and perky again.

As in July, August's daytime temperatures often park themselves in the 90s with stifling humidity to boot. It's the second hottest month in the mid-Atlantic region. August also is one of the region's drier months, although that can vary depending on whether your yard is in the path of sporadic summer thunderstorms or hurricanes and their remnants.

This month's moisture tends to come in dumpings instead of the gentle multi-day soakings of spring and fall rains. Be ready with the hose during those hot, dry spells, but don't be surprised by the occasional August gully-washer.

August gardening is much like July—more puttering than, say, the pruning and mulching frenzy of spring or the clean-up and cut-down marathon of fall. It's prime time for harvesting the vegetable garden, but also for admiring the coneflowers, serenely gathering cut-flower bouquets from the yard, and sipping a cool drink on the patio.

The annual flowers should be in peak form, too, *if* you've kept them fertilized, watered, and out of the mouths of rabbits, groundhogs, and deer. Plenty of perennials and shrubs flower in August, so there's no excuse if your yard is devoid of color. If it is, make note to get yourself some coreopsis, gaura, perennial sunflowers, Russian sage, tall phlox, goldenrod, caryopteris, dwarf butterfly bush, panicle hydrangea, and shrub roses.

If things are looking tired or baked around the yard, maybe you need more trees to nurse the plantings (and you) through the Mid-Atlantic's oven months. Temperatures can be 10 degrees cooler in summer under a shade tree than out in full sun.

Enjoy this semi-siesta month. Labor Day will be here before you know it, marking the de facto end of summer and the beginning of the year's second main window for planting, transplanting, dividing perennials, and similar jobs that the heat of July and August rendered impractical.

PLAN

ALL

Heat-beat August yards might be telling you that besides more trees, you need mulch, watering, or heat-tolerant plants.

Consider buying a chipper-shredder. These chopping machines turn that pile of tree- and shrub-trimmings into mulch and fall's coming fallen-leaf harvest into ideal compost fodder. Yeah, they're noisy and use gas. But chipper-spreaders recycle almost all yard waste and pay for themselves in disposal savings and less mulch to buy.

ANNUALS & TROPICALS

Heat-lovers such as celosia, lantana, vinca, and zinnias should be happy in the 90-degree weather. But if cool-preferring lobelia, osteospermum, nemesia, pansies, and such have fried in the heat, replace them later this month or early next with mums or a fresh round of fall pansies, violas, ornamental cabbage, or ornamental kale.

BULBS

Spring-flowering bulbs will show up at home-improvement and garden centers late this month. It's too hot to plant them yet. If you buy now, store them in a cool, dry area until the more optimal planting time in October and November.

If you're buying bulbs online or through a catalog, place your order now if you haven't already. They'll be shipped at the appropriate time.

■ *Prepare a bulb bed now by digging and adding amendments to improve the soil.*

Although now's early to plant bulbs, you *can* get a new bulb bed ready. Remove the turfgrass, loosen the soil 10 to 12 inches deep, and work in about 2 inches of compost or similar organic matter to create slightly raised beds. Rake smooth, top the soil with 2 inches of bark mulch, and you're ready to plant—later.

LAWNS

That lawn that looked so good in May can look so worn and weed-infested in August after the stresses of a hot, dry summer. Evaluate how much of your "lawn" is still desirable grass versus weeds or "junk grass." If you have at least 50 percent grass, it's worth rehabbing. If weeds are the majority, it might be easier to kill off everything, improve the soil, and start from scratch in September.

■ *If your lawn has more weeds or dead grass than live grass, a renovation is a better idea than trying to patch.*

Call now if you're hiring a company to do a major lawn renovation. Get on the calendar for September or October before others grab all of the time slots.

PERENNIALS & GROUNDCOVERS

Summer sun particularly bakes south- and west-facing slopes. Think about converting struggling south or west grassy slopes into no-mow, low-care mass plantings of heat-tough plants, such as shrub roses, ornamental grass, spreading juniper, daylily, sedum, and spreading sumac.

Some perennials, such as black-eyed Susan, purple coneflower, and gaillardia, self-sow. Decide whether you want that or not. Deadhead spent flowers before seeds mature if you don't want a plant to self-sow. Let them alone if you do.

SHRUBS

Many roses bloom continuously throughout summer, even before the more widespread rose "second wind" of September. Consider adding shrub-type roses or other long-blooming types if you need more August color.

Few flowering shrubs bloom in August. Among the choices are beautyberry, blue mist shrub (*Caryopteris*), butterfly bush, crape myrtle, rose-of-Sharon, panicle hydrangea, and vitex.

■ *Beautyberry is aptly named —and is one of the plants that bloom in August, later yielding spectacular berries.*

TREES

Trees not only make the patio more bearable in hot weather, they're also energy-savers. Trees planted to the south and southwest of homes block the hot afternoon sun, keeping rooms on those sides cooler and reducing air-conditioning need. When their leaves drop in winter, the sun's rays will get through to warm the house.

Evergreens make sense to the north and northwest of a house, where they'll block the prevailing cold winds in winter without blocking the south-originating sunlight.

Although they don't have quite the impact of a shade tree, vines planted along south- and west-facing walls do have some summer cooling effect on the sun-drenched structures there. Vine-covered trellises are especially useful to block the southern and western setting sun when you're trying to use a

HERE'S HOW

TO CONSERVE WATER

1. Start at plant-buying time by choosing varieties with low water needs.

2. Improve the soil with compost before planting. It encourages better rooting in clay soil, which helps plants withstand dry conditions better. In sandy soil, compost improves water-holding ability.

3. Group plants by water preference. That way you'll have all of the high-need plants together where you can target them. Locate high-water-demand plants near a hose.

4. Add more trees to cool and shade the soil.

5. Maintain adequate mulch over garden beds.

6. Consider a drip-irrigation or soaker-hose system to deliver water directly to the ground.

7. Add rain barrels to collect rain water so it's available when needed.

deck or patio in the evening. These take up very little horizontal space.

PLANT

ALL

August isn't an ideal month to plant because of the heat, but most container-grown garden-center plants do fine if kept watered. Conditions get less stressful toward the end of the month in Zones 5 and 6, then improve markedly throughout the region from early September on as temperatures cool, soil evaporation slows, and rain increases.

ANNUALS & TROPICALS

As summer winds down, garden centers replace heat-preferring summer annuals with a fresh crop of cool-preferring fall annuals. These can be planted starting in late August.

BULBS

Wait until October or November to plant spring-blooming bulbs. But several species of

■ *Once they're done, they're done. Pull up tired annuals and plant new ones.*

PERENNIALS, GROUNDCOVERS, SHRUBS & TREES

Minimize transplant shock by planting on a cloudy day or in the evening. Or erect a temporary shade structure for a few days after planting. Most important, keep the soil consistently damp.

Another option if you find a bargain that's too good to pass up during a hot, sunny spell: keep the plant in the pot, store it out of the afternoon sun, and water daily until oppressive heat subsides.

Avoid plants that are deeply discounted because they're so damaged or stressed that a recovery is doubtful. Dead and dying plants aren't bargains.

fall-blooming bulbs can be planted in late summer if you don't have any already. Choices include the resurrection lily, fall crocus (*Colchicum*), autumn daffodil (*Sternbergia*), and hardy cyclamen.

LAWNS

Those in Zones 5 and 6 can get busy overseeding or reseeding lawns toward the end of this month as temperatures cool. For warmer Zones 7 and 8, after Labor Day is better.

CARE

ALL

We're past peak weed-germinating time, but some species continue to sprout in the heat of late summer. Pull and spot-spray as long as weeds keep coming.

HERE'S HOW

TO SEED A NEW LAWN

Scratch the soil surface and add a light layer of compost to aid the germination of grass seed. A hand-spreader helps spread grass seed evenly over a bare patch. Scatter a light layer of straw over the area to help keep the soil damp. Grass seed must stay moist until it sprouts. Water the newly seeded area twice a day for ten minutes until the grass is at least an inch tall. Then water the newly seeded area three times a week for ten minutes. Don't mow the newly seeded area for at least two months. New grass is fragile, and foot traffic or mower blades could rip the seedlings out of the ground.

ANNUALS & TROPICALS

Remove fallen diseased leaves and any other rotting plant debris from flowerbeds. The cleanup lessens future disease problems.

Continue to stake "floppers," and snip back overly long stems.

BULBS

Snip spent lily flowers, but let the stems alone if they're green. Only cut lily stems to the ground after they brown. Keep the bulbs in the ground. These are hardy and will come back next year.

Continue to deadhead faded blossoms on dahlias, cannas, and other bulb flowers still producing.

LAWNS

It's probably time to sharpen the mower blade by now. Every twenty-five hours of cutting is a good guide. One sign of a dull mower blade is brown grass tips. Crisply cut grass blades heal well and stay greener, while ones that are bludgeoned off by dull mower blades are ragged and browner.

Continue to mow high and let the clippings lay so long as the grass is green and growing. Stay off the lawn to the extent you can if it's browning or already dormant in dry soil.

Pull or spot-spray lawn weeds so they're out of the way for new grass seed in the coming weeks. Allow six weeks between the time you last use a lawn weed-killer and when you seed.

■ *Keep mower blades sharp. Blades should be sharpened about once every 25 hours of cutting.*

PERENNIALS & GROUNDCOVERS

As summer wanes, the perennial garden may need some primping and clipping to look good again. Cut back leggy stems of catmint, artemisia, goldenrod, and others after they bloom. Clip off spent, diseased, or drought- and heat-injured browned foliage. Deadhead the tall phlox, coneflowers, Russian sage, black-eyed Susan, and anything else sporting browned flowers. And, of course, weed the beds to reduce competition for nutrients and moisture as well as to keep the garden looking tended.

Check the supports of large late-summer perennials. Are they still able to handle the full weight of grown plants, especially when rain and wind add to the burden? Shore up ones that got bigger than you thought with additional stakes or sections of fencing.

SHRUBS

Other than snipping spent flower heads off the ends of hydrangeas, butterfly bushes, and other summer-flowering shrubs, limit pruning to removing dead or injured branches. From now through late fall when leaves drop, shrubs are starting to prepare for cold-weather dormancy. Avoid shaping and other heavy cutting that will stimulate new growth at a time when growth should be slowing.

Many varieties of roses develop rose "hips," which are berrylike growths that form where flowers fade. By late this month, stop deadheading faded flowers, and allow hips to form. Later in the season, the hips will provide a nutritious meal for birds and other wildlife.

Check that summer storms haven't loosened climbing roses or vines from their supports. Re-tie them, and guide new shoots protruding beyond where you'd like. Or snip off overly long tips.

TREES

Be careful with the weed trimmer. Nicks in the soft bark of young trees allow pests and disease pathogens access to tender tissues. This is one reason why rings of mulch make good sense.

As with flowering shrubs, limit tree pruning from now through late fall to removing dead or injured branches. Trees also are starting to prepare for cold-weather dormancy and are slowing growth. Avoid shaping and heavy cutting that will cause new growth.

WATER

ALL

Getting tired of all of that bucket carrying, hose dragging, and sprinkler moving? Consider investing in an irrigation system, either a simple one that you rig up yourself or a professionally installed one with pop-up sprinkler heads and timers. Done well, it will save time and maybe even money and water in the long run.

■ *Drip irrigation systems are easier to install than they look, and make watering automatic.*

For watering small beds with a lot of plants, rubber soaker hoses are a work-saving option that allow water to ooze out along their length. For watering shrubs, pots, or a few large plants along longer runs, consider drip-irrigation systems. These use skinny plastic supply lines that can be tapped into as needed to insert emitters that drip water at the plant roots. Pop-up sprinklers are a good option for covering large areas, such as lawns. All of these can be rigged up to timers to make watering automatic.

Watering bags, tubs, and similar commercial products are other aids to apply water evenly and gradually. These are installed around young shrubs and trees and are filled once or twice a week. Holes in the bottom let the water seep out slowly, avoiding the threat of runoff from too-fast application. Seeing a big empty bag or tub around your new tree also helps you remember it's time to refill it.

Wilting foliage may mean a plant is hot, rather than sick or thirsty. To confirm this, check wilted plants after the sun and heat of the day have passed. If foliage recovers, the problem is heat. If it has not perked up, dryness is more likely.

Don't get faked out by summer downpours. A storm may look like it's dumping more than it really does. Or it may come down so fast that most of it runs off before soaking in. Use a rain gauge or stick your finger a few inches into the soil to assess whether a storm has just wet the mulch or supplied enough moisture where it's really needed, into your plants' root zones.

ANNUALS & TROPICALS

In-ground plantings are often root-developed enough by now to do well with a moderate soaking once or twice a week.

Figure on daily watering for flowers in pots and baskets. These need even more water now that they're grown and filling the pots with water-needy roots.

Annuals in small hanging pots out in full sun may need water twice a day in August's heat to keep from frying or ceasing to bloom.

BULBS

Bulbs growing in pots need daily (or more) watering, just like annual flowers. Summer bulbs growing in the ground can get by with a single 1-inch soaking a week or less, similar to perennial flowers.

Spring bulbs that have gone dormant (tulips and daffodils, for example) don't need or want moisture in summer.

LAWNS

Barring a widespread disease or bug outbreak, a browning lawn is usually due to dry soil. It's dormant, not dead. Once a soaking rain happens, the grass will "green up" in a day or two and resume growing. If you're okay with that, skip watering.

HERE'S HOW

TO WEATHER A SUMMER DROUGHT

1. Add mulch if you're down to bare soil, or close to it. Soak beds well before mulching. A 3- to 4-inch layer is plenty for trees and shrubs, 2 to 3 inches is ideal for perennials, and 1 inch is good around annuals.

2. Get rid of weeds. They're moisture competitors for your plants.

3. Monitor soil moisture regularly and look to "indicator plants" that tell you the soil's getting dry. Hydrangea, Japanese maple, redbud, astilbe, ligularia, and impatiens are among the first wilters.

4. Give highest watering priority to new or expensive plants and to plants you really don't want to risk losing. Save water on plants that can fend for themselves. (See July, Water, All.)

5. Minimize evaporation losses by watering early in the morning or early in the evening.

6. Make watering more manageable by dividing the yard into zones. Water a zone at a time instead of trying to water the entire yard all at once.

7. Water pots and ornamentals with recycled "grey water" from the house, such as from dehumidifiers, air conditioners, cooking, and dishwashing.

8. Avoid fertilizing and pruning. Both can stimulate growth at a time when plants should be conserving energy.

The time to think about watering a brown lawn is when a drought drags on, and the lawn is straw-brown for six weeks or more. Then, watering ¼ of an inch per week is enough to replenish moisture to the grass crowns without stimulating grass to resume growing.

PERENNIALS & GROUNDCOVERS

Moisture-sensitive perennials, such as astilbe, primrose, lobelia, and many ferns, benefit from soakings once a week or at the first sign of wilting or browning around the edges. First-year perennials also should continue to get weekly or twice-weekly soakings during August when rain doesn't happen.

Established perennials, especially drought-tough ones, can survive weeks without water and need hose help only in extended hot, dry spells.

Perennials in pots or baskets dry out quickly and benefit from daily watering.

SHRUBS & TREES

Focus on shrubs, woody vines, and trees that you've planted or moved within the past two to three years. Soak them deeply once or twice a week if there's no rain, enough to dampen the soil all around and to the bottom of the rootballs (most of which is in the top 10 or 12 inches). Check with your finger, a probe, or a soil-moisture meter.

Also pay attention to shrubs growing under trees. Those typically lose the moisture battle to bigger tree roots and may not get much rain in storms because the leaves block it. Soak these shrubs every few weeks if it's hot and dry.

Most other established woody plants need no supplemental water except in unusually long, hot, dry spells. When you do water, soak deeply.

Shrubs and small trees growing in planters dry quickly in August's heat, so check them daily. Soak well until water runs out the drainage holes.

New roses and ones that you're pushing for peak performance should continue to get soakings two to three times a week. Established roses are fine with a single, once-a-week, 1-inch soaking, and most will at least survive with less than that.

FERTILIZE

ALL

Virtually nothing needs or should get supplemental fertilizer again this month. It's counterproductive to fertilize plants that are coping with harsh heat and drought. More fertilizer doesn't help a plant deal with lack of water. Water solves that.

ANNUALS, TROPICALS & PERENNIALS

An exception to the August no-fertilize rule are flowers growing in pots or baskets. These use and leach nutrients so quickly due to daily waterings that they benefit from a water-soluble flower fertilizer at half-strength once a week.

LAWNS

Wait until at least September for the next fertilizer application. The exception is warm-weather zoysia grass, which can get one last fertilizer treatment if it's been eight weeks since the last one. Zoysia goes dormant with frost and should not be fertilized after August as with cool-season grasses.

Do not fertilize any lawn that's brown or flirting with dormancy.

Test your lawn soil so you know what kind and how much fertilizer to use in advance of fall. Kits are available from county Extension offices and most home-improvement and garden centers.

SHRUBS, TREES & VINES

Most don't need fertilizer anytime, but summer through early fall is the wrong time to apply it. Woody plants start preparing for winter dormancy in the coming weeks and don't benefit from fertilizer that encourages new late-season growth that might not harden sufficiently before winter.

Fertilize woody plants only if poor growth and a soil test indicate there's a nutrient deficiency. Wait to apply it when the plants drop their leaves and go dormant, or until early next spring. Never fertilize a shrub stressed by heat or pest problems.

July was the end of the line for rose fertilizing for the year. The exceptions are if you're shooting for peak performance, and in the cooler Zone 5 and 6 areas, it's okay to apply one last scattering of a granular, slow-acting fertilizer formulated for roses early in August. From here on out, roses should begin focusing more on storing energy in their roots than pushing new top growth.

PROBLEM-SOLVE

ALL

Some unusual growths appear in the mulch over summer. Most are nuisance wood-decaying organisms that are harmless to people, pets, and plants. Tops on the list is the artillery fungus, which is notorious for the black, tarry, pinhead-sized flecks the mulch-dwelling fruiting bodies shoot onto light surfaces. When these spore masses stick and dry, they're almost impossible to remove from siding, fences, white cars, and so on. This fungus grows best in shredded hardwood mulch, the most commonly used type. Inspect your mulch-side surfaces over summer for new spores and wipe them off as soon as possible before they dry. Artillery fungus doesn't grow as well in bark mulch, leaf mulch, or pine needles.

More noticeable is slime mold, commonly called "dog vomit fungus" because that's what it looks like

■ *Slime mold is a common but harmless fungal growth that often occurs on mulch in summer.*

in its early stage. The blobs start out pale yellow to yellow-orange on the mulch surface and dry into darker blobs that spew a dry gray powder when opened. Bag and toss the blobs if they bug you. No spray or treatment will stop them from forming; hot, dry weather will.

Among the weirdest is the "stinkhorn" fungus that sends up slender orange hollow stalks about the size of a pinky with a mushroom-like cap on top. It's harmless and typically blackens, shrivels, and disappears in a matter of days.

Fungal diseases are in their heyday this month because of the warm, humid conditions so many of them favor. Plant-damaging ones cause spots, blotches, or sunken patches on plant foliage, killing the tissues and threatening the stems with dieback. Others clog the "veins" of plant stems, and some rot roots.

Fungicides don't cure diseases but can protect uninfected foliage before or in the early stages of a threatening leaf disease. Different ones work best for different diseases, so it's important to diagnose the specific disease before turning to a spray.

While some plant diseases are potentially fatal, plants often grow through leaf diseases, especially ones that occur later in the season. Good sanitation helps. Clip off infected leaves or stems, and put them in the trash to prevent the spread of the disease. Also, remove fallen diseased leaves, which harbor fungal spores that may overwinter to reinfect next year.

ANNUALS & TROPICALS

Petunias, calibrachoa, nicotiana, and geraniums often suddenly stop blooming this month, leading gardeners to blame hot weather or lack of water. Look closely for small, green caterpillars called budworms that bore into the base of flower buds, causing them to abort. Also look for small holes at the base of flower buds that didn't open. Hand-pick budworms you can see, or spray with spinosyn or an insecticide labeled for budworm control.

Powdery mildew is a common disfiguring threat to zinnias, annual phlox, and some verbenas in August. The leaves develop a whitish-gray coating and

eventually brown and die. Snip off infected leaves, and water the ground, not over the leaves. At planting, space far enough apart for good air circulation. Fungicides can slow outbreaks. A homemade, organic recipe is 1 tablespoon of baking soda and ½ tablespoon of horticultural oil to 1 gallon water, sprayed every three or four days. The best solution is to plant mildew-resistant varieties in the first place, such as the Profusion and Zahara series.

BULBS

Powdery mildew is also fairly common on tuberous begonias and sometimes on dahlias. The same treatment options apply as to annuals.

LAWNS

Beetle grubs hatch this month and cause feeding damage in the lawn. The telltale sign is browning patches that pull up like loose carpet. That's because the young grubs have eaten the roots out from underneath. Dig up a square foot of turfgrass and examine the root zone for grubs. If you count more than four or five in a square foot, that's enough to cause noticeable damage and warrant treatment.

Grub-preventing insecticides that work well when applied late May through early July don't work as well in late summer and fall. Look now for products

■ *Powdery mildew affects all kinds of plants, from annuals to perennials to edibles. You can plant resistant varieties or try a fungicide to manage outbreaks. Better air circulation also helps.*

that *kill* grubs. An organic option is predatory nematodes (*Heterorhabditis bacteriophora* and/or *Steinernema carpocapsae*), which are microscopic worms that enter the soil and parasitize grubs. Mid-August through mid-September is good timing to buy and apply these.

A slower-acting, longer-term organic lawn-grub option is milky spore, a disease that sickens and kills grubs of Japanese beetles. It can be applied any time the ground isn't frozen. It's had mixed results, however.

Rust is a common lawn disease that strikes in late summer. Grass blades develop reddish-brown pustules that produce orange-red powder that puffs up as you walk through an infected patch (hence the nickname, "orange shoe disease"). Rust usually resolves on its own without lasting lawn damage, so treatment isn't recommended.

Powdery mildew can affect grass as well as garden plants, causing the same whitish-gray coating on grass blades. It occurs mostly on Kentucky bluegrass in shaded areas. Treatment usually isn't needed, but fungicides can control severe outbreaks.

Chinch bugs are small, black, beetle-like bugs that pierce grass blades in hot weather and suck out chlorophyll, causing brown patches in bad enough infestations. Several generations can hatch per year. If they're bad enough to warrant action, insecticides will kill them.

PERENNIALS & GROUNDCOVERS

Peony foliage often looks beat up by now due to several late-summer diseases, including botrytis, phytopthora, and powdery mildew. Cut off and dispose of leaves that are looking bad enough to detract from the landscape, including cutting back the entire plant to the ground.

Some black-eyed Susan varieties are prone to fungal leaf spot disease that some years is bad enough to warrant cutting down and removing all of the foliage. Plants usually grow a new set of leaves until frost kills those. In minor or early outbreaks, pick off spotted leaves as soon as you see them.

Perennial or groundcover leaves that are browning around the edges or turning a bleached, pale color could be suffering from sun scorch. These symptoms happen to young or shade-preferring plants getting more sun and heat than their genetics allow. A leading example is variegated hosta. Those planted along sunny driveways look fried around the edges this month. The best solution is to move them to a cooler, shadier spot. Excess salt in the soil (from winter ice-melt runoff) can compound this scorching damage.

Mites continue to threaten a variety of plants with their sucking damage as they thrive in the dry heat. Watch for pale, stippled leaves and fine webbing on stems. Wash mites off infected plants with forceful sprays of water from the hose, or in severe, persistent cases, spray with insecticidal soap or a pesticide labeled for mite control.

If you're seeing dead or yellowing patches in groundcovers near sidewalks, that's likely due to visits by local dogs. Their urine, which is high in nitrogen, "burns" plant foliage. Scent repellents can encourage passing dogs to pick a telephone pole instead. Consider a low fence if that fails.

SHRUBS

Old-fashioned lilacs are prone to powdery mildew, but it's also somewhat common on dark-leafed ninebarks, Exbury azaleas, shrub dogwoods, some hydrangeas, and occasionally on butterfly bushes. It's mainly cosmetic (especially on lilac), but severe or repeated infections can kill branches. Watch for the symptoms, and evaluate whether a fungicide treatment is warranted.

Browning tips on junipers, especially the low and spreading types, may look like heat or drought injury, but it's often the symptom of two common fungal blights. Look for tiny pepperlike spores under a hand lens. Early infections can be slowed by snipping the infected tips; pruning will aid air circulation. Otherwise, a continuing series of fungicide applications may be needed.

Junipers, spruce, and many other conifers are targets of mites as well. If you're seeing loss of color (usually the first sign), a good mite test is to place a piece of white paper under suspect branches and bang them. If you see little "dots" scurrying around on the paper, you're likely watching mites in action.

Boxwoods sometimes suffer slow deaths from "boxwood decline," which involves gradual branch dieback. A new, deadlier threat called "boxwood blight" (caused by the *Cylindrocladium buxicola* fungus) is spreading throughout the East Coast. It starts with concentric brown spots on the leaves and black streaking on the stems, followed by a fairly quick brownout of the entire plant. This blight is thought to spread mainly from infected nursery stock as opposed to blowing around in the wind or being spread by birds and bugs. Both of these diseases are difficult to control in a home landscape.

Mites, aphids, and Japanese beetles are bugs that still may turn up on rose foliage. Insecticidal soap can control both of the first two bugs, while hand-picking or spraying Neem oil or a beetle-killing insecticide are options for the latter.

Blackspot is the main rose disease threat, but powdery mildew often shows up, especially if it's humid. Most fungicides control both of those diseases if hand-picking infected leaves doesn't keep a lid on outbreaks.

More serious are rare but usually fatal viral diseases such as rose mosaic virus and rose rosette disease (see April, Problem-Solve, Shrubs.) These stunt rose growth and lead to symptoms such as disfigured, splotchy leaves and malformed buds. Viral diseases don't respond to fungicides either. If you suspect a virus, get an accurate diagnosis. If your hunch is right, you'll likely have to dig and remove the infected rose. Disinfect your shovel and tools after digging to prevent spreading the virus to other roses.

TREES

Late summer is when you might notice orange-striped oakworms stripping the leaves of oaks (and maybe hickories, maples, or birch trees). Because these insects are late-season feeders, they're not a big threat to the long-term health of a tree. They're more of a nuisance, dropping small gobs of oakworm waste over driveways, patios, and sidewalks. Ignore them, or for intolerable outbreaks, spray with Bt (*Bacillus thuringiensis*). Or hire a tree company to apply an insecticide.

Just because a tree is dropping something doesn't mean it's in trouble. Some species routinely drop twigs, fuzzy balls, seeds, flower bracts, last year's leaves, or excess fruit. Some slough off strips or patches of bark. Evergreens shed older leaves and needles from the inside as the tips grow. Know what's normal for your species, then worry only when something is dropping outside of that realm.

Lightning is attracted to tall, isolated targets such as telephone poles, tall buildings, and, of course, trees. Big, old shade trees are frequent victims. Lightning hits can cause large splits in the trunk and branches as the sap inside super-heats. Cells can rupture inside from the electrical charge as well. If you want to protect a valuable specimen tree, consider hiring a company to install a lightning protection system. Cables run down from the tree's top to a buried metal grounding rod.

Fat "bumps" about the size of a half-pea on magnolia branches are a sign of scale insects. Magnolia scale is the largest member of the scale family and is best controlled in August. Inspect your branches, and if needed, treat with horticultural oil or a spray labeled for magnolia scale.

■ *Older evergreen needles will drop off naturally after they brown.*

September

May is hard to beat as the mid-Atlantic region's top month in the garden, but September gives it a run for its money.

The daytime heat of July and August usually backs off into the 70s to low 80s, although last-gasp, mid-90s heat flashes can never be ruled out, especially down Tidewater way. Toward the end of the month, the coolest Zone 5 reaches of western Maryland and the West Virginia mountains can even start to flirt with borderline frosts.

Rain happens more often, too—usually. Although thunderstormish and hurricane-remnant dumpings occur, so do gentle daylong dousings. It's refreshing to see heat-beat plants perk up following a cool, September soaking rain, just when you thought the landscape was ready to call it quits.

The outlook of cooling temperatures and more frequent rain adds up to a month that's perfect for patching a thin lawn or starting a new one. It's also a great time to plant most plants or move ones you've realized are in the wrong spot. September planting is less stressful than midsummer planting and usually allows a minimum of eight to ten weeks of root growth before winter's approach shuts down the season.

A Cornell University study found that fall-planted plants survive best when they have at least six weeks of root growth before the soil temperature in the root zone drops below 40 degrees Fahrenheit. In the mid-Atlantic region, that translates into an ideal-planting cutoff of late October in Zones 5 and 6 and early to mid-November in the warmer Zones 7 and 8. September planting gives a buffer of several additional weeks.

Fall planting offers one other plus: reduced weed competition. Far fewer weeds germinate in fall than spring, so when you dig that soil and start watering your new plants, you won't get more dandelions than dianthus.

We're still a month or so away from fall-foliage glory, but in the meantime, enjoy the mums, asters, goldenrod, sedum, and the year's second-best bloom time for roses.

PLAN

ALL

Most gardeners rate four-season interest high on their wish list. Some strategies for achieving that include:

Add more variety. Plant more plants and different kinds of them. You'll get multiseason change and interest just by the odds and dumb luck.

Make a conscious effort to plan for all four seasons. Think what each part of the yard will look like in each season, and seek plants that will add interest to any boring gaps.

Move beyond two-week wonders. Many overused favorites are one-dimensional plants that peak only for a few weeks of the year (azaleas, rhododendrons, lilacs, peonies, forsythia, and burning bush, for example).

Look for hard-workers. These are plants that do more than one thing in one season. Example: oakleaf hydrangea blooms white in late spring, gets burgundy foliage in fall, then shows off peeling bark in winter.

Don't plant-shop only in May. You'll tend to buy only what's looking good then—or on sale. Shop in different seasons. Make it a point to go whenever your yard is looking particularly barren.

Visit public gardens. They're great for getting ideas and seeing what's doing what at any given time. Visit these in different seasons too.

Pay attention to what other people have planted. If you see plants nearby doing something interesting at a time when your yard is snoozing, find out what those plants are, and add them to your list.

Watch for deals on new plants. Many garden centers hold "Fall is for Planting" sales. As fall rolls on, even deeper discounts show up on both plants and garden supplies as retailers clear inventory before winter.

ANNUALS & TROPICALS

Don't wait too long to take tender tropicals and houseplants back inside. Some of them start to

■ *Oakleaf hydrangea* (Hydrangea quercifolia) *in fall color.*

■ *Oakleaf hydrangea in spring blooms.*

suffer when nighttime lows dip below 50 degrees Fahrenheit. Most will die if a surprise early frost hits. Think about this move late this month in Zones 5 and 6 and around mid-October in Zones 7 and 8. (See "Here's How To Overwinter Tropicals.")

While it's fresh in your mind, make post-season notes about how your flowers performed this year. What annuals were most successful? Where do you wish you had planted more of them? Fewer? What problems did you encounter this year and with what species? Has anything changed in the yard that will affect which annuals you plant where next spring?

BULBS

Late September is the beginning of prime spring-bulb planting, so finalize your plans for what you're adding where. Buy or order as soon as possible before the choices get picked over or sell out.

Spring bulbs can be used in a variety of landscape settings, not just massed by themselves. Some ideas are:

Interplant with perennials. Bulbs will poke up and bloom while the perennials are just waking up. Then the perennials take over the space and hide bulb foliage as it's yellowing.

Poke in among groundcovers. Taller bulbs such as daffodils, tulips, and hyacinths can be inserted into low plantings of vinca, pachysandra, hardy ginger, and such. Their shoots are strong enough to poke up through the groundcover foliage and bloom over top.

Mix and match randomly to create a "bulb meadow." This is a great way to take advantage of year-end bargains of two-packs of this and three-packs of that.

Plant under trees and tall shrubs. Many bulbs get sufficient sunlight before the trees and shrubs leaf out to recharge themselves for the following year's bloom.

Cluster in key spots around the yard. How about lining the front walk? Around the mailbox or front light post? Maybe some fragrant hyacinths around the back patio? Or how about some golden daffodils at the base of an arbor or in front of a fence?

Plant in foam, plastic, and other winter-hardy pots that can be left outside all winter. Come spring, the bulbs will emerge and flower in the pot. This is less expensive than buying already-flowering bulb plants in spring.

Plant in the lawn. Short, early bulbs work best for this. They'll poke up and flower before the lawn greens. If possible, hold off mowing until the foliage yellows. Good choices for lawn planting are snowdrops, winter aconite, and tommasinianus-type crocuses ("tommies").

Bulb growers grade bulbs by size. Since larger-sized ones usually perform best, they're typically more expensive than bags of bargain-priced smaller ones. Weigh the price versus their intended use. You may decide, for example, to pay more for bulbs you're planning to "force" for inside bloom or use out front, but opt for a bargain bag of dwarf daffodils that you're going to naturalize in the back yard.

Check bulbs for firmness and plumpness. A touch of blue mold on the surface is not a problem; neither is a peeling tunic or dry skin. What *is* a problem is soft or rotting bulbs, or ones that are dry and noticeably lighter in weight.

LAWNS

Labor Day weekend opens the window for major lawn work. September and October are the year's best two months for seeding or sodding new lawns and for rehabbing sad existing lawns.

Like any other plant, grass performs best in good soil with adequate nutrition. Unfortunately, many lawns are trying to grow in the heavily graded, compacted soils common to housing subdivisions. A good way to gradually improve poor soil without digging it up is "topdressing." This involves raking a light layer of sifted compost or similar fine, organic-rich topsoil over the soil surface. A ¼-inch layer is enough to begin helping without smothering the existing lawn. Topdressing can be done early each fall until your lawn is thriving.

■ *Fall is an ideal time to topdress a lawn.*

PERENNIALS & GROUNDCOVERS

Trying to reduce maintenance? Think about areas to convert to groundcover, such as bare areas around trees, hard-to-mow slopes, or mulched beds under shrubs. The traditional "big three" are ivy, pachysandra, and vinca (myrtle), but many others are good options. For shade, consider sweet woodruff, barrenwort, lamium, moss, ferns, Pennsylvania sedge, hardy ginger, or variegated Solomon's seal. For part shade, consider liriope, leadwort, foamflower, hellebores, or mazus. For sun, consider creeping sedum, thyme, dianthus, creeping phlox, or hardy geranium.

Mums aren't the only perennials that peak in September. Others that add color to the fall landscape are agastache, aster, boltonia, catmint, goldenrod, Japanese anemone, Joe-pye weed, lavender, leadwort, liriope, reblooming daylilies, Russian sage, salvia, sedum, toad lily, and turtlehead.

A good reason to leave at least some seedheads on late-season perennials is to provide food for visiting wildlife in fall and winter. Weigh that against whether you want any self-sowing.

SHRUBS

September is the year's second showiest month for roses. Are you taking advantage of that? Lean toward low-care shrub, landscape, and antique types if you like the idea of the color but not the pests, diseases, and fertilizer effort.

A few flowering shrubs bloom in September. Besides roses, take a look at blue mist shrub (*Caryopteris*), butterfly bush, abelia, dwarf crape myrtle, and panicle and reblooming hydrangeas.

Berries and fruits are an even showier feature than flowers on the shrub front in September. Choices worth including are bayberry, cotoneaster, nandina, beautyberry, chokeberry, St. John's wort, skimmia, holly, juniper, and viburnum.

Need some privacy or some sun protection on a second-floor deck or balcony? A vine-covered trellis inserted in a window box on the floor is a colorful solution that takes up very little precious floor space.

Pyracantha fruits are maturing into bright reddish-orange clusters (or should be if they didn't rot from summer disease). These are at their showiest in fall and early winter and are durable choices that prune well into any size or shape you like. Just be aware they have large, pointy thorns.

Another fall- and winter-fruiting vine is American bittersweet, which is different from the invasive Oriental bittersweet. This native vine gets red berries in fall that birds love, but that are poisonous to people. American bittersweet can twine its way up about 20 feet.

TREES

Several tree species sport eye-grabbing fruits by September. The native American dogwood and the Kousa dogwood are two of the best. Also take a look at crabapple, hawthorn, and the evergreen American holly.

Is your tree lineup diverse? When everyone plants the same few species, decimation can occur when something comes along to threaten those species. It's happened with American chestnuts, American elms, and most recently, ash. A diversity of trees spreads out the risk of widespread loss and helps the ecosystem and its inhabitants that keep nature in balance. Just because you've never heard of a species doesn't mean it's a bad choice. And just because everyone plants flowering pears and flowering dogwoods doesn't mean you should plant them, too.

Some diversity questions to consider include:

- Does your yard have conifers (pine, fir, and spruce, for example) that provide shelter to birds in storms and cones to feed them and the squirrels?
- Does it have flowering trees to attract pollinators and add fragrance over multiple months?
- Does it have fruit- or nut-bearing trees that support wildlife?
- Does it have any/many regional natives, such as redbud, American fringe tree, blackgum, river birch, red maple, serviceberry, American dogwood, and sweetbay magnolia?

PLANT

ALL

"Fall is for planting" isn't just garden-center hype to get rid of plants the stores don't want to overwinter. Fall really *does* offer some planting advantages, such as:

- The soil temperatures are warm enough to support good root growth at least through the end of October.
- The shorter days, less intense sunlight, and cooler temperatures of early fall mean less stress ("transplant shock") for plants being evicted from their cozy pots into the untamed ground.
- Newly planted plants lose less moisture through their leaves in fall than summer, which lowers water demands.
- Rain usually increases from summer, further reducing the hose duty that new plantings need.
- Fall-planted plants will have two growing seasons under their belts instead of one (now

and next spring) before facing a grueling hot mid-Atlantic summer.
- The bugs are mostly gone.
- A lot of plants go on sale from here on out.
- It's more pleasant for the gardener to be out digging in September than in the furnace called July.

Before digging a new bed (especially when using power equipment), find out where your buried utility lines are. Gas and electrical lines are usually deeper than shovel or tiller depth, but cable and Internet lines might be only a few inches down.

ANNUALS & TROPICALS

Replace tired summer annuals with cool-season color plants. The colorful foliage of ornamental cabbage and ornamental kale are two popular choices, but there's also a fresh supply of pansies, violas, snapdragons, and more, some of which are cold-hardy enough to survive winter and bloom again next spring.

Or pick from a plethora of mums. Most of those are winter-hardy enough to qualify as perennials, but some people treat mums like annuals. They'll display them in a pot or bed until the flowers brown, then toss them.

BULBS

The cooling soil of October and early November is the year's best for spring-bulb planting, but late September also is fine, at least in Zones 5 and 6. (See October's "Here's How To Plant Spring Bulbs.")

As you empty your pots of summer annuals, replant a few winter-durable pots (foam, plastic, or concrete) with spring bulbs this month and next. Plant at the same depth as in the ground, two-and-a-half to three times as deep as their height. Set the pots where they'll get winter snow and rain. The bulbs will chill, root, and then flower on cue next spring.

Existing bulb plantings can be dug, divided, and replanted this month if you have a patch that's overcrowded or if you want to "expand the flock." Be careful not to slice into the buried bulbs while digging.

Fall-blooming bulbs such as resurrection lilies and sternbergia can be planted this month.

■ *Scatter bulbs to naturalize in your lawn. Short, early bulbs work best.*

LAWNS

This is the year's best month for planting a new lawn and for overseeding and rehabbing an existing lawn. See "Here's How To Overseed a Thin Lawn" if you're rehabbing. See "Here's How To Start a New Lawn from Sod" if you're sodding instead of seeding.

However you seed, good seed-to-soil contact is very important. If you're dealing with a large area that's too labor-intensive to rake by hand, do your seeding after aerating and/or dethatching the lawn. Both of those procedures disturb the soil. For large areas, use a tractor to drag a heavy doormat or section of chain link fence to both prepare beds and to incorporate scattered seed into the soil surface.

Another seeding alternative for large areas is to rent a "slit-seeder" or seeding machine. This power equipment has vertical blades that cut shallow slits in the soil. It then inserts seed from hoppers behind the slits.

Match the type of grass seed to the area you're planting. Grass-seed mixes are usually formulated by the light conditions (sun or shade) or use (normal versus high traffic). Sunny blends are typically highest in Kentucky bluegrass and

perennial ryegrass. Shadier mixes have a higher percentage of fine fescues. High-traffic options are often 100 percent turf-type tall fescue, a coarser grass that's best able to tolerate soccer games and Labrador retrievers.

To zero in on the best specific varieties of each grass type, check out the ratings done regularly by universities in various states. Results are posted online on the National Turfgrass Evaluation Program website at www.ntep.org. Select the State Data button, then select your state on the map.

Adding superior seed varieties each autumn or two gradually improves your lawn quality as the older grasses age and die out.

PERENNIALS & GROUNDCOVERS

September planting and transplanting allows two good months of root growth at a time when plants can focus on roots instead of splitting energy demand with flower production and top growth.

As with trees and shrubs, loosen and fray out tightly matted or circling roots before planting. It's okay to remove the soil as needed. Try not to damage or remove any more roots than necessary to free them.

Perennials with long taproots, such as baptisia, balloon flower, globe thistle, columbine, and butterfly weed, are more difficult to transplant than perennials with spreading and clumping root systems. Dig deeply to get the entire root of these, or better yet, plant them and leave them alone.

Mums overwinter best when they're planted in late summer or early fall. The roots have more time to establish before winter. Those have a higher survival rate than ones planted in late October and beyond.

SHRUBS & TREES

This month and next are two excellent months to plant and transplant almost all container-grown shrubs, trees, and woody vines for the reasons listed above under Plant, All. (See March's "Here's How To Plant a Tree" and "Here's How To Plant a Shrub.")

Be careful not to damage new plants on the way home from the nursery. An underrated woe is when people toss leafed-out trees and shrubs in the back of an open pickup and drive home on the highway. To a tree, that's the equivalent of enduring a 65 mph windstorm. Cover plants with plastic or fabric if they'll be exposed to moving air. Loosely tie or wrap branches to minimize snap-offs. And secure plants so they're not rolling around in the trunk.

Some say spring is better to plant roses than fall, but most gardeners have good rose-planting success in September.

HERE'S HOW

TO START A NEW LAWN FROM SOD

1. Prepare the soil by removing all vegetation and loosening to a depth of at least 6 inches.

2. Add an inch or two of organic material, such as compost, mushroom soil or peat moss, and incorporate it thoroughly into the existing loosened soil. If your soil already is good, skip this step. (See "Here's How To Check the Quality of Your Soil" in the Introduction.)

3. Rake smooth or drag large areas with a mat. It's okay to lightly dampen the soil the evening before sodding, but avoid working on wet soil.

4. Unroll and lay strips of sod, butting them up against each other and in a staggered pattern, similar to the way bricks are laid.

5. Fill in any gaps with cut pieces and fill small cracks with topsoil. Tamp down the pieces or go over larger areas with a roller.

6. Water well so that both the sod and the top 2 inches of soil are damp. Keep the planting damp with daily or more watering, if necessary, for the first four to six weeks.

CARE

ALL

Stay on top of the weeds. Dig, pull, spot-spray—whatever it takes. The rate of new weeds slows from here on out, but existing ones will try to produce mature seeds before frost kills them. If those drop, you're looking at future work.

September mulching is fine if your mulch layer has deteriorated.

Edge the landscape beds if they're getting ragged.

ANNUALS & TROPICALS

Besides taking tender plants back inside that you want to keep for another season, now's a good time to take cuttings of favorites before frost kills them. (See "Here's How To Start New Plants from Cuttings.")

Pull out dead and bug- and disease-ridden annuals, but give the remaining annuals a chance to rebound. As temperatures cool and rain returns, many annuals get a second wind, especially cool-hardy plants such as alyssum, osteospermum, nemesia, and snapdragons. Help them by clipping brown tips or leggy stems, giving them a dose of liquid

HERE'S HOW

TO OVERSEED A THIN LAWN

Mow the grass shorter than usual, to about 1 or 2 inches. Rake up any debris.

1. Scratch the surface of bare areas with a garden rake. Or plan on overseeding after you aerate or dethatch the lawn or otherwise disturb the soil surface. Germination is low (if at all) if you just toss seed on top of a compacted surface.

2. Scatter seed over the bare or thin areas, lightly rake, and lightly tamp to achieve good seed-to-soil contact.

3. Water enough to wet the soil about 2 inches deep, then keep the soil

■ *Sprinkle seed over a prepared bed and lightly tamp and water it to patch a dead spot in the lawn.*

■ *Small dead patches of lawn can be spot-repaired with mixes that come with seed, fertilizer, and mulch in one bag.*

surface consistently damp with frequent light waterings until the seed sprouts. Figure on daily waterings or more if it's hot and dry or if you have sandy soil.

4. Optional: Cover larger areas with a thin layer of straw to help retain moisture. Products also are available that combine seed with paper mulch.

5. Once the seed is up, cut back on watering to every two or three days. Wait until the grass is 3 inches tall to begin mowing.

HERE'S HOW

TO START NEW PLANTS FROM CUTTINGS

Many annuals, perennials, and even shrubs can be propagated by rooting cut stems. Some of the easiest are coleus, geraniums, perilla, plectranthus, ivy, purple-heart, and Persian shield.

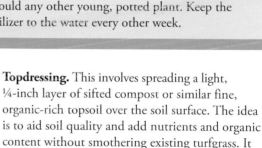

1. Cut 4- to 6-inch tips off of the end of healthy stems or branches of non-patented varieties.

2. Remove the lowest leaves so that at least one—and preferably two—nodes are bare. Nodes are the point from which shoots emerge. They're also where new roots will emerge from cuttings.

3. Dip the cut end into a rooting hormone powder (available at most garden centers and home-improvement stores).

4. Insert a pencil into a pot filled with lightweight potting mix or seed-start medium to create a small hole. Insert the powdered end of the cutting into the moist rooting medium, covering the nodes.

5. Water well, and loosely cover the pot with clear plastic wrap or a plastic bag to maintain moisture.

6. Set pots in light, but not direct sun. Make sure they don't dry out. When small leaves emerge, that's a signal roots are establishing.

7. Remove the plastic, and treat the "start" as you would any other young, potted plant. Keep the potting mix damp, and begin adding a dilute fertilizer to the water every other week.

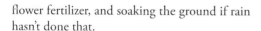

flower fertilizer, and soaking the ground if rain hasn't done that.

Cut off maturing seedpods on species that you don't want to self-sow.

BULBS

Take in last year's potted amaryllis, or dig and pot any you've been growing in the ground. Store these bulbs dry so they're dormant for six to eight weeks before starting a new growth cycle. Room temperature is fine. (See December's "Here's How To Grow Amaryllis Inside Over Winter.")

LAWNS

All sorts of lawn improvement steps are best done this month. Most are geared toward overcoming the lousy soil you've likely got underneath and toward providing more ideal cultural conditions. Jobs to consider include:

Topdressing. This involves spreading a light, ¼-inch layer of sifted compost or similar fine, organic-rich topsoil over the soil surface. The idea is to aid soil quality and add nutrients and organic content without smothering existing turfgrass. It can be done annually.

Aerating. Most effective are machines that remove cores or finger-sized "plugs" from clay soil and deposit them on the surface. This opens air space in the soil and aids compaction. Machines work best after a rain softens the ground (they'll largely bounce across a hard, dry lawn) and when four to six passes are made.

Dethatching. Thatch is the spongy layer of mostly dead roots at the soil surface. A layer ½-inch-thick or less is fine, but thicker thatch begins to impede fertilizer and rain penetration. The solution is to rip it out with a dethatching rake

■ *Cores of soil have been removed from this lawn by a core aeration machine.*

■ *A dethatching machine has tines that tear through the lawn surface to remove excess thatch.*

or dethatching machine with rotating vertical blades. It's best done after a rain (and best in early spring for zoysia grass). Rake and compost the removed thatch.

Maximizing growing conditions. Now that punishing summer weather is retreating, grass will resume growing and focus on root growth—the key to a healthier lawn. Get the soil tested if you haven't done that lately, and put down the fertilizer and/or lime that's recommended.

Seeding. New grass seed germinates well this month, and root growth gets off to an ideal start in warm soil, rainier weather, cooler temperatures, and less weed competition. (See "Here's How To Seed a New Lawn" and "Here's How To Overseed a Thin Lawn.")

A common question is, "Does it matter in which order I do all of those things?" For starters, you may not need to do all of the ones mentioned, or at least not every year. You may not have a thatch problem, for example, or your lawn may be at a good acidity level and not need lime. But if you're tackling the whole regimen, start with the jobs that roughen the soil, such as the dethatching and/or core-aeration. Then scatter the grass seed, some of which will fall into the opened holes and slits. Then apply any fertilizer that's recommended by the soil test. Then topdress with compost, which will lightly cover the seed and fill some of the holes and slits. A good soaking is the perfect curtain call.

Some research suggests that lime and fertilizer together can reduce the effectiveness of the nitrogen in fertilizer. To alleviate that possible conflict, apply the fertilizer first and wait until a soaking rain dissolves it into the ground before applying any recommended lime. Lime can be applied anytime throughout fall before the ground freezes.

Continue to mow grass at 3 to 4 inches tall (2 inches for zoysia) until the last cut or two of the season.

PERENNIALS & GROUNDCOVERS

Dig and divide perennials that are spreading beyond where you want them. Ones that divide best now are those that already have bloomed for the season. Cut or separate the dug clumps into fist-sized pieces. Put one back, and plant the rest in new sites or give them away. Perennials that are flowering now are best transplanted early next spring. (See April's "Here's How To Divide Perennials.")

Groundcovers also are easy to divide and transplant this time of year. Dig up dense sections, pull or cut apart into smaller pieces, and plant them in additional areas. Replant one of the pieces where you removed the clump.

It's hard to stake tall, flopping perennials "nicely" at this point, but prop them up and/or tie them

TO OVERWINTER TROPICALS

1. Tropicals that you've planted in the ground should be dug and returned to pots with fresh potting mix.

2. Before moving the repotted, dug-up tropicals and ones that stayed in their pots all summer back inside, eliminate bugs trying to hitch a ride inside. Either hose off the plants with a stiff spray of water, or spray them with insecticidal soap or a similar bug-killer.

3. Once the plants dry, move them inside to appropriate light settings; ones that prefer bright light near south- or west-facing windows or under plant lights, and ones that can take less light by your east- or north-facing windows, or in other dimmer spots.

4. If your pots have holes in the bottom for drainage, place containers under them to keep water off the carpets and floors.

5. Use no or only limited fertilizer over winter (growth needs are low). Water when the soil goes dry and the pots become noticeably lighter. Do not overwater to the point of soggy soil, which is the leading killer of indoor plants.

■ *Tropicals being grown as potted houseplants need to go back inside when overnight temperatures dip into the 40s.*

with stakes and jute as best as you can to prevent stems from snapping and bending.

Ornamental grasses can start to flop apart by now. Bundling their midsections can improve the appearance, as can cutting off the worst floppy-stem offenders from around the perimeter. Grasses that are hulking messes should be divided early next spring. (See February's "Here's How To Cut Ornamental Grasses.")

Deadhead late-summer bloomers. Snip off the seedheads of species that you don't want to self-sow. Leave others to feed birds.

SHRUBS
Tender shrubs that you're growing outside in pots (palms, citrus, and jade plant, for example) need to go back inside before frost. (See "Here's How To Overwinter Tropicals.")

Other than snipping spent flower heads off the ends of hydrangeas, roses, butterfly bushes, and other late-flowering shrubs, limit pruning to removing dead or injured branches.

Besides cutting fresh roses for bouquets, dry rose petals for potpourri. Some gardeners spread the petals on a rack (out of bright light) to air-dry them, while others spread them on a cookie sheet in a warm oven with the door slightly ajar.

TREES
Check the ties on staked spring-planted trees to make sure they are still lax but firmly fastened around the expanding tree trunk. Loosen ties that are starting to make indents in the wood, or worse yet, starting to grow into the bark. Remove supports from trees planted last fall. One year is enough.

Other than removing broken or dead branches, avoid pruning now at least until the leaves drop.

SEPTEMBER

WATER

ALL

Plants' water needs go down this month as the weather cools, evaporation losses drop, and average rainfall goes up. That doesn't mean you can put away the hose. You'll need to regularly soak new fall plantings and keep an eye on soil moisture.

Be alert for "sneaky" early-fall dry spells. Things may not *look* as dry as during a July or August heat wave, but it's still possible the soil is dry in the root zones if soaking storms haven't happened. Sometimes those shallow rains are enough to keep the lawn green and the mulch damp without wetting plant roots.

ANNUALS & TROPICALS

Continue to water annuals in pots and baskets; check daily. In-ground annuals and tropicals should be fine with a weekly soaking when rain isn't doing the job.

BULBS

Bulbs growing in pots also likely need daily watering. Dahlias, tuberous begonias, and other summer bulbs growing in the ground are usually fine with a weekly soaking when the weather's dry.

Soak bulb beds right after planting new ones to settle the soil, but there's no need to water existing beds where dormant spring bulbs are already nestled.

LAWNS

Newly seeded lawns and overseeded thin patches should be sprinkled daily or more to keep the seed moist until it sprouts. Once the grass is up, water two or three times a week so the soil is consistently damp 4 to 6 inches deep. That encourages root penetration.

Keep the soil underneath new sod damp. You may need to water two to three times a week if rain isn't keeping the soil moist down 4 to 6 inches into the root zone.

PERENNIALS & GROUNDCOVERS

Water new perennials, ornamental grasses, and groundcovers twice a week if rain isn't happening.

Soak enough so the soil is damp to the bottom of the rootballs.

Most established perennials need little to no water in September, unless it's been unusually hot and dry. Insert your finger 2 or 3 inches into the soil of your perennial beds to test for dryness. If it's not moist, soak.

If it's been a dry late summer, moisture-loving perennials may need regular soakings once or twice a week. Pay particular attention to turtlehead, lobelia, astilbe, Joe-pye weed, ligularia, swamp milkweed, and hardy hibiscus. No wilting allowed!

SHRUBS & TREES

Water this season's new plantings two to three times a week, directing most of the water close to the main stem(s) and applying enough that it dampens the soil all around and to the bottom of the rootball. Check with your finger, a probe, or a soil-moisture meter.

Established shrubs, trees, and woody vines are usually fine without supplemental water in a normal September. The exception is an extended hot, dry spell, during which a deep soaking once a week is helpful.

Existing roses that you're pushing for peak performance should continue to get soakings two to three times a week, although that might taper off with cooler weather and more rain. Otherwise, a once-a-week soaking is fine if it's hot and dry.

FERTILIZE

ALL

If you're digging a new garden, test your soil to see what fertilizer (if any) is needed and in what amounts. Work it into the soil as you're preparing it, in advance of planting.

With a few exceptions, this is another no-fertilize month throughout most of the landscape. Between nutrients being released by decaying mulch and those slow-acting fertilizers you applied in spring, most plants are good to go.

ANNUALS & TROPICALS

This is one of the exceptions: annuals and tropicals still growing in pots and baskets benefit from a half-strength flower fertilizer once a week.

BULBS

New bulbs don't need fertilizer (their nutrition is already built in), but existing bulb beds benefit from a fall scattering of an organic or slow-acting fertilizer formulated for bulbs. Apply it this month or next, ideally right before a soaking rain. Otherwise, water it in after scattering.

LAWNS

If you're fertilizing a lawn only once a year, this is it. Late-summer nutrition helps the lawn recover from the stresses of heat and drought and helps grass plants manufacture carbohydrates essential to root growth that peaks in the coming weeks.

If you're fertilizing twice a year, your second treatment should go down either late this month or in October.

If you're following a three-treatment regimen, early September is prime time for the second dose. (Early to mid-November is the last.)

If you're following a commercial four-step program, early September is the time for the third application.

The general advice is to use a fertilizer that's higher in nitrogen than the other two main nutrients (phosphorus and potassium). Phosphorus often is not needed at all, and Maryland now bans lawn fertilizer that contains phosphorus unless a soil test indicates it's needed. The most accurate plan is to have your soil tested every few years so you know exactly which nutrients your particular lawn needs and in what amounts. Do-it-yourself test kits are available at County Extension offices and most home-improvement and garden centers.

PERENNIALS, GROUNDCOVERS, SHRUBS & TREES

For new fall plantings, the compost or other organic amendments you worked into the soil during bed preparation are usually enough to supply adequate nutrition. A soil test tells you if you have any specific nutrient deficiencies that can be corrected by working in a targeted fertilizer before planting.

For established plantings, unless growth is poor and a soil test nails down that a nutrient deficiency is to blame, no fertilizer is needed.

PROBLEM-SOLVE

ALL

Not everything flying is bad. Pest insects normally account for only about 10 percent of the insects in a typical yard. The others are either beneficial or benign. Lesson 1: Lots of insect activity doesn't necessarily equate with lots of plant damage. Lesson 2: Relatively few insects cause landscape damage, and much of that is cosmetic or temporary.

If you're seeing unacceptable levels of plant damage and trace it to pest insects, one problem could be a lack of beneficial insects keeping a lid on the pests. Some reasons for that:

- Frequently used general insecticides have killed off many of the resident beneficials. Consider switching to more targeted controls and use only when necessary.
- Your yard lacks sufficient plant diversity to attract and support a healthy population of beneficial insects. Remedy that by planting a wider variety of plants, especially natives and others that attract bug-eating birds and beneficial insects.
- You hit a down cycle in key beneficials. The population of beneficial insects drops when their main food source (pest bugs) is low. As beneficials dwindle, the pest population can expand, and there's a lag until the beneficials catch up again. This natural cycling explains why some bugs are worse some years than others.

Deer think you've planted all of those nice, new trees and shrubs with the tender bark just for them. To be on the safe side, erect cages, fences, or other protection around new plantings if you're gardening in deerland. Ditto for spot-fencing plants commonly targeted by rodents.

ANNUALS & TROPICALS

You may see all sorts of insults on annual flowers, such as discolored leaves from mites or lace bugs, wilting stems from aphids, a whitish-gray cast on leaves from powdery mildew, and so forth. It's late in the season to invest in controls, especially since annuals don't have much longer to live with frost around the corner. Yank dead plants, and neaten damaged ones until they go downhill enough to detract from the landscape.

BULBS

Rodents such as squirrels, voles, and chipmunks love some bulbs (mainly tulips) and will dig them up almost as soon as you plant them. One defense is to top the planted bed with chicken wire. Bulb shoots will poke through but rodents can't tunnel down. If your rodents are smart enough to move over, tunnel down beside the wire, and go in sideways, line the bottom of your planting bed with wire, bend the sides up to the surface, plant and backfill with soil, then top with a sheet of wire to essentially create a chicken-wire box.

Don't advertise that you've planted tulips by leaving dried skins over the soil. That's a scent attractant.

If you know you have a rodent problem, plant bulb species that they (and deer and rabbits) don't bother. Daffodils and alliums top that list, but others include fritillaria, dogtooth violet, glory-of-the-snow, tommasinianus-type crocus ("tommies"), snowdrop, snowflake, Siberian and striped squills, winter aconite, and Spanish bluebells.

Cover bulb-planted pots with chicken wire to keep rodents from digging those over winter.

LAWNS

Grub damage becomes very noticeable now. If lawn patches are browning and pulling up rootless like pieces of carpet, that's the likely problem. You'll probably even see the fat, white, C-shaped, wormy things in the soil underneath pulled-off dead patches.

Grub preventers applied in late May through early July won't do much good now. Quick-acting insecticides are more effective. Look for products that say "grub killer," not "grub preventer," if you

take action. An "organic" option is buying predatory nematodes that parasitize the grubs. A longer-term organic option (if your grubs are the larval stage of Japanese beetles) is milky spore, a disease that's applied in powder form.

Holes in the lawn usually mean that birds or skunks are digging for grubs. You could just let the animals have at it and patch the holes with a little grass seed. If you kill the grubs with an insecticide, the digging eventually will stop as the grubs decay.

A black dust on the lawn is likely sooty mold, a fungus whose reproductive spores are black and powdery. Sooty mold isn't harmful to people or pets, won't hurt the lawn in the long run, and will go away when the weather turns colder and/or drier. Outbreaks often follow a rain.

Assorted mushrooms and related fleshy fungi appear in many lawns in late summer. Most are harmless and can be kicked over or ignored. They're growing on decaying organic matter in the soil. However, a few are poisonous when eaten, so if you have small children or pets who might sample these growths, bag and remove them as you see them (unless you've positively identified that they're non-poisonous). There are no sprays or treatments to prevent fungal growths from popping up.

PERENNIALS & GROUNDCOVERS

If rabbits, deer, or other animals are sampling your new perennials, spray scent repellent. Or erect a temporary fence until the enticing young, tender foliage matures.

Borers are the bane of iris. The adult is a moth that lays eggs on iris leaves in late summer to early fall. The eggs hatch into larvae that tunnel down iris leaves in spring and into the underground rhizomes, potentially killing whole plants. Short-circuit the cycle by cutting iris foliage before the borers reach the rhizomes. Otherwise, insecticides control this pest. Watch for notches or pinholes in the leaves and "sawdust" (borer poop) at the base of the plant. Infested rhizomes have small "worms" tunneling in them.

SHRUBS

Shrubs and trees sometimes grow strange-looking shoots, almost as if it's a different plant growing out of the existing one. These are called "witches' brooms" or "reversions," which are either genetic mutations or growth that's returning to an original form of the plant. This growth is often more vigorous than the desired plant (especially if the desired plant is a dwarf variety), so prune off these oddities as soon as you see them. Cuttings from mutations are often how breeders develop new and unusual plant varieties in the first place.

Bagworms are full-sized now, and their cone-shaped, hanging sacs are brown, making them far more noticeable than earlier in the summer. Chemical controls don't work very well this late in the season. June applications are much more effective. Remove and destroy as many of the bags as you can to get rid of eggs inside that will hatch into next year's bagworms.

■ *This bagworm case looks like an evergreen cone, but it's actually protection for the feeding caterpillar inside.*

Powdery mildew and blackspot are common rose diseases in September. It's getting late enough now that roses won't suffer much harm if the diseases defoliate plants. Pick off and clean up diseased leaves if you opt to avoid spraying. Otherwise, continue spraying a fungicide.

Woody vines such as wisteria, trumpet vine, and sometimes climbing hydrangea are notorious for failing to bloom. Most of the time, it's the age of the plant. Wisteria can take five to seven years from planting to bloom for the first time. Other explanations include pruning after flower buds have formed but not yet opened and soil that's out of balance nutritionally, often from excessive nitrogen. Training vines to horizontal positions also can stimulate flowering.

TREES

Baglike webs toward the end of tree branches are the fall webworm at work. Caterpillars are feeding on leaves inside the webbing. This late-season chewing damage is almost harmless and can usually be ignored. If webworms bug you, poke open their bags with a stick to give the birds a caterpillar feast.

Twigs and branches dropping from your trees could be the work of a slender, long-horned, brown beetle called the twig girdler. Adult females chew all the way around small branches after laying eggs, apparently because larvae don't develop well when sap is flowing. The weakness gradually causes the branches to snap off. Pick up and destroy branches; the larvae are inside. Damage is usually mild and cosmetic, so spraying isn't normally warranted.

Bagworms are common on many trees in addition to shrubs, especially arborvitae. Hand-picking is your best option since sprays aren't very effective now. (See Problem-Solve, Shrubs.)

If you're controlling woolly adelgids on hemlocks with horticultural oil, now through early October is good timing for the year's second application.

October

Although fall officially arrives in late September, October is when it really starts to feel like fall in the mid-Atlantic landscape.

Daytime highs start dipping into the 50s and 60s, and nights turn noticeably cooler. Frost usually ends the annuals, tropicals, and warm-weather vegetables by early to mid-October in the cooler areas of Zones 5 and 6, by late October to early November in Zone 7, and by mid-November in Zone 8. That means a good bit of October's garden work involves preparing for a return of colder weather such as moving tropicals back inside, covering annuals to milk them through that first borderline frost, taking cuttings from tender plants before frost zaps them, and so on.

The best part about October in this part of the world, though, is the fall foliage. The mid-Atlantic region has four distinct seasons, and fall is legendary for its blazing leaf color, especially in the tree-adorned Allegheny and Blue Mountain ranges with the Shenandoah Valley nestled between. Tourists come from afar to see these forests in their red, orange, and gold fall glory. Maple, sweetgum, blackgum, birch, oak, dogwood, and serviceberry are among the native tree species that are particularly vibrant in autumn.

If you play your cards right, your own yard can be a riot of rich fall color, too. Many of those same tree species make excellent landscape specimens—including serviceberry, dogwood, and the smaller maples in small yards. Often overlooked are the many shrubs that turn color in fall. Fothergilla, Virginia sweetspire, summersweet, oakleaf hydrangea, witch hazel, ninebark, viburnum, nandina, and blueberries are some of the best choices to make your fall garden go out in a blaze of brilliance instead of a dribble of drabness.

And don't forget about next spring while you're out there ogling the fothergillas and sweetspires. October also is prime time to plant spring-flowering bulbs so next year can open with a blaze of brilliance of another sort.

PLAN

ALL

Falling leaves, pulled plants, and end-of-season grass clippings make a perfect compost "harvest." If you don't have a compost bin or three, now's a good time to get busy building. If you're already composting, empty existing bins of finished compost to make way for this year's new "crop" of ingredients. (See "Here's How To Compost.")

HERE'S HOW

TO COMPOST

1. Choose an open spot that's ideally out of view and on soil or grass instead of concrete or asphalt.

2. Erect bins that allow piles at least 4 feet tall, wide, and deep. Material options include wood slats, skids, concrete blocks, or wire fencing. Ones that allow airflow are best. Note: bins aren't absolutely necessary; their job is to contain the compost materials and keep them from blowing around.

3. Start adding ingredients. The ideal mix is a blend of high-nitrogen "greens" and high-carbon "browns." A good proportion is 3 parts browns to 1 part green. Good browns include shredded paper, fallen leaves, pine needles, sawdust, and wood chips. Good greens include grass clippings, fresh weeds from the garden (ones that haven't gone to seed), pulled or frost-killed garden plants, and assorted non-meat, non-dairy kitchen waste, such as coffee grounds, banana peels, carrot shavings, salad leftovers, and eggshells.

4. Wet the pile to get it "cooking." Re-wet the pile during unusually hot and dry weather during the growing season.

5. Ways to speed decomposition: shred or chop materials into small pieces; turn the pile frequently; add worms called "red wigglers"; and add occasional the shovelful of garden soil or finished compost.

■ *Early fall is a good time to start a new composting area.*

■ *Grass clippings are a valuable source of nitrogen in a compost bin.*

■ *Unused produce from the kitchen can be added to the compost pile.*

■ *Shredded newspaper is an excellent high-carbon composting material that blends well with grass and other green materials.*

■ *Straw makes good mulch during the growing season, and it can also be added to the compost pile.*

■ *Leaves blend well with grass clippings to make an ideal composting mix.*

When plant-shopping in October, you'll run into fresh fall stock as well as spring leftovers. Check the leaves and branches for signs of bug damage or disease. Think twice about those. But if the leaves are just tired and browning, or if the spent flower stems just haven't been snipped, that's not a problem—especially if the price tag says 40 or 50 percent off.

Assess roots by gently slipping plants out of their pots. Healthy roots are fleshy and white or creamy, not black and mushy or brown and shriveled. Some circling or matted roots are fine. But if the roots are so badly circled that you can't even get the plant out of the pot, that's more of a drawback. It doesn't mean the plant won't live happily ever after, but it lowers the odds.

ANNUALS & TROPICALS

Get those tender tropicals back inside if you didn't already do it.

Drape lightweight fabric over still-blooming annuals if an overnight frost is forecast. That might be enough protection to keep them going through warm-ups that often follow the first cold snap or two. The *average* first fall frost in the region's coolest Zone 5 region is late September, ranging to mid-November for the average first fall frost in Zone 8. Watch current forecasts because each year's dates can occur significantly earlier or later.

How can you tell if you had a light frost? Check the impatiens, vinca, or nasturtiums in the morning. Those are three of the most frost sensitive annuals and will wilt at the first sign of 32 degrees Fahrenheit.

BULBS

It's possible to have spring bulbs blooming from late January through June. The key is choosing a variety of bulb species with differing bloom times. Here's a guide:

January/February: Snowdrop, winter aconite, early crocus, *Iris reticulata*

March: Spring snowflake, most crocuses, early daffodils, early tulips (*Tulipa kaufmanniana, tarda,* and *fosteriana* types)

April: Glory-of-the-snow, Siberian squill, Grecian windflower, most daffodils, striped squill, hyacinth, mid-season tulips, grape hyacinth, spring starflower

May: Spanish bluebells, camassia, crown imperial and most fritillary, late tulips, late daffodils

June: Allium

It helps to map where spring bulbs are going in the yard. Keeping track of them is easy in the spring when the leaves and flowers are up, but after they die back in summer, that's when they tend to get sliced by shovels or dug up.

Bulbs aren't just for full sun. Many species flower well in shady to partly shaded locations, helped by the fact that bulb foliage can take in early-season sunlight before tree leaves emerge. Good choices for wooded areas and under trees are snowdrops, Siberian squill, glory-of-the-snow, striped squill, Grecian windflowers, and winter aconite.

LAWNS

October is still a good month to rehab a crummy lawn or plant a new one. Get to it as early in the month as possible to give new grass its best shot of germinating and rooting before the ground freezes.

PERENNIALS & GROUNDCOVERS

Some perennials have foliage that turns color in fall. At the top of that list is threadleaf bluestar (*Amsonia hubrichtii*), which has fine foliage that turns bright gold in fall. Another good one is the groundcover leadwort (plumbago), which turns crimson red as its blue flowers fade for the season. And most ornamental grasses take on tan, russet, or burgundy shades in fall in addition to providing textural plumes or seedheads.

Deer will eat almost anything rather than starve to death over winter. If you're doing some fall planting in deer country, consider varieties low on the deer-favored menu. Good choices include plants that are toxic to mammals (helleborus, cimicifuga, foxglove), plants with fuzzy or silver leaves (lamb's ears, catmint, lavender), and plants with strongly aromatic foliage or stems (anise hyssop, artemisia, and most herbs).

■ *Hellebores (Lenten rose) are* not *deer favorites and are wonderful landscape plants.*

Don't overlook moss as groundcover, especially in wooded areas. Most types prefer shade, acidic soil, coolness, and humidity. To encourage moss, clear the area of weeds, and sprinkle granular sulfur to acidify of the soil (a pH of 5.5 is ideal). Keep the soil damp. Moss usually will start to appear "magically" from existing spores. Or transplant patches from elsewhere in the yard, or buy starter patches of moss that are available online or from some garden centers.

SHRUBS

Burning bush is the best-known shrub for fall color. Its leaves turn fire-engine red in fall, but the show is often short, plus it's a species that often seeds invasively into unwanted areas. Other better fall-foliage shrubs for mid-Atlantic landscapes include fothergilla and panicle hydrangeas (gold or gold/red); Virginia sweetspire, crape myrtle, sumac, nandina, and blueberry (blood or bright red); oakleaf hydrangea, viburnum, PJM rhododendron, and ninebark (deep red to burgundy); summersweet, spicebush, winterberry holly, and bottlebrush buckeye (gold); chokeberry (red to red/gold); and spirea 'Ogon' (rusty orange-red).

A few vines also end the season aglow with brilliantly colored foliage. Two of the showiest are Boston ivy and Virginia creeper.

TREES

Maples are the best known of the fall-foliage trees, a reputation that is well deserved. Almost all of them turn glorious shades of red, gold or red/gold blends in October. Match your pick to your yard size—shade-tree-sized red maple, sugar maple, or Freeman maple Autumn Blaze® for larger yards, and

more compact Japanese maple, trident maple, and paperbark maple for small to mid-sized yards.

Some other good landscape trees for fall color are:

Over 30 feet: assorted oaks (gold or red/gold); ginkgo, river birch, and katsura (gold); and blackgum and sweetgum (deep red).

Under 30 feet: dogwood (deep red); serviceberry and flowering pear (bright red); stewartia (red/gold blend); and witch hazel, parrotia, and American fringe tree (gold).

PLANT

ALL

How late is too late to plant in the fall? Cornell University researched that by planting sets of the same plants progressively later in the season, then assessing their performance over several years. The conclusion is fall-planted plants survive best when they have at least six weeks of root growth before the soil temperature in the root zone drops below

■ *The Mid-Atlantic has spectacular fall foliage trees that grow well here, such as this ginkgo.*

40 degrees Fahrenheit. In the mid-Atlantic region, that translates into an ideal-planting cutoff of late October in Zones 5 and 6 and early to mid-November in Zones 7 and 8.

This finding doesn't mean you can't plant later. Landscapers will tell you they've planted trees and shrubs in winter and had them survive. The takeaway is that your odds of success start to drop once you plant past the above guidelines, if Cornell's findings are correct.

Check those plant guarantees before buying. Garden centers often guarantee most plants for a year, but year-end closeouts and borderline-hardy species might *not* be guaranteed this time of year.

October is a good month to prepare new beds, even if you don't plant until next spring. The soil is reasonably dry and workable, and temperatures are more pleasant than trying to dig a bed in July. Prepare the soil, mulch the ground, and walk away. (See April's "Here's How To Turn Lawn Into a New Garden Bed.")

ANNUALS & TROPICALS

Pot a few annuals now, such as impatiens, geraniums, coleus, and wax begonias, and a few tender herbs, such as rosemary and basil, for a sunny windowsill. These may not make it all winter, but you can milk a few extra weeks out of them inside.

It's not too late to fill beds vacated by yanked annuals with a fresh planting of cool-preferring pansies, violas, snapdragons, or ornamental cabbage and kale. Pansies and violas usually survive winter to bloom again in spring, but cabbage and kale die back when seriously cold snaps appear. Yank those when that happens because they'll rot and start to smell like, well, rotting cabbage.

BULBS

This is the year's best month to plant spring bulbs. The cooling soil triggers bulbs to put down new roots and start the biological clock ticking. Once each variety's genetic chilling time is met, and the weather signals a new season, leaf shoots and then flower shoots will emerge. (See "Here's How To Plant Spring Bulbs.")

Now's also a good time to begin "forcing bulbs" so they'll bloom inside over winter. (See "Here's How To Force Bulbs for Inside Blooms.") The easiest bulbs to force are daffodils and early bloomers such as crocus, scilla, *Iris reticulata*, grape hyacinths, Dutch hyacinths, and species tulips.

Outdoor bulb plantings look best in clusters or masses as opposed to lined up single-file. You'll also get far more impact by planting in larger amounts, especially when you're using smaller bulbs. A six-pack of daffodils doesn't go very far across the whole front of a house.

Plant spring bulbs in a few winter-durable pots (such as foam, plastic, or concrete). They can stay out all winter. No special care or protection is needed. Just make sure the pots have drainage holes in the bottom. Set the pots where they'll get winter snow and rain.

It's time to pot and water amaryllis bulbs if you want them to flower in December. Depending on the variety, they'll need six to ten weeks of lead-time before blooming. (See December's "Here's How To Grow Amaryllis Inside Over Winter.")

LAWNS

Grass-seed germination slows as the soil and air temperature drop. Try to get your seeding done by mid-October in Zones 5 and 6 and by the end of October in Zones 7 and 8. Beyond that, seed germination slows, and young grass is increasingly at risk of dying off if a cold spell comes along.

PERENNIALS, GROUNDCOVERS, SHRUBS & TREES

All of these can still be planted in October but the sooner the better to give young roots the maximum time to establish before the ground freezes. Soak the ground well after planting to settle the soil, and cover the ground with mulch to retain moisture and keep the ground warm as long as possible.

All can also be transplanted this month, although most roses would rather move in early spring. Again, the sooner you can get to it this month, the better.

HERE'S HOW

TO PLANT SPRING-FLOWERING BULBS

1. Loosen the soil to 10 to 12 inches deep, and incorporate 1 to 2 inches of compost, chopped leaves, mushroom soil, or similar organic matter. The resulting slightly raised beds are ideal for the excellent drainage that bulbs need. Fertilizer is not needed.

2. Set the bulbs on top of the raked ground where you want to plant them. When the layout and spacing looks good, go back and plant them one by one at a depth that's two-and-a-half to three times as deep as the bulb's height. Space small bulbs 3 to 4 inches apart, larger ones 6 to 8 inches apart. The pointy end goes up.

3. Smooth and soak the ground after planting to settle the soil around the bulbs. Top the soil with 1 to 2 inches of bark mulch, pine needles, or chopped leaves. (Note: factor the mulch layer into your total planting depth.)

4. If you've had trouble with rodents eating your bulbs, cover the soil surface with a sheet of chicken wire, then mulch over top of it.

5. An option for planting bulbs in blocks or rows is: dig a trench to the correct depth, set the bulbs in the bottom, then cover the whole planting with the excavated soil instead of inserting them one by one.

CARE

ALL

Non-gardeners look at all of the falling leaves as a raking nightmare. Gardeners view them as free mulch! Leaves are useful in lots of ways around the yard:

- Let them lie underneath trees and shrubs as winter insulation and free nutrients as they break down. If you don't like the look, top them with a light coating of wood or bark mulch in the spring.

- Chop or shred them as mulch over garden beds. Save a few bags for use next growing season.
- Mix them with spent garden plants, organic kitchen waste, and season-ending grass clippings to make the perfect compost blend.
- Chop them and incorporate them into the soil while preparing a new bed. They'll mostly break down by planting time next spring.
- Run over light layers on the lawn. The fragments break down quickly and add nutrients and organic matter to the soil.

TO FORCE BULBS FOR BLOOM INDOORS

Here's the regimen recommended by New Jersey bulb-forcer extraordinaire Art Wolk, author of the book *Bulb Forcing*:

1. Fill a mid-sized plastic pot, with drainage holes in the bottom, two-thirds to three-quarters full with moistened, lightweight potting mix.

2. Press bulbs into the mix so tightly that they touch. Add more potting mix to the top, then press down to firm it.

3. Begin chilling bulbs any time from October through early November to trigger the blooming process. Most bulbs need soil temperatures at or below 48 degrees Fahrenheit for eight to thirteen weeks. The earliest bloomers, such as crocus, scilla and *Iris reticulata*, need the least amount of chill time. Later-blooming varieties, such as Dutch hyacinths and mid- to late-season daffodils and tulips, need the most.

4. One chilling option is burying the potted bulbs in an 18-inch-deep pit outside covered with 2 feet of leaves to keep the ground from freezing. (Use a stick to mark your site.) Another option is storing the pots in a leaf-insulated cardboard box in an unheated garage or in a window well. A refrigerator (ideally one you're not using to store food) also works well.

5. When the appropriate chill time passes, retrieve the pot, hose it off, and move inside to a cool, bright location (55 to 68 degrees Fahrenheit is ideal). Water when the soil starts to go dry, and turn the pots a quarter of a turn each day so the flowers grow uniformly. Flowers should emerge in one to five weeks.

■ *Instead of using a leaf blower to remove every last leaf from the lawn, chop thin layers of leaves with a mower and let them decay into the ground.*

The seed of most plants is mature by now, meaning it's a good time to collect seeds to save and start next season. One caveat: some plants (many annual flowers in particular) are hybrid varieties and may not produce the same new plants as this year's. (See "Here's How To Save Seed.")

Some of the best candidates for seed-saving are marigold, zinnia, larkspur, cosmos, ageratum, browallia, celosia, cleome, hyacinth beans, impatiens, nicotiana, petunia, portulaca, salvia, snapdragon, sunflower, gloriosa daisy, and ornamental peppers.

October is a good month to mulch. It's actually easier than summer, when full-grown plants are in the way. After frost-killed annuals are yanked and browned-out perennials are cut back, you'll have easier access to open ground.

If you have space, store a pile of extra mulch in case you need it over winter, such as if a heavy rain washes a gully or you plant a live Christmas tree. Mulch may not be available from garden centers and vendors over winter.

Continue to pull weeds from outdoor planting beds to prevent them from going to seed and causing problems next year.

Deal with poison ivy before birds carry its berries away to start even more plants. Cover all exposed skin before pulling plants. Spray larger vines with a weed-killer labeled for poison ivy control. **Note**: even dead poison ivy vines have active oil that can cause a skin allergy. And fumes from burning poison ivy can get into your lungs and cause an even *worse* and potentially fatal reaction.

HERE'S HOW

TO SAVE SEED

1. Select seedheads or seedpods that are browned and mature. Pinch with your fingers to release the seed.

2. Air-dry the seed for at least several days if it hasn't already dried on the plant.

3. Place the seed in marked envelopes so you'll know what's what.

4. Store the saved seeds in a cool, dry place until you're ready to start them. A jar in a refrigerator is perfect.

ANNUALS & TROPICALS

Bag and discard bug- or disease-infested frost-killed plants to minimize the risk of reinfesting/reinfecting next year's plants. Clean but dead plants can go in the compost pile.

Don't till the ground after you yank your dead annuals to "get it ready" for next year. Research shows that tilling increases weed problems, speeds the loss of organic matter, and can harm soil composition, especially if wet soil is tilled or pulverized. Top existing beds with chopped leaves or a light layer of bark mulch, and let them alone.

Some tender plants survive winter in a sort of "hibernation" state in a freeze-free indoor location, such as an unheated sunroom or basement. Pot the plants (if they're not already in pots), and cut back the foliage to about a foot before stowing. Let

them die back or go semi-dormant. No need to fertilize. Add just enough water every few weeks to keep the roots from drying without pushing new growth. Next May, move the plants into light, begin watering and fertilizing, and in a few weeks you should have a reborn survivor. Good candidates include bougainvillea, mandevilla, some euphorbias, fuchsia, gardenia, tropical hibiscus, princess flower (*Tibouchina*), alternanthera, and many salvias.

Self-sowing annuals leave behind lots of seeds in the soil. If you like that idea, disturb the soil as little as possible. To discourage it, clip off seedheads before they mature and/or remove plants still sporting seedheads. Annuals that frequently self-sow are snapdragon, browallia, calendula, bachelor's button, cleome, larkspur, cosmos, California poppy, impatiens, toadflax, sweet alyssum, money plant, four-o'-clock, bells of Ireland, forget-me-not, corn poppy, nigella, portulaca, and Johnny-jump-up.

Cuttings that you took last month probably have roots by now. Pot them in small containers filled with potting mix. Grow under bright light indoors, and keep the mix consistently damp.

BULBS

Tender bulbs/tubers/corms, such as dahlia, gladiola, caladium, elephant ear, tuberous begonia, canna, crinum, and calla, need to be dug and stored after the first light frost damages their foliage. A few of those (dahlia and crinum, for example) are winter-hardy in Zone 8 and warmer parts of Zone 7. In those areas, cut the browned foliage to the ground and cover the bed with 2 or 3 inches of mulch. (See "Here's How To Overwinter Tender Bulbs.")

A common bulb fake-out is when grape hyacinths send up leaf shoots in fall. This is normal. That's just what this species does. There's no need to mulch it or cut it. The flowers will happen next spring.

LAWNS

Mow fallen leaves into the lawn, assuming you're cutting often enough that the leaf quantity isn't so great as to clog the mower or leave behind so many leaf fragments that they smother the grass. Small leaf fragments are beneficial, but you should see mostly grass when you're done.

HERE'S HOW

TO OVERWINTER TENDER BULBS

1. Tender bulbs/tubers/corms, such as dahlia, gladiola, caladium, elephant ear, canna, calla, and tuberous begonia, can be stored dormant inside over winter. Just before or immediately after fall's first light frost browns the foliage, cut the plants to ground level.

2. Dig the bulbs and let them air-dry for a week or so. Brush off soil, and discard any bulbs that are injured or diseased.

3. Store the dried bulbs in a container of ever-so-slightly moistened peat moss, sawdust, or perlite in a cool, dry, rodent-free spot, ideally with temperatures in the 40s. You can store the whole clump now and separate them later, or separate them now.

4. Check the medium throughout winter, and remoisten if it's dry or if you're seeing signs of bulbs shriveling. If it's too wet and bulbs are rotting, immediately remove them, toss the rotting ones, and store the rest in new, drier medium. The goal is to walk that fine line between too dry and too wet.

For large quantities of leaves that you can't mow into the lawn, rake or blow them off. Leaf coverings shut off sunlight to the grass. That's not a big issue over winter when grass is dormant, but it *is* detrimental in the shoulder seasons of fall and spring when grass needs light to grow. Matted leaves also trap moisture, increasing the odds of springtime fungal disease.

As grass growth slows and ultimately stops for the season, cut it short for the last time. A 2-inch height dries quicker and heads off snow mold and other cool-season, moisture-related fungal diseases. Step down in two phases. Lower the height a notch on the next-to-last cut, then lower it to 2 inches for the final cut.

October is an excellent month to add lime to the lawn, but only if a soil test indicates this alkaline mineral is needed. Lime isn't a routine need. If your lawn's soil already is neutral or alkaline, liming is a waste and maybe even counterproductive.

It's not too late to kill broadleaf weeds in the lawn. Like other plants, they're attempting to store carbohydrates in their roots for winter, which makes herbicide sprays more effective than in slow-growth periods.

PERENNIALS & GROUNDCOVERS

You don't have to cut every last perennial to the ground as soon as it browns. For one thing, birds appreciate the seeds and nest-building material. For another, many perennials—mums in particular—benefit from the insulation of dead top growth that collapses around the roots. Get rid of foliage that's diseased or bug-ridden, but it's okay to save some of your perennial foliage for cutting at winter's end.

■ *As perennials die back for the season, clip off and compost the browned-out foliage.*

Don't cut back perennials that are still green. Some perennials stay green all winter and add to the winter landscape, such as hellebores, dianthus, creeping sedum, yucca, and many coral-bells. You can always snip off browned-out leaves as they happen later, or cut back and/or neaten these still-green perennials at winter's end.

Some plants that stay green in winter aren't true perennials, but are biennials because their life cycle spans two seasons. Examples include foxglove, sweet William, hollyhock, forget-me-not, and poppy. These grow vegetation the first season, then send up flower spikes or stems that drop seed to produce the next generation. Then they die. For first-season biennials, let them alone. If it's their second fall (meaning they bloomed), they'll die with frost, and you can pull them.

One exception to the leave-the-leaves advice is to rake dense leaf droppings out of the evergreen groundcover beds. Thick layer of leaves can shade and smother plantings of vinca, pachysandra, creeping sedum, foamflowers, and other low-growers that hold their leaves all or most of winter.

Ornamental grasses can be cut when they brown if you like (the plants won't care), but many gardeners enjoy the texture, the sound and motion of them swaying in the wind, and the winter interest. Let them stand all winter, and cut them back to a stub in early spring before new growth occurs. Or cut them anytime over winter when blades start blowing around the yard.

SHRUBS

Other than removing dead or injured branches, early fall is a bad time to prune for two key reasons: You'll stimulate new growth that won't harden off in time before cold weather, opening it to dieback, and your plants (especially evergreens) will look chopped all winter until new growth starts in spring. Shrubs need to prepare now for winter dormancy. Let them do it. If you really can't wait until end of winter, at least wait until the leaves drop, signaling dormancy has begun.

Another issue with fall pruning is that you might cut off flower buds that already have formed on spring-blooming flowering shrubs. If you prune shrubs such as forsythia, lilac, weigela, and azaleas now, you'll cut off next year's flowers.

To prevent pest eggs or disease spores from overwintering and causing problems again next year, clean up fallen leaves and fruits from under shrubs that ran into bug or disease issues. Put them in the trash, not the compost.

Many winter-hardy roses will continue blooming through the season's first light frost. Drape a light fabric over your plants if a freeze is forecast to help nurse buds and blooms through the cold snap, possibly buying several more weeks of color.

TREES

As with shrubs, hold off on the pruning for the reasons listed above. Trees that "bleed" sap in spring are best pruned during winter, but most others are best pruned at the end of winter or in spring after they've flowered. Limit tree-pruning now to removing dead or injured branches.

Wrap or get fencing around tree trunks—especially young ones. That protects not only against rodent gnawing (which picks up once green vegetation dies off), but fall is when deer use trees to rub their antlers.

WATER

ALL

It's still not time to put away the hose. Water demand may be headed downward, but those newly planted plants need to be kept consistently damp until the ground freezes. That might not happen until late November or early December and beyond in Zone 8.

Be especially vigilant to keep new evergreens damp because their foliage continues to lose moisture throughout winter. You'll lower your first-winter survival odds if you let their roots head into frozen-soil time already dry.

Be especially, *especially* vigilant with new broadleaf evergreens, which lose even more moisture than needled evergreens in winter. And be especially, especially, *especially* vigilant to keep the first-fall moisture levels up with new broadleaf evergreens that are marginally winter-hardy in parts of the region, such as cherry and schip laurels, sweetbox, hardy camellia, osmanthus, some hollies, skimmia, and nandina.

Check moisture regularly in the root zone with your finger because the ground may be drier than the top growth indicates. Soak as needed to keep the soil damp all around and to the bottom of rootballs.

ANNUALS & TROPICALS
Soak annuals once a week if they're still blooming and rain is scarce. Continue checking pots and baskets daily. Watering frequency may be a little less, but don't assume you're done just because it's cooler.

BULBS
If rain isn't happening, soak newly planted bulb beds once a week. Their fledgling roots don't need a lot of water, but they appreciate some dampness. Existing bulb beds are usually fine without fall watering.

LAWNS
Sprinkle newly planted lawns up to two to three times a week to keep the soil damp in the top 4 to 6 inches. You want those young roots to penetrate as quickly and as deeply as possible before the ground freezes.

Existing lawns seldom need water in the fall, so long as they're green and growing. If it's an

unusually dry fall and grass is wilting or browning, water once or twice a week to prevent lawn roots from going into freeze season already dry.

PERENNIALS & GROUNDCOVERS
Continue watering new perennials, ornamental grasses, and groundcovers twice a week if it's dry. Established ones should be fine, unless it's very dry, in which case a weekly soaking is helpful.

Also keep an eye on moisture-loving perennials (astilbe, ligularia, lobelia, and so on), and water those if they're showing signs of wilting.

SHRUBS & TREES
Continue soaking new trees and shrubs two to three times a week if it's dry. Pay particular attention to keeping new evergreens damp until the ground freezes, especially broadleaf ones.

Established trees and shrubs are usually fine without water in fall, unless it's been unusually dry, in which case a deep, weekly soaking is helpful.

Continue soaking new roses two to three times a week if it's not raining. Established ones should be fine with a once-a-week soaking.

FERTILIZE

ALL
Not everyone agrees whether fall is a good time to fertilize most landscape plants or not. One school says fall fertilizer, especially when applied in late fall, is the best time of year. Another school says that fall fertilizing, especially when it's done toward early fall, is a bad idea because it can stimulate new growth that won't harden in time for winter. The agreement overlap seems to be late fall after plants go dormant. So if your plants need nutrition, apply it toward the end of October in Zones 5 and 6 and in early to mid-November in Zones 7 and 8.

ANNUALS & TROPICALS
Keep fertilizing still-blooming annuals and tropicals growing in pots and baskets once a week with a half-strength flower fertilizer. There's no need to fertilize ones growing in the ground now.

BULBS

New bulbs don't need fertilizer (their food supply is already built in), but existing bulb beds benefit from a fall scattering of an organic or slow-acting fertilizer formulated for bulbs. Apply it this month if you didn't already do it in September. Water it in well.

LAWNS

Most turfgrass researchers now recommend against so-called "winterizer" fertilizers that are high in phosphorus and potassium, which are the last two numbers on the fertilizer label. Current thinking is that most soils already have sufficient phosphorus for growing grass, and that nitrogen (the first number on the label) is still the most important nutrient. Maryland limits nitrogen amounts and bans phosphorus in lawn fertilizer unless a soil test indicates a need. (See March, Fertilize, Lawns.)

So far as timing, if you're only fertilizing twice a year, May and then again in either late September or October are the two recommended times.

If you're following a three- or four-treatment regimen, you should've applied an early-fall dose in September, and then will be applying the last treatment in mid- to late November. That means nothing goes on this month. Note: Maryland bans homeowners from applying lawn fertilizer after November 15.

PERENNIALS, GROUNDCOVERS, SHRUBS & TREES

An early-spring application of a granular, slow-acting fertilizer is usually enough for all of these, if even that is needed. More fertilizer in the fall usually is not needed, unless growth is lagging or symptoms of nutrient deficiency are showing up. In that case, first test the soil to nail down exactly what's needed and in what amount.

It's past time to fertilize roses now; wait until spring.

PROBLEM-SOLVE

ALL

As winter approaches, some bugs that overwinter as adults seek warm shelter, and our houses look very inviting. The big three are boxelder bugs, lady beetles, and stink bugs. These hard-shelled bugs are more nuisance than threat, but when their numbers swell, they can become a vexing nuisance.

The best solution to the bug-in-the-house problem is to look for holes and openings that let the bugs in. Look for cracks around windows, openings between walls and pipes, and holes in screens. Seal or caulk openings. Some people try killing congregating bugs on outside walls with a soapy spray or quick-kill insecticide, and others use vacuum cleaners, hand-picking, and light traps to deal with populations inside. A drawback of indoor insecticides is that they result in lots of dead bug

■ *(Left) Boxelder bugs can often be seen swarming outside houses in early fall as they look for ways to get inside. (Middle) Lady beetles are excellent bug-eaters outside in summer, but they can become a nuisance when they get inside the house during winter. (Right) Stink bugs have become a common pest in the Mid-Atlantic region, especially when they invade homes over winter.*

bodies in places where you might not be able to remove them (inside walls).

ANNUALS & TROPICALS

It makes no sense to treat bug or disease problems on plants that are going to die soon from frost. For tender plants you're taking inside, hose them off and/ or spray with insecticide to avoid allowing aphids, whiteflies, spider mites, and such inside. Eggs could be under the leaves even if you don't see any bugs.

BULBS

Discourage tunneling rodents by topping bulb beds with chicken wire. (See September, Problem-Solve, Bulbs for more on that.) Another option is working about 10 percent sharp gravel, ground slate pieces, or similar jagged minerals into the soil before planting. This adds enough jagged texture to make it uncomfortable on rodents trying to tunnel in it.

LAWNS

Grub feeding tapers off as grubs dig deeper to spend the winter in the warmer underground. You may notice dead turf but not see the grubs anymore for that reason. The deeper refuge also makes them very difficult to kill now. You're better off reseeding the dead grass, and making note to apply a grub preventer next June to disrupt a repeat of this year's damage.

Stiff, yellowish grass sticking up above the rest of the darker green lawn grass is likely a weedy grass look-alike called nutsedge. Broadleaf weed-killers don't kill it. If you have just a few patches, pull it up. Loosen the soil so you get the little bulblet underground. For widespread trouble, pros have access to herbicides (including halosulfuron and bentazon) that control nutsedge without harming turfgrass.

PERENNIALS & GROUNDCOVERS

Voles threaten plant roots again as aboveground vegetation dies back. Cages around susceptible plants (foamflowers, dianthus, hosta, lilies, and foamybells) help, or set out cage traps or snap traps baited with peanut butter.

SHRUBS

Do you have no or few berries on your hollies? That's a common dilemma, especially with the deciduous winterberry holly, which is grown primarily for its brilliant fall fruits. One explanation is that you have male plants. Only female hollies produce fruits. A second problem could be you have females but no male nearby to pollinate the flowers. You'll also need the right male to pollinate the right female, specifically, ones that overlap flowering times. Winterberry hollies are picky about this one. Other explanations include lack of pollinating insects; the plants are too young to produce fruits; you've cut off the pollinated, forming berries with a summer pruning; or plants have been seriously stressed, such as by extreme heat or a bug or disease problem.

Deer may nibble on rose canes and foliage that remains on shrubs prior to a hard freeze. If you're seeing damage, spray a deer repellent or cage the plants for winter.

TREES

Some needled evergreens shed their older needles this time of year. White pines are notorious for dropping copious quantities of these needles, which turn yellow before dropping, making many homeowners think the tree is dying. If needles are falling only from the inner sections of branches and not the tips, this is normal. There's no need to do anything. These needles make excellent mulch.

One way to reduce winter-storm damage risk is by thinning out overly dense branching. That means a more open structure that lets wind blow through better, reducing the "sail effect" of a dense canopy. Wait until after trees lose their leaves to do thinning.

■ *Female hollies need a male pollinator to produce red fruits like these.*

Back to cold weather. Even Virginia's balmy Hampton Roads in Zone 8, the southern end of the mid-Atlantic region, usually sees a killing frost by mid-November, officially ending another growing season. For much of our region, that's already happened by late October or early November.

The arrival of frosty nights turns tender annuals into brown blobs, causes leaves to drop from the deciduous trees and shrubs, and sends perennials into winter dormancy. By late November or early December, the soil's root zone has dropped to below 40 degrees Fahrenheit, slowing root growth to a crawl—if even that. Above ground, the season's first few wet snows appear, or worse yet for plants, a branch-snapping freezing rain.

The first visit of winterish weather doesn't mean it's time to run inside and close the blinds until April. Warm reprieves often follow the first cold burst or two, making for a fair number of pleasant days to get outside and finish some of the cleanup that October's fast demise didn't allow. A bonus is that weeds and bugs for the most part have called it quits.

The landscape should be far from bare, though. Some tree and shrub species (parrotia, stewartia, fothergilla, and Virginia sweetspire, for example) are late to turn color and long to hold onto their colorful leaves. They still look pretty good into Thanksgiving many years. Fruiting species also are key late-fall pleasures, in particular winterberry holly, viburnum, crabapple, dogwood, bayberry, nandina, juniper, rose hips, and the BB-sized metallic purple fruits of beautyberry.

And November is a time when colorful-leafed evergreens really come into their own, ranging from woody species such as golden false cypress, variegated boxwood, and blue juniper to perennials such as golden creeping sedum, variegated liriope, and lime-green or burgundy coral-bells.

Take advantage of those last few warm days to get a good, long look at what's left of this season's landscape color. Anytime now, things could turn white.

PLAN

ALL

As plant work ends, turn to yard jobs that can be done in cool or cold weather. Repair the fence or pergola. Re-do the patio. Dig that new bed. Waterproof or paint the arbors and trellises. Put in a new walkway. Terrace a slope with landscape timbers.

Cut a few berry-laden branches to display inside in a vase. Or scavenge the landscape for fall and winter outdoor decorating. (See December's "Here's How To Use Landscape Plants for Holiday Decorating.")

ANNUALS & TROPICALS

Jot down which annuals did well this year in case you want to grow them again next year. Also note what fizzled so you don't make *that* mistake again.

HERE'S HOW

TO PREPARE YOUR LANDSCAPE FOR WINTER

A checklist of season-ending jobs:

1. Clean and take inside anything at risk of winter breakage, including terra-cotta pots, ceramic statuary, gazing globes, ornaments, and fountains.

2. Take in anything not needed now that might weather, rust and/or blow away, such as lawn furniture, metal plant supports, stakes, and flags.

3. Blow leaves out of evergreen groundcover beds and off the lawn if there are too many to mow/chop into fragments. Otherwise, let leaves in place to mulch bare soil or insulate trees and shrubs.

■ *To prevent your birdbath from completely freezing over, float a tennis ball in it.*

■ *Before winter hits, paint wooden structures to protect them.*

4. Double-check to make sure you've brought in all tender plants that you want to keep.

5. Either now or at winter's end, remove dead foliage from perennials as frost knocks it back. Compost clean foliage; bag and toss diseased and bug-ridden leaves.

6. Weatherproof, paint, or stain wooden trellises, arbors, pergolas, fences, and decks.

7. As the ground freezes and watering ends for the year, disconnect, drain, and take in hoses. Also drain and shut off sprinkler systems so they don't freeze and break. Disconnect, drain, and invert or store rain barrels.

8. Once you're done with the shovel, pruners, mower, and other outside tools, clean and sharpen them for next season.

9. Keep the birdbath water from freezing. Put baths in the sun, and float a table tennis ball to keep a small area open during a mild freeze. Or invest in a birdbath heater.

Many tropicals are adept at cleaning dust, bacteria, mold spores, and even chemical toxins out of indoor air. NASA tests of nineteen species found that philodendron, spider plant, and golden pothos were the best at removing formaldehyde. Gerbera daisies and potted mums were tops for removing benzene. Other plants that filter one or more indoor air pollutants are: English ivy, peace lily, Chinese evergreen, bamboo or reed palm, snake plant, red-edged dracaena, cornstalk dracaena (corn plant), Janet Craig dracaena, Warneck dracaena, and weeping fig. To clean the air in an average 1,800-square-foot house, NASA suggests fifteen to eighteen plants in 6- to 8-inch pots.

BULBS

Check the garage, basement, mudroom, or tool shed for bulbs you may have bought but forgot to plant. It's still okay to plant them.

Amaryllis and paperwhite narcissus potted bulb kits don't need chilling and can go right in a pot with moistened potting mix. Look for hyacinths listed as "pre-chilled" if you plan to grow them in a vase inside.

PERENNIALS & GROUNDCOVERS

Not all perennials and groundcovers die back with frost. Vinca, pachysandra, ivy, and European ginger are creeping groundcovers that hold their foliage all year. Dianthus, liriope, coral-bells, foamflowers, and some ferns and creeping sedums are perennials that look good through most winters. Hellebores even bloom toward the end of winter.

■ *Even though most everything else is dormant or colorless, pachysandra is evergreen—even in November.*

All of these are candidates for a winter garden or for spotting winter interest throughout the yard.

SHRUBS

Evergreen shrubs planted along roads, driveways, and sidewalks or near the coast are at salt risk. Some of the more salt-tolerant shrub species include arrowwood viburnum, bayberry, beautyberry, butterfly bush, forsythia, hydrangea, inkberry holly, juniper, lilac, mugo pine, potentilla, red chokeberry, St. John's wort, sumac, summersweet, spirea, and snowberry.

Several low shrubs are useful as groundcover plants where you want an evergreen over winter. Spreading juniper and bird's nest spruce are the most commonly used, but the spreading English yew 'Repandens' is a good choice in a shadier spot. Spreading euonymus and some cotoneaster are low broadleaf evergreen options. In Zones 6, 7, and 8, consider sweetbox, spreading Japanese plum yew, and box honeysuckle.

Roses might be history, but their red, yellow, or orange pea-sized fruits or "hips" offer fall and winter interest. Some varieties produce more and showier hips than others, primarily rugosa and other heirloom or antique varieties. Consider adding a few if you're missing this fall interest for roses.

TREES

Choose salt-tolerant tree species near roads, driveways, sidewalks, and the coast. Choices include American fringe tree, American holly, Austrian pine, bald cypress, blackgum, Bosnian pine, Colorado blue spruce, cryptomeria, elm, ginkgo, goldenrain, hawthorn, hedge maple, honey locust, Japanese black pine, Japanese tree lilac, Japanese white pine, Kentucky coffeetree, larch, sweetbay magnolia, sweetgum, white oak, willow, witch hazel, and zelkova.

If you're planning to buy a live, balled-and-burlapped evergreen to use as a Christmas tree, dig its ultimate planting hole now. The ground might be frozen later when you're ready to plant. Fill the hole with mulch, and cover with a tarp or board. Store the saved soil in the garage or other spot where it won't freeze. (See "Here's How to Protect Woody Plants over Winter.")

HERE'S HOW

TO PROTECT WOODY PLANTS OVER WINTER

1. Wrap the trunks of young trees and shrubs with paper or plastic tree wrap to head off animal chewing damage.

2. Erect a deer fence or start spraying deer favorites with a repellent if these four-legged plant-eating machines are nearby.

3. Protect foundation evergreens and shrubs from snow and ice sliding off the roof by erecting a burlap protector or a plywood lean-to over them.

4. Make sure the soil of newly planted plants is damp as the ground freezes.

5. Erect burlap barriers to protect vulnerable evergreens from cold winter winds, especially borderline-hardy broadleaf evergreens or newly planted ones.

6. Optional: Spray broadleaf evergreens in windy areas with an anti-desiccant to discourage winter winds from browning the leaf margins. Re-apply twice more over winter on above-40-degree days. Note: Some research indicates these have minimal to no effect.

PLANT

ALL

November planting isn't out of the question, but success rates go down approaching frozen-soil time. Broadleaf evergreens, which lose the most moisture over winter, and borderline-hardy species in your zone are most at risk from late-season plantings. Nurse November plantings by keeping the soil consistently damp until the ground freezes and topping the soil with 2 or 3 inches of insulating mulch.

One risk of late-planted plants is that rootballs are prone to being shoved up and partially out of the ground during alternate freezes and thaws, which can dry the roots. Check these regularly over winter, and tamp any "heaved" rootballs back into the ground immediately.

ANNUALS & TROPICALS

As long as the ground remains unfrozen, it's okay to plant pansies and violas (if you can find them).

BULBS

It's fine to plant year-end bulb bargains or ones you bought and forgot to plant. If the ground is frozen, hack through the frozen crust. Or watch for an afternoon thaw to plant them.

Spring bulbs also can be planted in winter-durable pots if you can't get them into the ground.

Amaryllis and paperwhite narcissus bulbs will root and bloom without a chill period. Just pot and water them to start growth. Paperwhites usually bloom within four to six weeks of potting, while amaryllis take more like six to ten weeks. Start some every few weeks to spread out the flowering over winter. Toss paperwhites when they're done, but save your amaryllis for future years. (See December's "Here's How To Grow Amaryllis Inside Over Winter.")

LAWNS

Wait until early next spring to renovate a lagging lawn. However, if you're stuck with bare soil or a thin lawn, scratch new seed into the surface, water well, and cover with a light layer of straw. Depending on weather, you might get the seed to germinate, especially early in the month and in the warmer Zones 7 and 8. Better yet, lay sod.

PERENNIALS, GROUNDCOVERS, SHRUBS & TREES

Get these in the ground immediately, or if the ground is already frozen, use the insulated-pot option outlined in December, Plant, All.

CARE

ALL

Add fallen leaves, year-end grass clippings, frost-killed garden plants, and other non-diseased, non-bug-ridden yard waste to the compost pile. Now is still a good time to start a pile or two. (See October's "Here's How To Compost.")

If you've been "cooking" compost all season, empty the bins and use the finished compost to top vegetable gardens, annual beds, or the lawn. Or incorporate it into new beds you're digging to break up clay. Emptying now clears the space for all of the incoming compost ingredients.

Add mulch to the beds if it's thin or gone. Even if the ground has frozen, mulch keeps it frozen to limit the alternate freezing and thawing that causes young rootballs to "heave" out of the ground.

Mow moderate leaf layers on the lawn. Blow or rake dense leaf covers that threaten to smother lawns or evergreen groundcover plantings.

Continue to dig or yank weeds.

ANNUALS & TROPICALS

Pull dead annuals as frost kills them. Some go down at the first hint of 32 degrees Fahrenheit, while others hang in there until a really hard freeze comes along. Don't yank annuals that are still blooming or that have live foliage, such as sweet alyssum, blue salvia, dusty miller, snapdragon, and pansies. These might give you color into December or even survive winter altogether.

BULBS

Dig, clean, dry, and store tender bulbs such as dahlias, cannas, callas, gladioli, and elephant ears if you haven't already done that. (See October's "Here's How To Overwinter Tender Bulbs.")

Clip fallen foliage from fall-blooming hardy bulbs, such as sternbergia and colchicum. Or get rid of it at winter's end.

Make sure the bulb beds are covered with 2 inches of mulch. It minimizes alternating freezes and thaws that can push newly planted bulbs toward the surface.

LAWNS

Gradually reduce the mowing height so the final cut of the season takes the grass down to about 2 inches.

Once you're done mowing for the year, drain any remaining fuel; change the oil, fuel filter, and spark plug; clean the deck; and sharpen the blades.

Add lime if the lawn needs it. A soil test will tell you.

■ *Clean the mower, change the oil and air filters, and drain the gas at season's end.*

PERENNIALS & GROUNDCOVERS

Cut frost-killed perennial foliage to (or almost to) the ground if you're a neatnik. If you're leaving some seedheads for the winter birds and nest-building materials for the mammals, postpone cleanup until winter's end. A few perennials, such as mums, borderline-hardy species and anything planted late in the season, appreciate retaining the collapsed, dead foliage as insulation over winter.

Cut and remove diseased or bug-ridden foliage from the garden to reduce overwintering bugs or bug eggs and disease spores.

Don't cut perennials or groundcovers that are still green. Some, such as coral-bells, hellebores, and dianthus, are evergreen and need just a neatening cut at winter's end, if even that.

SHRUBS

Protect shrubs that need it. That includes broadleaf evergreens in windy sites (especially borderline cold-hardy ones), and shrubs in the line of snow or ice sliding off roofs. Erect burlap screens to block prevailing winds, or snow fencing if drifting snow is a problem. Erect a small lean-to over top of shrubs in danger of being flattened by snow slides.

Once the leaves are off the shrubs and trees, it's okay to prune summer-flowering shrubs and some evergreens. Some gardeners like to get a jump on spring work or are concerned that too-big shrubs are more prone to blowing over in winter. The flip side to cutting now is that evergreens might look chopped all winter until new growth resumes, and shrubs that suffer winter damage will need further pruning (maybe more than you would've wanted) at winter's end. Definitely do *not* prune spring-flowering shrubs now, or you'll cut off the flower buds that already have formed. (See April's "Here's When To Prune Which Shrubs and Trees.")

It's fine to prune off dead or damaged shrub wood anytime.

There are two schools of thought on late-fall pruning of hybrid tea, floribunda, and grandiflora roses: Some say let them alone, and prune once at winter's end. Others say remove about one-third of the ends to minimize whipping around and breakage over winter, then finish the job next spring. If pruning in fall, either November or December is fine.

After a hard frost, winterize roses by insulating the base of the plants (to about 6 to 10 inches up) with

■ *Crossing branches can be removed from trees after the leaves drop for the season.*

soil, bark mulch, chopped leaves, pine needles, wood chips, shredded bark, or prunings from overly long-needled evergreens. This needs to be pulled back at winter's end.

Check nametags that are wired on rose bushes. Loosen them if any are strangling the growing canes.

Fasten the stems of large woody vines such as kiwi, wisteria, and climbing roses securely to their supports for winter. Make sure ties on this season's growth aren't so tight that they're strangling their branches.

TREES

Most of the same pruning considerations that apply to shrubs also apply to trees. Excess or crossing limbs can be pruned out once leaves drop.

It's fine to prune off dead or damaged limbs and to harvest boughs or berried clusters from hollies or needled evergreens to use in holiday decorating.

WATER

ALL

Fall can be sneaky-dry. It's important to keep newly planted plants consistently damp until the ground freezes, *especially* new broadleaf evergreens. Don't let roots head into winter bone dry.

ANNUALS & TROPICALS

Keep the soil damp around potted annuals and tropicals that you've moved inside for winter. But also be aware that water demand drops in winter, leading to potential overwatering, the leading killer of indoor plants. Water these plants when the soil goes dry and the pot's weight becomes noticeably lighter. Once or twice a week may do it. Avoid soggy soil.

BULBS

In an unusually dry fall, you may need to soak newly planted bulb beds once or twice so the soil isn't going into winter dry. Again, no sogginess!

If you're forcing bulbs outside and have buried pots where rain can reach them, you'll likely not need to water those, except in an unusually dry fall. Forced bulb pots stored out of rain's reach will need moisture help from you, though. Check weekly and add just enough water to keep the soil damp but never soggy.

LAWNS

Established lawns are fine without water now, except possibly in very dry autumns in which the grass is wilting or browning. Continue to water newly planted lawns so the top 4 to 6 inches of soil stays damp. Knock it off once the ground freezes.

PERENNIALS, GROUNDCOVERS, SHRUBS & TREES

Established plantings should be fine as temperatures cool and normal rainfall happens. Just watch for very dry autumns in which you might need to do a deep soaking or two so roots don't go into winter dry.

Give special attention to anything you've planted this season, especially earlier this fall. The roots haven't gone out into the soil much yet and might need moisture aid from you and your hose. New plantings benefit from soakings about twice a week when rain isn't doing the deed, right up until the ground freezes.

FERTILIZE

ALL

Landscape plants are going dormant or at least slowing growth this month, so fertilizing isn't a high priority. The need for fast-acting, water-soluble fertilizers, if you're even using those anywhere other than on potted plants, especially drops now. If anything needs a shot of long-acting fertilizer, apply it before the ground freezes. After the ground freezes, there's a risk that a cold rain on top of frozen ground will wash fertilizer away.

ANNUALS & TROPICALS

Annuals and tropicals need little fertilizer inside during their slow-growth winter period. A small amount of slow-acting granular fertilizer scratched into the potting mix will likely suffice. Overfeeding can encourage leggy growth and a buildup of salts. (See Problem-Solve, Annuals & Tropicals.) Resume a dilute fertilizer in late winter as growth picks up again.

BULBS

Scatter a granular bulb fertilizer over existing, unfrozen bulb beds if you didn't do it earlier. New beds don't need it. Neither do bulbs you're forcing in pots or paperwhites and hyacinths you're growing for indoor winter display.

If you're planning to save amaryllis for future years, fertilize it once a month with a balanced granular fertilizer, starting now and continuing throughout winter.

LAWNS

If you're fertilizing once a year and missed your ideal late-summer time frame, it's okay to do the application now, but before the ground freezes. Ditto for twice-a-year feeders. If you missed the fall-application window of late September or October, do it immediately.

■ *More and more lawn fertilizers are being made without phosphorus, which can pollute waterways if excess amounts run off the land.*

If you're following a three- or four-treatment regimen, mid- to late November is the time for your final application of the year. Marylanders, state rules ban homeowner-applied lawn fertilizer after November 15, so do the deed before then, if your lawn needs it.

Current advice is to use a fertilizer rich in nitrogen, the same kind that's recommended for earlier applications and not a high-phosphorus, high-potassium "winterizer." The best plan, though, is to have your soil tested so you know exactly what nutrients your particular lawn needs and in what amounts.

PERENNIALS & GROUNDCOVERS

November is good timing for topping perennial beds with a light layer of compost since the bins can be cleared out for incoming ingredients and plants have been cut back for winter.

SHRUBS & TREES

Most woody plants get the nutrition they need from reasonably healthy soil, especially if you're fertilizing the lawn or garden beds nearby. Low-care-leaning gardeners usually get away with no supplemental fertilizer, opting to watch for signs of poor growth and fertilizing only if/when a soil test indicates a nutrition deficiency.

Others opt to fertilize young plants (or all landscape plants) with an annual application of a balanced, granular, slow-acting fertilizer. That can be applied either in late fall before the ground freezes or early in the spring before growth resumes.

Soil tests also will tell you if you need to alter the soil's acidity level (pH). Either lime (alkaline) or sulfur (acidic) can be applied this month.

Outdoor roses don't need fertilizer now, but if you're using manure, November is a good time to apply it, before the ground freezes.

PROBLEM-SOLVE

ALL

Deer trouble shifts into high gear as the natural food supply dwindles. One line of anti-deer action is to use scent or taste repellents. Numerous commercial products are available as well as homemade concoctions using assorted ingredients, such as rotten eggs, hot pepper sauce, blood meal, ammonia, urine, human hair, or bars of soap. Repellents should be reapplied regularly, *especially* after rain and snow. They're most effective when different ones are rotated.

A second deer option is spot-fencing or caging targeted plants. Deer (at least the smarter ones) generally won't jump into narrower confined areas from which they might not escape. For widespread, ongoing problems, the best solution is to do what public gardens in deer country do: erect a tall fence around the entire perimeter, 8 to 10 feet tall. Electric fencing is another option.

Bag and trash the fallen or cut-off foliage of bug- and disease-ridden plants to limit overwintering bug eggs and disease spores. Compost clean foliage.

Stink bugs, lady beetles, and boxelder bugs are still trying to get inside your house for winter—or they may be there already. (See October, Problem-Solve, All for options.)

ANNUALS & TROPICALS

Salt damage is second to overwatering as the cause of indoor-plant death. Symptoms are browning leaf edges and wilting, much like lack of water. Excess salt typically comes from softened tap water and excess chemical fertilizers. Solve the problem by repotting in fresh potting mix, and/or rinsing out the salt by copious watering with unsoftened water. Limit future salt buildup by using unsoftened water and fertilizing with organic or slow-release plant foods.

Aphids, mites, whiteflies, and scale are all possible indoor-plant bug problems in this less-than-ideal growing environment. Minimize plant stress with adequate light, humidity, and soil moisture. Inspect for bug eggs, and wipe them off with an alcohol-dampened soft rag. Or knock back infestations with bug-killers labeled for indoor control of pests.

BULBS

Place a sheet of chicken wire over bulb beds and top with mulch if you're seeing holes in the ground or other signs of rodent exploration.

Bulbs being grown indoors will lean and bloom toward the window side where the light is. Rotate your pots a quarter of a turn daily (or as often as you can remember) for more even growth.

LAWNS

Dog urine "burns" grass and creates brown patches, usually surrounded by dark green perimeters where the nitrogen is enough to help instead of burn. Messing with the dog's diet doesn't solve this. Either water urine-soaked spots immediately, or train your dog to "go potty" in a selected area, such as a mulched spot or stone bed—maybe adorned with a faux fire hydrant.

■ *Dog urine can burn grass and cause brown spots like these on the lawn.*

Nimblewill is a grass imposter that blends in with turfgrass during the growing season. When frost arrives, this dense, wiry, upright, grassy weed turns brown and becomes very apparent. It's a problem on three fronts: it's perennial (comes back year after year), it overruns desirable grass, and it's difficult to control without harming the "good" grass. Early infestations can be pulled or sprayed with a selective herbicide. Crabgrass preventers head off new infestations. But for large, existing nimblewill patches, you may need to use a kill-everything herbicide and reseed with new grass.

Crabgrass browns with frost, making its wiry, groundhugging habit readily noticeable. The seed has matured and dropped, so rather than trying to remove spent crabgrass now, consider applying a crabgrass preventer at the end of winter.

Herbicide sprays become less effective in cold weather. Digging still works fine, though, until the ground freezes.

PERENNIALS & GROUNDCOVERS

Cage still-green perennials and groundcovers to guard against rabbit, rodent, and deer damage. These stand out now after so much else has dropped leaves or gone dormant. Or start applying repellents and set out traps.

SHRUBS

Besides deer, rodents such as mice, voles, and chipmunks often chew on the roots and base of shrubs. Rabbits may "girdle" stems; they chew the bark in a band the whole way around, usually killing the plant. Tender young transplants are particular targets. Wrap or cage trunks, up as high as 3 to 4 feet to account for snow accumulation that can elevate varmints' reach. Or get traps and repellents in place if you're going that route.

TREES

Install plastic wraps and/or cages around trees, especially young ones. They face the same animal threats as shrubs.

Now that trees have dropped their leaves, it's a good time to check for trouble. Are there dead branches or "hangers" that might drop? Does the tree have cavities or rotting branches? Are mushrooms growing at the base? Are cracks or splits developing in the trunk or large branches? Is the tree starting to lean? Did the leaves this year drop or turn color early or grow smaller than usual?

The above aren't all signs of impending doom, but they're worth investigating. An arborist or experienced tree expert can evaluate. Pay particular attention to big trees that have targets nearby if they should fail (people, cars, or your house).

Not all "evergreens" are evergreen. Larch, dawn redwood, and bald cypress are examples of needled trees (technically "conifers") that turn color in fall and then drop their needles for winter before growing a new set the following spring. The lesson is: don't be alarmed if your larch, dawn redwood, or bald cypress is now, well, bald.

■ *Nimblewill is a grassy weed that can choke out desirable lawn grass. It browns over winter.*

December

The calendar declares it's officially winter late this month, but much of the Mid-Atlantic's weather feels winterish from Thanksgiving on. December can treat us to a few light-jacket days, but more often than not, nights are consistently below freezing, and snow can come at any time.

Consider it a bonus anytime you can get outside this month to finish fall's jobs. If you're *really* on the ball and luck out with a few nice December days, you might even get a jump on next season with some dormant-season pruning or bed-edging.

For the most part, conditions are more comfortable inside. There you can feed your gardening habit by sharpening the mower blade, getting the seed-starting station ready, and starting the annual winter ritual of planning how to make next season's garden the best yet. Sure, you'll have to trade your petunias for poinsettias and your amsonia for amaryllis, but hey, they're all colorful and involve soil. If your own indoor potted plants aren't quite cutting it for you, December is an excellent month to visit a public conservatory.

The mid-Atlantic region has a quality collection of glasshouses filled with tropicals, including Baltimore's Rawlings Conservatory; Lewis Ginter Botanical Garden Conservatory in Richmond; Maryland's Brookside Gardens Butterfly House (which converts to tropicals and trains in December); Norfolk Botanical Garden's Tropical Display House; and the granddaddy of them all, D.C.'s U.S. Botanic Garden Conservatory, which offers an annual Season's Greenings exhibit of blooming holiday plants, model trains, and D.C. landmarks made out of plant parts.

Most of the region's public gardens remain open through winter, showing off such outdoor winter-interest plants as winterberry holly, redtwig dogwood, nandina, and camellia.

Even though there's always something to do if you're a gardener, this month marks the beginning of the gardening off-season.

That's just as well because December usually turns out to be one of our most hectic months otherwise. Plus, it's a good time to give your back a rest.

PLAN

ALL

Assess your yard's warmer microclimates best suited for borderline-hardy plants. Examples can include a walled-in courtyard, south- or west-facing masonry walls that absorb heat in winter, and east-facing sides of dense evergreens that block cold, northwesterly winds. Spots where the snow melts first are usually sunniest. Spots where the snow piles up are wind tunnels.

Place winter-interest plants so you can see them out a favorite window. Options include colorful evergreens, shrubs with winter fruits, trees with great bark, and evergreen perennials and groundcovers. Hardscaping features (such as walls, benches, arbors, boulders) add to the winter effect.

Re-do lost or fading plant labels. Make them for new plants you planted this season.

Check your pesticides and safely dispose of any beyond their useful life.

ANNUALS & TROPICALS

Inventory leftover seeds, and make a list of what you'll need. Seed catalogs start showing up online and in the mail this month.

Contrary to popular belief, the poinsettia is *not* poisonous. Eating the leaflike bracts might make you nauseous, or you might get a skin rash from the milky sap, but people or pets don't keel over dead after eating a piece.

BULBS

Garden centers and mass retailers have an increasing array of already-flowering amaryllis, paperwhites, hyacinths, freesias, and other bulbs if you didn't start your own last month.

LAWNS

Get your mower ready for next season. Replace the spark plug. Clean gunk and grass clippings from the engine and undercarriage. Clean and sharpen the blade. Replace the fuel filter. Clean or replace the air filter. Change the oil, and drain old gas for winter.

SHRUBS

Low-heat, low-voltage LED light strings pose no harm to woody plants that you're decorating. Just be careful not to snap branches wrapping them—or fall off the ladder and break one of your limbs. Secure lights loosely, not tightly, and remove them after the holidays so they don't grow into the bark.

TREES

If you're planning to buy a live, balled-and-burlapped evergreen as a Christmas tree and plant it afterward, prepare the hole early this month. The ground may be frozen later. Fill the hole with mulch and cover with a tarp or board. Store the saved soil where it won't freeze when you need it.

■ *Cleaning the blades of mowers and garden tools is a good winter job.*

PLANT

ALL

It's not the ideal time to plant outside, but if you find yourself with a plant in a pot, go ahead and get it in the ground. Water well, and cover the soil with mulch. Or set the potted plant in a larger container insulated with leaves, foam packing peanuts, or mulch. Place it in a protected spot over winter, such as along a heated wall, in a walled-in courtyard, in a cold frame, or in an unheated garage. Check regularly, and keep the soil damp.

ANNUALS & TROPICALS

Besides poinsettias, add color inside in December with choices such as Christmas cactus, cyclamen, tropical kalanchoe, red anthurium, or orchids. Growers are even producing white-flowering euphorbias (an outdoor annual) and forcing hellebores (a perennial) into bloom for holiday sales.

Houseplants add indoor interest now, and then can go outside in summer. Some, such as palms, croton, snake plant, and dracaena, make good centerpieces.

When picking indoor plants, look for stocky leaves and no signs of wilting, bugs, disease, or browning around the leaf edges. A good sign is plants that are pushing new leaf buds.

Be careful taking new plants home. Most winter-sellers are tropicals that don't like anything under 50 degrees Fahrenheit. On cold days, the seller should place live plants in a plastic or paper sleeve before you leave the store. Keep the plant in the car with you with the heater on—not in the cold trunk.

BULBS

Get any last remaining spring bulbs in the ground immediately. Don't wait until spring or next fall. They'll dry out and die by then. December-planted spring bulbs still have a decent chance of growing, although maybe shorter in size and later to bloom.

Stores still may be selling discounted spring bulbs. If the bulbs are firm and not rotting or drying, the odds are good. Hack through the frozen crust to plant them if you must, or wait for an afternoon thaw. Or plant your bargains in winter-resistant pots.

HERE'S HOW

TO GROW AMARYLLIS INDOORS

1. Set the bulb, pointed end up, in a pot nearly filled with potting mix. Plant so that half of the bulb is above the soil line.

2. Firm potting mix around the bulb and water. Move the pot to a cool, bright location (60 to 65 degrees Fahrenheit is ideal), and keep the soil damp but never soggy.

3. Turn the pot regularly as the leaves and then the flower stalks emerge. This produces more even, balanced growth. Blooms should occur in six to ten weeks.

4. After flowers fade, cut off the flower stakes at the base. Fertilize every two to four weeks with a diluted bulb or flower fertilizer, continue watering when the soil dries, and continue displaying in a bright location.

5. After danger of frost is past, gradually acclimate the plant to the outside over seven to ten days, then either continue to grow it as a potted plant outside or plant it in the ground over summer. Fertilize monthly.

6. Stop watering and fertilizing in late August. In early September, move the pot back inside and let foliage die back. Or dig up the bulb and store it bare and dry. Cut off foliage when it browns.

7. After about eight weeks, repot in fresh potting mix and begin watering again for a new cycle.

LAWNS

Grass-seed germination is unlikely this late. If you're stuck with bare soil, lay sod, which can be installed anytime the ground isn't frozen. Otherwise, wait until early spring for seeding.

SHRUBS

A winter-decorating trend is to flank doorways with light-adorned, narrow, upright evergreens in pots. Good plant choices include young arborvitae or holly, upright boxwood, narrow juniper, dwarf Hinoki cypress, dwarf blue spruce, and sheared upright yew or Japanese plum yew. Use foam, heavy plastic, or otherwise winter-tough pots, and keep these damp all winter when the soil isn't frozen. When the plants outgrow the pot, repot into a larger size or plant them in the ground.

CARE

ALL

If weather permits, bed-edging can be done in December. The ground is typically soft and cuts easily. Yank winter weeds while you're there.

Get out the chipper-shredder and chip that pile of yard prunings, cut-down ornamental grass, and other yard waste that can be composted or used as mulch.

Switch to more plant-friendly ice-melters this winter instead of the cheapest choice—rock salt. Salt runoff can lead to excess sodium in lawns and planted beds, which can translate into browning of leaf tips and edges in hot, dry weather. Alternatives are calcium magnesium acetate, calcium chloride, or potassium chloride. Better yet, just scrape off ice or put down sand or wood ashes for traction.

Top off thin mulch. Bare soil really should have *some* mulch over winter to prevent erosion.

Just because poison ivy has dropped its leaves doesn't mean you can pull it off trees barehanded. The oil in the stems is still very much active all year long, and you can get a rash even in December by handling leafless poison ivy plants.

ANNUALS & TROPICALS

Yank any remaining cold-tolerant annuals when they finally bite the dust and start to rot.

Inside, maximize light to your potted annuals and tropicals by cleaning the windows. Dust and grime cut down a surprising amount of light. Move leggy plants to sunnier windows or closer to the windows. Don't let them touch cold glass, though, or you might freeze the tender leaf tissue.

Skip leaf-shine products. They make plants look clean and shiny, but they clog plant pores. A better, cheaper idea is lukewarm water and a sponge to clean dust off leaves.

■ *Wipe dust off houseplants with a damp, soft rag to maximize light's effect inside.*

The poinsettia does best in bright but indirect light, at temperatures between 55 to 70 degrees Fahrenheit. Make sure water can drain out the bottom. Either poke holes in the foil and set a saucer underneath, or transfer the pot into a slightly larger decorative pot. Water when the pot is noticeably lighter and the top inch or so of the soil is dry. There's no need to fertilize unless you plan to keep the poinsettia for another year. Fertilizer isn't needed until early spring.

BULBS

Regularly turn indoor bulb pots (amaryllis, hyacinths, and paperwhites) so all sides are exposed to light evenly. That prevents the growth and the blooms from leaning to one side.

Check tender bulbs (cannas, gladiolas, dahlias, for example) being stored inside over the winter. If you're seeing signs of rot, replace the storage medium with dry sawdust, sphagnum moss, or shredded newspaper in ventilated bags, and look for a cooler, drier storage location. If the medium and storage location is so dry that bulbs are shrinking and shriveling, lightly dampen the medium.

LAWNS

Turfgrass is dormant now; there's no care needed. Stay off frozen and wet grass as much as you can to avoid crushing the crowns and compacting the soil.

PERENNIALS & GROUNDCOVERS

If weather permits, continue cleaning frost-killed foliage out of the perennial beds.

SHRUBS

If you haven't set up protection for shrubs against wind, snow, critters, and other winter threats, do so now. That includes root insulation for borderline-hardy figs, roses, and camellias in the form of 3 or 4 inches of bark mulch, fallen leaves, or pine needles.

Harvest shrub branches for holiday decorations.

TREES

Snow and ice storms can rip off limbs or even topple whole trees. After a storm, remove broken branches you can safely reach, cutting back to the little ring

■ *When pruning, cut back to the branch collar, which is the ring that can be seen at the juncture of two branches (or at the juncture of a branch and the trunk).*

HERE'S HOW

TO USE LANDSCAPE PLANTS FOR HOLIDAY DECORATING

1. Evergreen prunings make ideal boughs, garlands, roping, and winter arrangements. Take branches you'd remove anyway, such as crossing or overly long branches. Cut back to joints, where smaller branches attach to longer ones or to the trunk.

2. Use landscape gleanings to make a winter pot or window box display. Look for berried twigs of holly, winterberry, crabapple, and beautyberry; branch prunings from evergreen trees and shrubs; bright red stems of redtwig dogwood; rose hips; lime-green fruits of osage orange; dried flower heads of red celosia and red amaranthus; and seedheads from ornamental grasses.

3. Use dried flowers such as hydrangea, baby's breath, allium, strawflower, or celosia to add a natural look and a spot of color to Christmas trees and evergreen arrangements.

4. Spray-paint pine cones, seedheads, sweetgum balls, and assorted nuts, and display them in baskets or use as accents on larger decorations.

5. Use grapevines, clematis vines, or willow branches to make wreathes.

6. Make a "kissing ball" (an alternative to mistletoe) out of boxwood cuttings stuck into a potato and decorated with ribbon and berries.

just outside where the branch attaches (the "branch collar"). Cleanly carve off torn bark with a sharp knife. No tar or tree paint is needed on wounds.

For large, hanging limbs and other bigger and/or off-the-ground work, call a tree company. As legendary USDA tree expert Alex Shigo often said, a dangerous combination is a homeowner, a chainsaw, and a ladder.

Recycle your Christmas tree after the holidays. Cut off the branches and intertwine them as insulation around the base of rose bushes; grind the branches into mulch with your chipper-shredder; or rub off the dried needles for mulch and compost, and sink the bare tree in the ground as a vine support. If you have a stream or brushy area on your property (or have the permission of someone who does), toss the tree where birds and small mammals can use it for shelter.

WATER

ALL

Inside, nothing kills more plants than too much water. Some pointers:

- Be sure your pots have drainage holes.
- Use lightweight, porous, well-drained potting mix for indoor plants.
- Don't be fooled into thinking it's time to water just because the surface dries. Most houseplant roots are in the bottom two-thirds of the pot. Stick your finger into the soil 1 to 2 inches deep to check the moisture there.
- Tip or lift the pot to check its weight. Dry soil is noticeably lighter.
- When you water, add enough so that it drains out the bottom, ensuring that water has reached the entire depth of the rootball. Dump excess water to avoid hindering additional drainage.

Outside, once the ground freezes, watering is done except for the following specific exceptions.

BULBS

One exception to the December no-water generality concerns bulbs being chilled in pots for indoor winter forcing. Bulb pots buried in

the ground or in spots that get winter rain are fine. But if you're storing pots in an unheated garage, covered window well, refrigerator, or similar no-rain spot, check regularly and add moisture as needed.

LAWNS

If it's been an unusually warm and dry late fall, and the ground isn't frozen, newly planted grass benefits from a sprinkling. Established lawns can fend for themselves.

PERENNIALS & GROUNDCOVERS

Newly planted perennials benefit from an occasional December soaking if it's been a warm, rainless fall and the soil is unfrozen and dry.

SHRUBS & TREES

Another exception to the December no-water generality is for evergreens (and to a lesser extent, flowering shrubs) growing in pots. The soil in these should be kept damp whenever it's not frozen.

In-ground evergreens are usually okay over winter. The exception is newly planted or borderline-hardy broadleaf evergreens (sweetbox, skimmia, camellia, osmanthus, and so forth), which benefit from an occasional soaking if the soil is dry and unfrozen.

FERTILIZE

ALL

Wait until the end of winter to feed perennials, groundcovers, roses, shrubs, trees, and the lawn. Don't fertilize over frozen ground. Winter rains and runoff from snowmelt may carry it off site. Maryland bans fertilizing lawns after November 15.

ANNUALS & TROPICALS

A light application of slow-acting granular fertilizer once a month is plenty to meet the slow-growth demands of potted annuals, tropicals, houseplants, and rooted cuttings spending the winter indoors.

BULBS

Indoor-flowering bulbs don't need fertilizer this month, especially ones you're going to toss after bloom, such as paperwhite narcissus. Start fertilizing amaryllis with a balanced, granular fertilizer every two to four weeks after it finishes blooming.

PROBLEM-SOLVE

ALL

Deer will eat almost anything rather than starve. If deer live nearby, lean toward plants that are their least favorite. That may help if your neighbors have tastier fare. One of the best deer-resistant plant lists is published online by Rutgers University at www.njaes.rutgers.edu/deerresistance.

ANNUALS & TROPICALS

Dry air is an underrated detriment to indoor plants. Static is a sign that your air is dry, a common side-effect of home heating. Water-filled pebble trays beneath plants don't help much. A better idea is a room humidifier that puts moisture into the air.

Avoid placing overwintering plants near outside doors or heating vents. Even short blasts of cold outdoor air can harm tender tropicals, while regular doses of dry, warm air can brown leaf margins.

Examine your plants regularly. The sooner you catch a problem, the easier it is to deal with. Look for shiny, sticky coating on the leaves; new foliage that is twisted or discolored; fine webbing on the stems; pale or speckled leaves; leaves that are turning yellow; stems that are discolored near the soil line; and a gray or white coating on the foliage.

BULBS

Voles are mouselike rodents and highly underrated plant pests. They're active all winter, and they *love* bulbs. It's not too late to cover bulb beds with chicken wire to discourage voles from tunneling down.

LAWNS

Under protection of snow cover, voles venture out into the lawn in search of food. Their movement makes surface tunnels in the lawn that look like curvy roads built by drunken road crews. Fight voles now and scatter grass seed in the curvy roads in spring.

PERENNIALS & GROUNDCOVERS

Voles also pick on many perennials and groundcovers, feasting on the tender roots underneath. If your foamflowers suddenly look wilted or disheveled, see if the roots aren't gone.

SHRUBS

Animal damage is the main threat this month. Deer especially target azalea, rhododendron, yew, and arborvitae. Rabbits gnaw the bark of young, tender shrubs, and bite off branch tips, making sharp, clean, angled cuts that look like the work of scissors. Underground, voles, chipmunks, and mice could be eating roots. Install or reinforce your barriers, and set out traps and repellents if you're seeing any of this.

Watch for browning on the street side of evergreens caused by road salt from passing snowplows. Erect a burlap barrier to head off further injury.

TREES

That greenish-gray crust growing on tree trunks isn't some kind of ominous disease. It's lichen, a fungus and algae growth that's harmless to the plant. Just ignore it. Or admire it.

Trees run into the same animal risks in winter as shrubs. See Shrubs for threats and options.

Strong winter winds threaten young and newly planted trees in exposed sites. Either stake them for the winter or erect wind barriers of burlap (not plastic) to block the worst of its force.

■ *Surface tunnels in the lawn like these are a sign of vole activity.*

How Much Soil or Mulch Do I Need?

To determine how much soil or mulch to buy for a gardening project, you'll need two figures. One is the number of square feet of the area to be covered. The other is the depth, in inches, of soil or mulch that you plan to put down. To calculate the total square feet of a rectangular or square garden, measure the length and width in feet, then multiply those two. That total is the number of square feet to be covered.

- **For irregular areas**, divide the space into a series of smaller, approximate rectangles, and calculate the square footage of each. Then add the totals.
- **For circular beds**, measure the distance from the center to the perimeter (the radius). Then multiply that number by itself. Then multiply that by 3.14 to get total square footage.

Once you have the square foot total, multiply that by the number of inches of soil or mulch needed.

A guide for mulch depth: 3 to 4 inches for trees and shrubs, 2 to 3 inches for perennials, and 1 to 2 inches for annuals. If you're buying by bulk, vendors generally sell by the cubic yard. To determine how many cubic yards you'll need, divide your total of inches of mulch needed by 324.

Here's an example: You want to add 2 inches of mulch to a bed that's 8 feet wide by 20 feet long. Multiply 8 × 20 to get 160 square feet, then multiply by 2 inches. The total is 320. Divide that by 324, and you get almost 1 cubic yard.

Buying by the bag is significantly more expensive, so that option makes sense only for smaller jobs. Soil and mulch is typically sold in either 2- or 3-cubic-foot bags. One cubic yard is equal to 27 cubic feet, so in the above example, you'd need to buy fourteen 2-cubic-foot bags or nine 3-cubic-foot bags to get the job done.

Math overload? Numerous online calculators let you plug in square footage and inches needed, then give you totals in cubic yards and/or bags needed.

One is available at the National Gardening Association website at www.garden.org/calculators. Another is available on the Landscape Calculator website at www.landscapecalculator.com/calculators/mulch.

How Many Plants Do I Need?

Figuring out how many plants you'll need for a planting project is a product of the area size to be planted and how far apart you're planting. Here's how to come up with a total. Start by calculating the total square feet of the area by measuring the length and width in feet, then multiplying those two figures to get total square feet.

- **For irregular areas**, divide the space into a series of smaller, approximate rectangles, and calculate the square footage of each. Then add the totals.
- **For circular beds**, measure the distance from the center to the perimeter (the radius). Then multiply that number by itself. Then multiply that by 3.14 to get total square footage.

To determine plant spacing, plan for the size a plant is *going* to get, not the size at planting time. Keep in mind that the "mature" sizes listed on plant tags are estimates that will vary by weather, your particular site, and how far in the future you're planning.

- When planting next to a wall or property line, divide the mature width in half. Plant no closer than that distance. (Example: a holly that will get 8 feet around should be planted a minimum of 4 feet away from a wall.)

- For plants of the same size, plant them at a minimum that size apart. (Example: plant 4-foot-wide spireas and 4-foot-wide boxwoods no closer than 4 feet apart.)
- For plants of differing sizes, add the two mature widths and divide in half to determine minimum spacing. (Example: a 6-foot-wide viburnum and a 4-foot-wide spirea should be planted no closer than 5 feet apart. 6 + 4 = 10. Then 10 divided in half equals 5.)
- A good average for spacing perennials is 2 feet apart. Compact ones can go 15 to 18 inches apart. Bigger ones can go 2½ to 3 feet apart. Large ornamental grasses can go 4 feet apart.
- A good average for spacing annual flowers is 1 foot apart. Compact ones (wax begonias or pansies, for example) can go as close as 8 inches apart. More vigorous ones (lantana or petunias, for example) can go 18 to 24 inches apart.
- A good average for groundcovers, such as vinca or pachysandra, is 12 inches apart, although if you're patient, 15 to 18 inches (or more) is fine.
- For planting large blocks of small plants, calculate the total square feet to be covered, decide on spacing, and use the following chart:

PLANT SPACING

SPACING (Inches)	25 sq. ft.	50 sq. ft.	100 sq. ft.
8	57	114	227
10	36	72	143
12	12	50	100
15	16	32	64
18	11	22	44
24	6	13	25

Glossary

Acclimate: To become gradually accustomed to a different environment.

Acidic soil: Soil that has a pH reading of 6.0 and lower. Mildly acidic is 6.0 to 7.0. Lime counteracts overly acidic soil to make it more alkaline.

Aerate (aeration): To introduce oxygen into the soil. In lawns, it's commonly done with equipment that pulls cores of soil out of the ground, depositing them on the surface.

Alkaline soil: Soil that has a pH greater than 7.0. Sulfur counteracts overly alkaline soil to make it more acidic.

Annual: A plant that lives its entire life in one season and dies at the end of that year.

Anti-transpirant/anti-desiccant: A product that reduces a plant's moisture loss by coating the foliage with a thin film, usually a type of oil, resin, or wax.

Arborist: A person trained to care for trees. Certified arborists have met the qualifications of professional organizations.

***Bacillus thuringiensis* (Bt):** A bacterium that kills caterpillars by attacking the digestive system. Available as a dust or powder that's mixed in water and sprayed on plant foliage when caterpillars are feeding.

Balanced fertilizer: A granular or liquid fertilizer with approximately equal proportions of the three key nutrients listed on product labels—nitrogen (the first number), phosphorus (the second number), and potassium (the third number).

Balled-and-burlapped: Describes trees and shrubs grown in the field, then dug with roots wrapped with protective burlap and twine for transport and sale.

Bare root: Plants that are shipped dormant, without being planted in soil or having soil around their roots.

Basal: Refers to growth emerging from around the base, trunk, or main origin of a plant.

Beneficial insects: Insects or their larvae that prey on pest organisms and their eggs. Examples: ladybugs, parasitic wasps, soldier bugs, predatory nematodes, and spiders.

Biennial: A plant that grows over two seasons, usually growing foliage only in the first year, and then flowering, setting seed, and dying in the second.

Bract: A petal-like modified leaf structure of a plant stem, growing near its flower. Often, it is more colorful and visible than the actual flower, as in dogwood or poinsettia.

Broadleaf evergreen: A plant that holds its leaves all season and has wider leaves, as opposed to needles. Examples: boxwood, holly, rhododendron, and cherry laurel.

Bud union (graft): The point on the stem of a plant where a desirable branch or stem (scion) is attached to a plant growing in the ground (rootstock). Roses are commonly grafted.

Canopy: The overhead branching area or "reach" of a tree, including foliage.

Cell packs: Multi-compartment containers, usually made out of thin plastic and used to sell small plants, most often annual flowers and vegetables.

Chlorosis: A nutritional deficiency in plants, usually indicated by yellowed foliage with green veins. Most common in plants that require acidic soil, it's a sign that plants are unable to take up sufficient iron from the soil.

Climber: A plant that grows vertically by means of elongating stems. It may twist or cling to surfaces to pull itself up, or it may need ties to help guide it upward.

Cold hardiness: The ability of a perennial plant to survive the winter cold in a particular area. The

U.S. Department of Agriculture assigns cold-hardiness ratings by zone based on winter's average lows in a given area.

Compost: Organic matter that has decomposed into a spongy, fluffy texture. It adds nutrition to soil and aids its ability to hold air and water and to drain well.

Corm: A fat, flat, scaly underground stem that's planted underground similar to a bulb. Leaves and flowers emerge from nodes on the corm. Examples: crocus, gladiolus, freesia.

Crown: The part of a plant at or near the soil surface from which the stems emerge. Sometimes referred to as the "growth point" of a plant.

Cultivar: A CULTIvated VARiety. A plant that has been bred or selected for having one or more distinct traits from the species and then given a name to set it apart. 'Pardon Me,' for example, is a cultivar of daylily.

Damping off: A fungal disease that targets young seedlings. Spores in the soil cause their stems to blacken and collapse. Using sterile potting medium helps prevent this problem.

Deadhead: To remove dead flowers in order to encourage further bloom, neaten the plant, and prevent the plant from self-sowing.

Deciduous: A plant that loses its leaves seasonally, typically in fall or early winter.

Direct-seed: To sow seeds directly into the garden rather than starting them in small pots ahead of time.

Division: Splitting apart plants to create two or more smaller, rooted sections. Useful for controlling a plant's size and for acquiring more plants.

Dormancy (dormant): The period, usually winter, when perennial plants temporarily cease active growth and rest. Some plants, such as spring-blooming bulbs, go dormant in the summer.

Drip irrigation: A water-delivery system that uses supply lines (usually plastic) and emitters that slowly deliver water directly to the soil around plants or pots.

Drip line: Can refer both to the outer reaches of a tree's branching canopy where rainfall drips from branch tips or to a line that's part of a drip-irrigation system.

Establishment: The time needed for a newly planted or transplanted tree, shrub, or flower to produce enough growth (especially roots) that it's adapted to its new environment. An "established" plant no longer requires the additional care needed immediately following planting or transplanting.

Evergreen: A plant that keeps its leaves year-round, instead of dropping them seasonally. These can be needled plants as well as broadleaf ones.

Fertilizer: Any material that, when added to the soil, contributes one or more nutrients required by plants. These include nitrogen, phosphorus, nickel, potassium, sulfur, magnesium, calcium, manganese, boron, chlorine, zinc, copper, molybdenum, and iron.

Floating row cover: A lightweight blanket, often made out of spun-bonded polyester or similar woven fabric, that's draped over plants to protect them from light frost or bug damage. The covers are porous enough to let in light and rain.

Foliage: The leafy tissue of a plant, including needles as well as wider leaves.

Forcing bulbs: The process of potting dormant bulbs, then giving them the necessary chilling time before taking them into warmth to encourage earlier-than-usual bloom.

Frost: Ice crystals that form when the temperature falls below freezing. Tender plants die when frost kills their leaf cells.

Fungicide: A product that acts to prevent, control, or eradicate plant diseases caused by fungi.

Germinate: To sprout. Usually refers to the initial growth of seeds.

Girdling roots: Roots that circle around the base of a tree or shrub rather than growing outward into the soil.

GMO: Refers to genetically modified organisms, which involves altering a plant or animal's genetic makeup by inserting or removing genes.

Grubs: Fat, off-white, worm-like larval stage of an insect, most often beetles and especially Japanese beetles. They hatch in the soil and feed on plant (especially grass) roots until transforming into adults.

Habitat: The living environment of a plant or animal. A native habitat of a plant or bug refers to the setting in which it's found naturally.

Hand-pick: To eliminate pest insects, slugs, or caterpillars by plucking or knocking them from plant foliage into a container or jar of soapy water.

Hardening off: The process of gradually acclimating seedlings and young plants grown in an indoor environment to the outdoors.

Hardscape: The permanent, structural, non-plant parts of a landscape, such as walls, sheds, pools, patios, arbors, benches, and walkways.

Hardware cloth: A stiff, metal fencing with small openings, usually used to protect trees and shrubs from rodent damage.

Herbaceous: Describes plants that have fleshy or soft stems that die back with frost.

Herbicide: A product designed to kill plants, typically weeds. Some act on foliage and stem tissues, some act on seeds.

Hybrid: A plant produced by crossing two genetically different plants, usually to achieve a desired trait, new color, or some other perceived improvement.

Hydrogel crystals: Also known as polymer crystals or water-absorbing crystals, these are clear or white, dry granules about the size of coarse salt grains that can absorb and hold up to 600 times their weight in water. They're typically sold as watering aids, especially for use in potted plants.

Insecticide: A product designed to kill insects.

Larva(e): An insect in its immature stage, after it hatches from an egg. Typically either a worm or caterpillar form of a butterfly, moth, or beetle.

Leader: The term for the center or main trunk of a tree.

Lime: Limestone processed as granules, pellets, or powder for use in adding calcium to soils, thereby making it less acidic and more alkaline (increasing the pH reading). Dolomite limestone also contributes magnesium.

Microclimate: Small sections of a property that deviate slightly from the prevailing, surrounding climate. A courtyard with stone walls, for example, likely will have warmer, less windy conditions than the rest of a yard.

Mulch: A layer of material placed over bare soil to protect it from erosion, to slow evaporation loss, and/or to suppress weeds. It can be inorganic (gravel, plastic, fabric) or organic (wood chips, bark, pine needles, chopped leaves).

Native: Indigenous. Native plants are those determined to have been growing in a particular region before the arrival of European settlers.

Naturalize: (a) To plant seeds, bulbs, or plants in a random, informal pattern as they would appear in their natural habitat. (b) The tendency of some non-native plants to adapt to and spread throughout their adopted habitats.

New wood: The current year's growth. Usually used in reference to a plant "flowering or fruiting on new wood," meaning the flower buds form on the new growth.

Node: A swollen joint or ridged scar on a plant stem from which a leaf or smaller stem will (or could) emerge.

Old wood: Growth that's more than one year old. Some plants produce fruits or flowers only on older growth, not that season's.

Organic matter: Gardening-wise, it's material or debris derived from plants. Technically, it's carbon-based material that's capable of undergoing decomposition and decay.

Perennial: A flowering plant that lives three or more seasons. Some die back with frost and generate new shoots in spring; others hold their stems and leaves throughout winter.

Pesticide: A product designed to kill pests, including bugs, disease pathogens, pest animals, or weeds.

pH: A figure designating the acidity or the alkalinity of soil as measured on a scale of 0 to 14, with 7.0 being neutral.

Pinch: To remove tender stems and/or leaves by pressing them between thumb and forefinger. It's a pruning technique used to encourage branching, compactness, and flowering, or to remove bugs or diseased leaves.

Photosynthesis: The process by which plants, collecting energy from the sun by means of the chlorophyll in their foliage, transform carbon dioxide in the air and water from the soil into carbohydrates that fuel their growth.

Pollen: The yellow, powdery grains in the center of a flower. A plant's male sex cells, they are transferred to the female plant parts by means of wind or animal pollinators, to fertilize them and create seeds.

Pollination: The transfer of pollen for fertilization from the male pollen-bearing organ (stamen) to the female organ (pistil), usually by wind, bees, butterflies, moths, or hummingbirds.

Pre-emergent: Acting prior to the germination of a seed. Describes a product that inhibits the sprouting of a seed (as in pre-emergent herbicide).

Rhizome: An underground horizontal stem that grows side shoots. Examples: canna, ginger, most iris.

Rootball: The network of roots and soil clinging to a plant when it is lifted out of the ground or pot.

Rootbound (or potbound): The condition of a plant that has been confined to a container too long, its roots having been forced to wrap around themselves and even swell out of the container.

Root flare: The point at the base of a tree where the trunk transitions into the roots. This point starts to widen and should be visible just above grade if a tree is planted at the correct depth.

Rootstock: The part of a grafted plant that's growing in the ground and providing the root system. A desirable stem or branch (scion) is attached to the rootstock.

Root zone: The area that the roots of a plant occupy or can be expected to spread to when mature.

Scion: The ornamental or desirable part of a grafted plant. Usually refers to a cutting, shoot, stem, branch, or bud that is attached to a rootstock, the in-ground plant that's supplying the root system.

Self-seeding (self-sowing): Describes the tendency of some plants to drop or distribute their seeds freely, which then sprout on their own. Can be a wanted or unwanted trait.

Shearing: A pruning technique in which plant stems and branches are cut uniformly with long-bladed pruning shears (hedge shears) or powered hedge trimmers. Used in creating and maintaining hedges and topiary.

Slow-acting fertilizer: Also sometimes called slow-release or gradual-release fertilizer, this is a product that's water-insoluble, releasing its nutrients gradually as it breaks down. Typically granular, it may be either organic or synthetic.

Sod: Sections of soil in which turfgrass plants are already growing.

Soil test: Chemical analysis of soil to determine its fertility, pH, and nutrients. This is usually done by private laboratories or state university facilities. Less-sophisticated tests can be done by gardeners using kits available at garden centers.

Spores: Microscopic particles that allow fungi to reproduce themselves, similar to the function of seeds in a flowering plant.

Sucker: A new growing shoot. Underground plant roots produce suckers to form new stems and spread by means of these suckering roots to form colonies. Some plants produce root suckers or branch suckers as a result of pruning or wounding.

Sulfur: An element that's both a plant nutrient and a key product in making soil more acidic (i.e., lowering the soil pH). Mixed with water, it's also used as a fungicide.

Stippling: A description of plant damage to leaves. Stippled leaves are discolored due to loss of chlorophyll removed by tiny insects that insert small feeding holes throughout the leaf.

Thinning: The process of removing selected sprouts from a crowded planting, or removing excess branches from a woody plant.

Transplant: The process of digging and relocating a plant. In noun form, it's a young plant that is mature enough to be planted outdoors in a garden bed or pot.

Transplant shock: The stress or damage a plant undergoes after it's been moved from one setting or location to another.

Tropical plant: A plant that's native to a tropical region of the world and typically not able to survive frost.

Tuber: Enlarged roots that send out shoots and roots from nodes along their surface. Examples: dahlia, cyclamen, perennial (tuberous) begonias.

Turfgrass: Short grasses that are mowed and used in lawns as opposed to ornamental grasses, which are left to grow as landscape plants.

Variegated: The appearance of differently colored areas on plant leaves, usually white, yellow, or a brighter green.

Water sprout: A vertical shoot that emerges from tree branches. These should usually be pruned off.

Weed preventer: A product distributed in advance of a weed outbreak that either stops weeds from sprouting or kills them before they develop. Also known as a pre-emergent herbicide.

Index

tuberose, 78
tuberous begonia, 61, 75, 78, 123, 138, 150, 151
tulip, 28, 39, 41, 45, 49, 53, 54, 55, 57, 70, 75, 80, 86, 96, 120, 129, 140, 145, 147, 149
tulip fire, 70
Tulipa
    T. fosteriana, 145
    T. kaufmanniana, 145
    T. tarda, 145
turtlehead, 10, 43, 60, 66, 90, 130, 138
twig girdler, 141

umbrella pine, Japanese, 24
USDA Plant Hardiness Zones, 8, 9–10, 19, 42

variety, 12
verbascum, 43, 66
verbena, 66
Veronica, 34, 43, 66, 112
    creeping, 43
veronicastrum, 43
viburnum, 50, 57, 60, 67, 75, 104, 130, 143, 146, 157
    arrowwood, 159
vinca, 58, 66, 116, 129, 130, 145, 152, 159
vines
    fertilizing, 28, 85, 122
    watering, 28, 53
Viola, 35, 44, 54, 58, 60, 77, 92, 93, 105, 116, 131, 147
    V. × wittrockiana, 44
violet, dogtooth, 140
Virginia bluebell, 43, 60, 73, 87
Virginia creeper, 146

Virginia sweetspire, 50, 91, 143, 146, 157
vitex, 67, 81, 117
voles, 29, 39, 55, 71, 86, 89, 140, 155, 165, 173

walnut, 12
wandering Jew, 90
Warneck dracaena, 159
water conservation, 117
water features, 104
water pollution, 53
watering
    after planting, 14
    basics of, 15–16
    measuring amount of, 113
wax begonia, 147
webworms, 112, 141
weeds, 49
weeping beech, 24
weeping fig, 159
weeping Norway spruce, 24
weigela, 37, 50, 66, 67, 75, 81, 94, 107, 152
white oak, 44, 159
white pine, 27, 155
    Japanese, 159
white pine weevil, 113
whiteflies, 29, 39, 155, 164
wild grape, 106
willow, 27, 34, 159, 171
wilt diseases, 101
wind, 12
windburn, 71
windflower, Grecian, 145
winter
    preparing landscape for, 158
    protecting woody plants over, 160

winter aconite, 22, 32, 34, 35, 45, 129, 140, 145
winter hazel, 60
winter jasmine, 67
winterberry holly, 90, 104, 146, 155, 157, 167, 171
wintercreeper euonymus, 29
winter-sowing seeds, 34
wisteria, 36, 54, 94, 105, 141, 162
witch hazel, 25, 41, 44, 66, 67, 143, 146, 159
witches' brooms, 141
Wolk, Art, 149
wood ash, 38, 53, 54
woodland phlox, 60
woodpeckers, 55
woodruff, sweet, 43, 58, 104, 109, 130
woods aster, 60
woolly adelgids, 71, 141
wrens, 55

yarrow, 34, 43, 66
yellow corydalis, 43
yellowing, 99
yellowwood, 27, 82
yew, 28, 50, 51, 52, 66, 67, 104, 107, 170, 173
    English, 159
    Japanese plum, 50, 67, 104, 159, 170
yucca, 43, 152

zelkova, 159
zinnia, 22, 58, 61, 64, 73, 77, 93, 111, 116, 123, 149
zoysia grass, 26, 58, 59, 64, 69, 70, 94, 97, 122

Photo Credits

Black & Decker: 107

Tom Eltzroth: 43 (both), 59 (all), 104, 114, 128, 137

Katie Elzer-Peters: 23 (both), 28, 29 (bottom), 32 (bottom), 38 (top), 39, 42 (bottom), 48 (both), 61, 62 (right, middle), 64 (top), 67, 71, 80, 81 (both), 83, 84 (both), 92 (bottom), 93 (both), 94, 95 (bottom), 99, 100, 109 (both), 116 (both), 118 (all), 121, 135, 136 (top), 144 (bottom), 148 (all), 152, 161, 165 (top), 170, 171 (top)

Bill Kersey: 19, 33, 46 (bottom), 50, 63, 160, 162

Tim Murphy, University of Georgia, Bugwood. org: 165 (bottom)

Jerry Pavia: 88, 117, 128, 146 (top)

Shutterstock: cover, 6, 8, 10, 12, 13, 14, 15, 20, 24, 26, 27, 29 (top), 30, 32 (top, both), 35 (all), 38 (bottom, both), 40, 44, 45, 56, 60, 66, 72, 74 (both), 78, 79, 85 (both), 86, 90, 92 (top), 98, 95 (top), 101, 102, 105 (all), 106, 111, 112, 122, 123, 125, 126, 132, 141, 142, 146 (bottom), 154 (all), 155, 156, 158, 159, 166, 169, 171 (bottom), 173

Neil Soderstrom: 11 (top)

Lynn Steiner: 77 (both)

George Weigel: 36

Meet George Weigel

George Weigel is a garden writer, garden designer, and frequent lecturer best known for his books and the garden columns he's written weekly for more than twenty years for *The Patriot-News* and Pennlive.com in Harrisburg, Pennsylvania.

Originally from Lancaster County, Pa., he earned a journalism degree from Penn State University and later became a Pennsylvania Certified Horticulturist through the Pennsylvania Landscape and Nursery Association.

Besides his newspaper column, Weigel has written for numerous magazines, including *Horticulture, Green Scene, Pennsylvania Gardener, Central Pennsylvania* magazine, and *People, Places and Plants.* He also posts a weekly "e-column" on his own web site, www.georgeweigel.net, which includes month-by-month garden tips, public-garden profiles, plant profiles, and a library of articles on a wide variety of gardening topics. Weigel is the author of *Pennsylvania Getting Started Garden Guide* and co-author of *Pennsylvania Month-by-Month Gardening* (both with Cool Springs Press).

During the growing season, Weigel offers garden design and consultations to do-it-yourselfers through his Garden House-Calls business. He also leads numerous trips to gardens, both regionally and internationally, and he gives dozens of talks each year to garden and flower shows and assorted garden clubs and Master Gardener programs.

Weigel is a member of the Pennsylvania Horticultural Society's Gold Medal Plant Committee, a long-time member of the Garden Writers Association, and a former board member of Hershey Gardens, where he helped design the 1-acre Children's Garden.

He's taught classes at Harrisburg Area Community College, Hershey Gardens, and the Garden Club Federation of Pennsylvania's Landscape Design School. Weigel says his best horticulture experience, though, comes from getting down and dirty with plants in the garden. He once designed and planted a twenty-theme-bed Idea Garden for Country Market Nursery in Mechanicsburg, Pa., and he's an avid (his brother would say "wacko") life-long home gardener who's still trying to figure out how to outsmart the groundhogs.

Weigel and his wife, Susan, live and garden in suburban Cumberland County, Pa.